THE CLASSING GAZE

Sexuality, class and surveillance

Lynette Finch

ALLEN & UNWIN

First published in 1993
Allen & Unwin Pty Ltd
9 Atchison Street, St Leonards, NSW 2065 Australia

National Library of Australia
Cataloguing-in-Publication entry:

Finch, Lyn.
  The classing gaze: sexuality, class and surveillance.

  Bibliography.
  Includes index.
  ISBN 1 86373 437 6.

  1. Working class—History. 2. Social classes—History.
  3. Middle classes—History. I. Title.

305.56

Set in 10/11 Plantin Light by DOCUPRO, Sydney, NSW
Printed by Kim Hup Lee Printing, Singapore

10 9 8 7 6 5 4 3 2 1

THE CLASSING GAZE

This book adds new perspectives to current historical scholarship, using Australia as a case study to illuminate broad international concerns. Using the insights of Michel Foucault, it directs historical work away from simplistic empiricist readings of documents concerning class and sexuality, and towards an understanding of the constructed character of categories of thought. The result is a fascinating discussion of middle-class and official discourses on the 'working class' and especially the intersections of class and sexuality: her examples include incest, childhood innocence, seduction, abortion, pregnancy and mothering. Lyn Finch's work enhances our historical understanding of how both class and sexuality were understood and thought about. Feminist post-structuralist history is making its mark.

Ann Curthoys

Other Titles

Contents

Acknowledgements

My colleagues Margaret Miles, Sharyn Pearce, Allison Cottrell and Gail Tulloch all helped me with this book. Kay Saunders, Raymond Evans, Carole Ferrier, Geoffrey Bolton, Gail Reekie and Ann Curthoys read sections of earlier drafts and made constructive comments, many of which I have incorporated into this final version. Responsibility for the end product, of course, rests with me. Jon Stratton deserves the greatest acknowledgement for his constant support and for his thorough reading of the final manuscript, exorcising many (and hopefully all) of the incomprehensible sentences.

Table

Abbreviations

AMG	*Australasian Medical Gazette*
AMJ	*Australian Medical Journal*
ANL	Australian National Library
AR	Annual Report
BCC	Brisbane Coroner's Court
BMJ	*British Medical Journal*
BPP	*British Parliamentary Papers*
Col.Sec	Colonial Secretary Reports
CPP	*Commonwealth Parliamentary Papers*
CSR	Crown Solicitor's Records
HRA	*Historical Records of Australia*
IR	Inquest Registers
JLC	Journals of the Legislative Council
JOL	John Oxley Library
LA	Legislative Assembly
LC	Legislative Council
LTL	La Trobe Library
MICC	Mt Isa Coroner's Court
MJA	Medical Journal of Australia
ML	Mitchell Library
mss	Manuscripts set
NSWLA	New South Wales Legislative Assembly
NSWPD	New South Wales *Parliamentary Debates*
NSWPP	New South Wales *Parliamentary Papers*
NSWSA	New South Wales State Archives
PD	*Parliamentary Debates*

PP	*Parliamentary Papers*
QPD	Queensland *Parliamentary Debates*
QPD	Queensland *Parliamentary Papers*
QSA	Queensland State Archives
RCDB	Royal Commission into the Decline of the Birthrate
RCEWS	Report of the Royal Commission to Enquire into and Report Upon the Operation and Effect of the Wine and Spirits Sale Statute
RCSDCF	Report of the Royal Commission on Secret Drugs, Cure and Foods
SAA	South Australian Archives
SAPD	South Australian *Parliamentary Debates*
SB	Special Bundle
SC	Supreme Court
SCCWCM	Report from the Select Committee on the Condition of the Working Classes of the Metropolis
SCLASM	Select Committee into the Laws Affecting the Solemnization of Marriage
SCLRPG	Report from the Select Committee of the House of Lords on the Laws Relating to the Protection of Young Girls
SCPVD	Select Committee into the Prevalence of Venereal Diseases
SMH	*Sydney Morning Herald*
V&P	*Votes and Proceedings*
VLC	Victorian Legislative Council
VPD	Victorian *Parliamentary Debates*
VPP	Victorian *Parliamentary Papers*

Introduction

Victor Hugo's classic mid-nineteenth century novel about the destitute and outcast of Paris, despite being translated into English several times, has always retained its French title, *Les Misérables*. The reason, Norman Denny explains in his 1976 translation, is that:

> *Les Misérables* . . . [is] untranslatable: the . . . meaning is utmost poverty, destitution; but Hugo's *misérables* are not merely the poor and wretched, they are the outcasts, the underdogs, the rejected of society and the rebels against society.[1]

In a way this book is about why there is no equivalent word in English. The class of people whose lives, language, attitudes and beliefs Hugo captured certainly did exist in Britain and British colonial cities and they were, indeed, the subjects of many mid-nineteenth century investigations. Yet, they dropped out of sociological investigations during a brief period spanning the 1880s to 1920, and there are no great English novels about them. As chapter two explores, there were some attempts in English investigations to give this class a name: the outcast, the intemperate, and the vicious were terms used to describe them. None have the totalising impact of either Hugo's sympathetic term or of Marx's condemnatory label—*lumpenproletariat*.

The twentieth century absence of this class-without-a-name forms a strong presence in this study. It is, however, not about them but, rather, explores the emergence of the other urban poor—this is a history of the emergence of the discursive

1

construct, 'the working class'. It investigates a process, dating from the middle of the nineteenth century, in which a particular understanding and a particular way of speaking about, acting upon, organising and reacting to—in short a discourse of—a section of society emerged. Because it discusses a discursive articulation this is not an empirical study in the traditional sense but is, rather, in a special sense, a history of an idea. It looks at the way in which one particular set of statements about a section of society came to be accepted and acted upon, but not other sets. From that time, at least in the consciousness of that section of society which we can call the educated middle class, the term, the working class, has carried an important and highly significant meaning and a whole range of knowledge has been collected, ordered, and acted upon in relation to a particular understanding of the subject.

It is clearly the case that the institutions through which articulation of, and intervention into the working class occurred— the law, medical science, philanthropy, the army, factories and schools—are bourgeois institutions. The categorisation of one section of society into the middle class, or the bourgeoisie, was also the product of discursive construction but it had already occurred before the period under investigation here. The particular processes analysed here are those through which the middle class made sense of another section of society.

Discourse theory does not imply that reality does not exist; there is no attempt here to deny that there were real people, living in real houses, in real cities. Neither is it suggested that these people were just an idea in the bourgeois collective mind. But discourse theory does take into account the fact that the group of people whom bourgeois observers called the working class could equally well have been described in a variety of different ways and that the categories which separated them from other types of people could have been placed elsewhere. The set of behaviours which were used to characterise them in a particular way could have been interpreted differently against a different set of measuring sticks and a very different group or, indeed, a whole range of different groups would have been the result. The emergence of the particular set of categories which resulted in their being articulated as the working class and the effect of this articulation is the subject of this book.

Since it uses discourse theory, this is a history which sits outside the dominant historiographical traditions of Germany and Britain (and, therefore, those of Australia) which have followed the path set by the nineteenth century German historian Ranke. Since the 1830s the influence of Ranke, whose assertion it was that historians should leave judgement aside and 'simply . . . show how it really was'[2], has been challenged, fine tuned, and modified, but has never been overturned. This empirical—its critics say empiricist—historiography has worked with an epistemology which assumes that the historian acts as a mirror, reflecting a true and accurate account of reality. Historians tend to debate the quality of the mirror, disputing the range of realities produced, without challenging the idea that the mirror itself is a possibility. This tradition was born of an epistemology which conceptualises reality as an immutable truth which exists and which is not dependent upon culture, history or interpretation, but forms a bedrock beneath the surface of social practice. Meaning, in this tradition, is not historically determined.

This Rankean legacy which, according to Jeffrey Weeks, has institutionalised the history of 'one damn thing after another'[3], forms an interrelated and complementary set of analytical tools with the Whig history of progress, which believes in a progression of time and narrative, with the ideas of the present representing a continuity and extension of the ideas of the past. This historiography is imbued with a faith that the present has emerged in a logical driving process from the past; accordingly, reading backwards from the present is a reasonable and logical thing to do. It sees the task of history as the chronicling of the processes through which the present was delivered out of the past.

The influence of French historian/philosopher Michel Foucault on historical traditions since the 1960s has tended to hover on the fringes of historiography; his methodological tools and his challenge to orthodoxy too threatening and too disruptive to be taken up by the mainstream as another useful approach. The Foucauldian challenge is to abandon the concern with the truth or falsity of particular theories, attitudes, knowledge and practice and concentrate instead on uncovering the conditions of their emergence. His history of the present turns historiographical methodology on its head, for:

> . . . if conventional historical analysis aims to render familiar a past that is thoroughly strange, and achieves this through the lens of the present, Foucault's writings . . . open up new possibilities for the present insofar as that present is rendered strange. It does this by throwing into question some of the features of the present that have come to be taken for granted as somehow natural and basic.[4]

This method, which Foucault called the genealogical method, uses the past to challenge the present by casting a spotlight on the obvious, the taken-for-granted way in which knowledge is organised within modern Western thought. It asks questions about the conditions which allowed the possibility of a subject, how it came to have meaning, and how some sets of questions and statements which describe the subject are accepted, but not others.

Neither Foucault nor his contemporaries invented this method. Early this century, an Italian historian, Benedetto Croce, argued that the past can only be known through the present and, therefore, what historians do is neither record nor capture the past, but construct it. Using the present as a point of departure, Croce argued that historians organise material about the past, evaluate its worth and decide what meaning, or significance, to attribute to it. All history, according to Croce, is therefore contemporary history, a construction of the present not a representation of the past.[5] Foucault's genealogical approach combines this conception of history with discourse theory, which has emerged from Marxist influence within French philosophy.

If this book were a Marxist study it would be concerned with ideology, rather than discourse, so the relation between the two concepts requires some explanation. Ideology, in the work of Marx, refers to the system of ideas, meanings and practices in which people think and act within material and economic structures. Beliefs and interpretations are formed through consciousness and are, therefore, the product of a state of mind. False consciousness, for example, is that state of mind where workers' interpretation of reality, their consciousness, does not accurately reflect the real conditions of their place in the social order, based on economic relations. This theoretical understanding of the relation between ideology and reality gives to ideas an abstract existence shaped by consciousness, for otherwise it would not be possible to have an idea that did not accurately reflect reality. Reality in this epistemological tradition is not subject to interpretation or historical specificity of meaning.[6]

The French structuralist Marxist Louis Althusser made a significant contribution to the relation between ideology and economic conditions by introducing a materiality to ideology. Ideologies, he argued, exist in Ideological State Apparatuses, such as the apparatuses of religion, law, the media, education, the political system, trade unions and the family. In this theoretical formulation, consciousness is constructed through ideologies which are tied to real structures, as opposed to the earlier view which states that ideology is formed by consciousness. Through this inversion, ideas no longer have an existence outside ideology. Althusser held that ideologies are the 'imaginary relations of individuals to their real conditions of existence'.[7] So, for

Althusser, there are 'real' material conditions, 'real' relations to those material conditions, and 'imaginary' relations to material conditions. 'Imaginary' relations are the ones which have effect for, through ideology, people actually relate to 'the real' through 'the imaginary'. In many cases their 'imaginary' relation to 'the real' may differ from their 'real' relations to 'the real'. This is false consciousness. So there is, in this theoretical formulation, economic order—real classes which are formed through relations to that order—and there are both real and imaginary (sometimes false) ways in which the classes relate to the reality of that economic order.

Foucault took the next step, asking if it is 'the imaginary' which has effect and not 'the real': what is relevant about 'the real'? Surely all that is important is how 'the real' is interpreted and understood and how social and political order is constructed in relation to that interpretation? Discourse is precisely this—the ways of understanding, interpreting, making sense of and reacting to a 'real', which is impossible to know. We can only know discourse and never reality. It is, therefore, not possible to have true or false discourses, although rational and irrational discourses are quite possible. Judgements about the truth or falsity of discourses would be measured against a real relation to reality and discourse theory is not concerned with real relations to reality, but only with ways of making sense of that reality.

This is a study about the emergence of a class grouping which combines discourse theory with a history-of-ideas style of study. The first three chapters focus upon the emergence of the idea, the working class, and the key categories which allowed its emergence—Man, society, population, morality and sexuality. They show how the category was first articulated through social and epistemological, rather than economic, determinants. Use of the term, Man, has been adhered to throughout this book. Efforts by other theorists to find a non-sexist way to label the construct, such as Jeffrey Minson's choice of the term, the individual, have been singularly unsuccessful.[8] Man was an historically specific object and was, in fact, male. Relabelling the object obscures the fundamental phallocentrism of Western philosophy which really did, and does still, generalise the human condition as male and which, therefore, specifically excludes the feminine.

Chapters four to seven look at the effects of this specific emergence and articulation of a class grouping, and although this includes evidence of resistance by those under observation, the central aim is to show why key bourgeois campaigns to organise and alter the working class seemed reasonable and logical to bourgeois reformers. These chapters are centrally about the campaigns which arose from a particular way of organising information about society. So it is, therefore, not a study of working class resistance but of middle class conceptualisations, although these chapters do look inside the category, the working class, at the people inside, for it was, of course, people who were affected by the campaigns, and not ideas. The concern, throughout, is to explain why the middle class thought it reasonable to act as they did, why they might even care about incest and youthful sexuality of another class and why they might consider abortion practices within this class to be their business.

Locating the family at the centre of a process of dividing society into classes (or the classing process as it is called in this book) places this study in the same academic orbit as Jacques Donzelot's *The Policing of Families*, while the emphasis on sexuality and morality within this family unit draws it near Kerreen Reiger's *The Disenchantment of the Home*. Donzelot points to the way in which the construction of 'the social' brought into being new constructions of the family. One hybridisation of the family constructed a new medico-political relationship between the mother and the state, and this, combined with the emergence of the new 'psy' organisations, were interrelated aspects of the 'emergence of new techniques of regulation'.[9] Reiger takes up Donzelot's link between the mother and societal regulators, arguing that the intervention that this way of thinking would logically bring about, modern technocratic strategies directed at the home, did not succeed in integrating passive mothers into the regulatory system as Donzelot implies though an allegation of 'collusion' but, rather, brought about a fundamental 'disenchantment with the home' among women. Although in disagreement, the two studies introduce key concepts of this book, namely the notion that the family played an organising role in modern society, that the mother was targeted to be the moral linchpin of the family, and hence of society, and that her role had to be taught through external rationalising education.[10]

This book looks at the same type of educational and medico-charitable interventions into families though the late nineteenth and early twentieth centuries. As most of the campaigns explored were the result of reasoning which was not meaningful to most levels of the working class until this century, they were mostly not resisted for, often, those being acted upon did not realise they were being targeted. For example, in chapter six it is shown that working class women, subject to campaigns by doctors to intervene in the entire conceptualisation and experience of pregnancy, then turned to these medical experts as if they were simple replacements for female midwives. Consequently both groups were confused at the clashing attitudes to abortion. Working class men, who had never been involved in so-called women's business, such as pregnancy, did not even know that a struggle to control their wives, lovers and mothers was going on.

By the end of the nineteenth century, following a series of social surveys which are described in detail in chapters one and two, a whole set of knowledges about 'the working class' had been accepted as meaningful and important. The information, presented in parliamentary inquiries, newspapers and novels, enabled reformers to ask a whole set of questions about what to do about the behaviours and beliefs revealed, necessitating decisions about a range of strategies by such institutions as parliaments. The establishment of the modern structures of prisons, factories, schools and a network of philanthropic institutions followed. The second half of the nineteenth century witnessed an explosion of discursive practices through which an understanding of the discursive construct, the working class, was arrived at and acted upon.

Through the influence of British utilitarianism, surveillance was the key method in both the collection of knowledge, and the management of discipline relating to this new grouping. Bentham, and other utilitarians, writing in the late eighteenth and nineteenth centuries, sought to use reason alone to explain the changes which were happening in social order. Their rejection of religion, superstition, and the entire realm of the metaphysical resulted in a way of seeing based upon the material evidence being perceived as 'speaking for itself'. One had only to observe and, using reason, one could understand. Everywhere, whether the evidence was clearly located, or needed to be prised out, there was a reality, and only the physical evidence—that which one could actually see—was relevant in understanding it. Bentham's Panopticon, his circular prison design which was adopted as the basis for most prisons in the Western world, was conceptualised as the material exemplification of the role of surveillance. Foucault quotes the French Minister of the Interior in 1841 who, in explaining the role of surveillance, stressed the necessity for easy and economical viewing:

> . . . surveillance will be perfect if from a central hall the director or head-warder sees, without moving and without being seen, not only the entrances of all the cells and even the inside of most of them when the unglazed door is open, but also the warders guarding the prisoners on every floor.[11]

In utilitarian methodology, this use of surveillance in discipline was matched by its use in collection of data. Until the end of

the nineteenth century, strategies of surveillance involved understanding how people interrelated with their environment.[12] This
is contrasted with the style of surveillance of the twentieth century
which is based upon a psychological style of reasoning, in which
individuals, or whole groups, are diagnosed as being a particular
type, based upon psychic traits, with debate then revolving around
appropriate methods for management of problem types. The shift
in reasoning, from environmentalist to psychological, brought into
play a strategic shift in policing from the law, to medical
science[13], a point which will be returned to throughout the book.

The nineteenth century environmentalist social surveyors acted
within an historically specific perception of the world, in order
to decide what was relevant and meaningful among all the
potential information there was to be observed about this as yet
unconstituted grouping. The borders of the grouping were located
through adherence to a notion of class—that is, they agreed that
some sections of the population were not the same as others,
and what made them different was that they were in different
classes. This particular meaning of 'class', in which groups of
people are understood to be united through economic and
political self-interest, emerged at the end of the eighteenth
century, and took almost all of the next century to dominate
social commentary.[14] Before that time, social categories were
based on ranks, orders, degrees, or interests, reflecting both a
different perception of society and the divisions within it.

Use of the word 'class' reflects a perception that bits of society
can be clearly demarcated from others and that the bits add up
to the whole. The less determinate terms—ranks, orders or
degrees—reflect a society roughly divided into overlapping,
unclearly bordered groupings, which did not then add up to the
whole. The nineteenth century view of a society divided by clear
demarcations based upon observable material conditions is one
which first conceptualised society as a unit, and as an understandable and describable entity. Chapter one will return to a
discussion of the importance of this view of society, showing
how it, and the discursive construct, population (a measurable
and mappable thing), were articulated and became crucial
organising categories of social control.

The first use of the term class, in its modern sense, was to
describe the middle class. Asa Briggs has shown that the term,
middle classes, antedates the term, working classes. Briggs argues
that the emergence of the phrase, middle classes, and the fact
that it became increasingly meaningful, was one of the many
pointers that the middle class was on its way to political
dominance.[15] Harold Perkin has added to Briggs' investigation of

the emergence of categorising terms. His analysis, which is located within Marxist empiricism, is based upon research which has located a change in categorising terminology. Perkin argues that long after the middle class became conscious of its own self-interest, all literature continued to speak of the middle *classes*, as well as the working or lower classes, each in the plural. Perkin explains this in terms of ideology, arguing that use of the plural form reflects:

> . . . the vagueness of the social facts, the existence of numerous layers and sections within the three major classes which only time and the experience of class conflict would hammer into something like compact entities.[16]

He dates this transcendence from being a class in itself, to a class for itself (to use Marxist terminology) at some time in the 1830s for, by the next decade, reference to a middle class in the singular was becoming common.

Building on this work, it can be seen here that the years immediately following the period denoted by Perkin (as a period of emerging class consciousness for, firstly, the middle class and then for the working class) were precisely those during which a range of social surveys of the urban poor began to be carried out. These surveys commenced the articulation of the urban poor as a distinct social grouping, with describable patterns of behaviour, speech patterns, and a distinct (and undesirable) morality. Through these surveys the middle class developed a way of talking about, and conceptualising, the working class. At the same time the information revealed provided the middle class with a set of standards against which they could measure themselves and understand their own emerging distinctiveness as a grouping. The surveys sketched out an 'abnormal' against which the middle class could explore the dimensions of their own 'normality'. This was, as chapter three shows, of most importance in establishing the sexual dynamics of the middle class family, as the only reasonable and socially permissible norm.

It was during the last quarter of the nineteenth century that bourgeois literature came to refer to *a* working class, showing the rise to dominance of the discursive construction of these people into *the* working class—a knowable, measurable and organisable category. During the early nineteenth century, terms which described the urban poor were used loosely and interchangeably: the lower orders, the working classes and the urban poor were all used to designate the same vague grouping of people. From at least the last two decades of the nineteenth century they were replaced in most literature by the term the working class. This term reflected the social fact that a way of understanding had emerged in which sections of society who had previously been understood as a loosely related overlapping range of different types or ranks were now conceptualised as a unified, if heterogeneous group.

Social surveys of the urban poor became common in the 1840s. Information in these mid-nineteenth century studies was organised around a set of key terms. Until the end of the nineteenth century the unifying notion of morality, which was, in turn, organised about a set of behaviours and attitudes—observable phenomena— formed the basis for choosing the categories. The range of chosen concerns through which middle class observers made sense of the behaviour of the observed, included references to: living conditions (in particular how many people lived in a single room); drinking behaviour (both male and female); language (including both the types of things which were spoken about, and the manner in which they were referred to—literally the types of words used); and children's behaviour (specifically how closely they were watched and controlled, and the types of things they were allowed to talk about). These were *moral*, not economic, references.

The range of surveys which predated Marx's location of the working class within the economic order of production capitalism, including Frederick Engels' survey[17], all organised the observed people through reference to morality not to political or economic order. These nineteenth century environmentalist surveys gave 'the proletariat' to the political economist, Karl Marx, as an already constituted grouping and it was a commodity owned by this discursive construct, labour power, which he located within economic structures. Although Marx has been credited as being a founding father of that section of what later became known as sociology which was devoted to studies of the working class, he was never concerned with who they were, what they really felt about their lives, or what their real attitudes were. Sociology as a discipline is discussed in detail in chapter one, but it is worth noting here that within the English understanding of sociology, Marx was *not* a sociologist, although Engels was. Marx never tried to relocate the boundaries, nor present a different working class to that already being formulated by the social surveyors. In fact, especially in his later work, Marx was not concerned with people at all. He was an analyst of structures who saw his task as investigating the economic system which was being created around him, and which was dependent upon the destruction of feudal social order and social ties, and locating the proletariat, as they were called in his works, within the power structures he described.

This is an aspect of Marxist class analysis which has been noted by R.W. Connell and T.H. Irving in their *Class Structure in Australian History*. 'Most class analysis since Marx', they note 'has taken it for granted that class relations form the basic or fundamental structure of any society in which they appear'.[18] Pointing to the historical inaccuracy of making this assumption, Connell and Irving set themselves the task of determining 'how far the "class principle" . . . dominates other forms of division and relations'. It was not, as they acknowledged, a simple task for:

> . . . class relations fill up, so to speak, the space of a given society, we nudge the circularity that plagues arguments in this field—for how do we mark out that space? . . . It would seem then that we cannot assess the dominance of a given set of social relations without also taking those relations as a means of defining the space that is dominated: which is, on the face of it, circular.[19]

Although it uses structuralist theory, *Class Structure in Australian History* is the direct antecedent of this book. The authors problematised the circularity of structuralist theories of class and, just as this book does, they noted that class is 'a constructed unity, and is only to be demonstrated by following out the process of construction and showing that its main dynamics follow class patterns'. Without a theory which allowed them to step outside the structure of class—and discourse theory is such a theory—they inevitably returned to overriding economic determinants to analyse the construction of class relations. This book does not do this. It discusses the conditions of emergence of a particular discursive class group and notes that they were articulated, not through economic ordering but, rather, through the use of moral and cultural categories.

The importance of the use of moral categories, within a feminist viewpoint, is that this process placed women at the centre of the discursive construction, whereas Marxist sociology defines the working class according to the labourers' relation to means of production. While not all labourers are, or have ever been, male, Marxist sociology has assumed them to be, and women's location in class has been by proxy. Women become identified as being in the same class as their husbands or fathers. This male dominated perception of class was challenged, but never resolved, in debates between feminists and Marxists from the middle of the 1970s.[20] These Marxist–feminist debates always took as a given, the assumption that it was Marx's intention to describe

11

and define a section of society when he discussed the oppression of labourers within capitalist economic order, and that the definition was dependent upon the relation of male labourers to the means of production. In fact, Marx's reference was not to labourers, but to that which they have to sell, labour power, and although his horror of the conditions under which labourers lived and worked was the driving force in his efforts to discern what was unique and different about the particular oppression of workers under capitalist industrialisation, his theories were about the treatment of the commodity, labour power, not about the labourers themselves. He inherited, and worked with, an assumption that the commodity, labour power, was owned by a grouping called the proletariat who, by the end of the nineteenth century, was reconceptualised as the working class, but his life's work was neither to identify, nor show the boundaries, nor argue about who was or was not working class.[21] It was, therefore, never relevant to him whether women who did not sell labour power were, or were not, true members of the proletariat.

The identification of a particular grouping in society as the working class occupied environmentalist surveyors from the middle to the end of the nineteenth century, and it was through their efforts that the category came to take on meaning. Environmentalist social surveys of the late nineteenth century divided the lower orders into two groups—those who were moral and those who were not—and it is the nature of this division which is discussed in chapter two. In the absence of an accepted name for one of the groupings, this book has labelled the two classes the respectable and the non-respectable working class. The environmentalist surveys categorised the urban poor into two distinct types using a division based upon particular questions: the alcohol test was not 'Did they drink?' but, in the case of men, 'Was their drinking the type which affected their ability to reason?' and, in the case of women, 'Did they drink enough to affect their sexual behaviour?'. The housing test was not 'Did large numbers live in crowded rooms?' but 'Would they still live that way given the choice?' and the answer to this question was determined by the efforts (interpreted by middle class observers) made by the mother to clean the room. The children's behaviour criteria were not based upon how often, or how long, the children played in the streets without adult supervision, but rather 'Was their lack of supervision the product of their mother's fatigue after battling to clean the room, or engaging in paid employment outside the room, or was it due to alcoholic stupor and a lack of motherly feeling on her part?'. There was even a chance to further dichotomise maternal drinking for, if the observer believed she drank out of despair rather than because she had a vicious nature, she and her family could be raised out of the non-respectables. In this instance they fell into a limbo class, awaiting salvation or damnation.

In this mid-nineteenth century round of surveys, the categorisation of the general population of the urban slums into two identifiable, knowable entities relied heavily upon an interpretation of the observable behaviour of women. More specifically, however, the behaviour of the women was contextualised in a particular way—in relation to how they operated within the social category, the family. At the core of all articulation of the working class is the discursive construct, the modern, or middle class family. The behaviour of women was made sense of in relation to their role as wives and mothers. The family unit had, by the end of the eighteenth century, been constituted, within middle class society, as a crucial site of social order and as the basic unit of society—a factor of bourgeois society criticised in the nineteenth century by John Stuart Mill who firmly believed that the individual should occupy that place.[22] The division of the observed grouping of people into the respectable and non-respectable preoccupied the environmentalist surveys of the last two decades of the nineteenth century for, by that time, after four decades of study it had been established as a reasonable way of relating to, and intervening into, the lives of those people increasingly being referred to as the working class.

The acceptance among middle class surveyors of the division was established by the time the next method of surveillance, with a different range of measuring tools, a different mode of policing, and a different basic scale of behaviours first appeared on the horizons of epistemology. Environmentalist, or utilitarian modes of seeing, relied upon interpreting observable behaviour. In a complete rejection of metaphysics, the only evidence accepted as reasonable was that which one could see, and the way of policing the behaviour was through constant vigilance. At the end of the nineteenth century a new way of observing and making sense of the world allowed a different set of evidence to be accepted, even if it was not visible. This psychological style of reasoning sought out new presences, devised ways of understanding knowledge through the measuring of an invisible concept, intelligence, and understood the drives of humans through a new invisible force, sexuality.

Sexuality replaced morality as the primary grid through which knowledge about society in general, but working class behaviour in particular, was organised and acted upon. In a sense, sexuality and the psychological style of reasoning which gave birth to it, represented a return of metaphysics, or certainly a move away from utilitarianism, and it is for this reason that Foucault speaks of sexuality as the new deity of the late nineteenth and early twentieth centuries.[23] Because the class was articulated at the same moment as sexuality was, the two discourses, the working class and sexuality, share a common, interwoven history of emergence.

A final point should be made about the range of sources used in this study. Parliamentary reports and private investigative surveys have already been detailed as sources which provided a great deal of material on how the middle class contextualised their observations about the working class. In some chapters these published accounts are joined by unpublished court records, including those of the coroner's court. Letters and diaries are also used and, in the last chapter, interview material is used as a source through which the processes described are illustrated. That chapter is about the ways in which one way of speaking was replaced by another and, therefore, in order to illustrate an absence in language, representatives of the middle and working class were asked to describe themselves. Their inability to do so, and their descriptions of the effect upon their lives of the absence of words relating to the body and to sexual intercourse, provides the core of one section of the chapter.

This is a study about the conditions of emergence of a grouping of people who did not articulate themselves. In the first place, their construction as a categorisable thing came into being through some other grouping's ideas and interpretations. How the people under observation interpreted their own behaviour was neither here nor there to the confident middle class nineteenth century social surveyors. They interpreted attitudes and behaviours for themselves; they took no notice of why urban poor women said they drank, or how they understood and related to their children's laughter and language. The urban poor were never called to give evidence to parliamentary inquiries to speak for themselves, because the only relevant material within these environmentalist surveys was how the enlightened observers inter-preted behaviour based upon a homogeneous range of measuring implements. Morality, and then sexuality, provided the grids through which information about behaviour was interpreted. While the interpretations of the poor were never given space within the classing process described in this study, it is undoubt-edly the case, conversely, that the subjects of this discursive articulation would have shaken their heads in total non-compre-hension at the interpretations placed upon their daily lives, and would not have recognised the two groups, the non-respectable and respectable working classes. No doubt this dichotomy divided families, friendships, enemies and social networks just as colonial national boundaries arbitrarily carved up tribal lands. What did it matter what an external group thought about their lives, attitudes, customs or language? The nomads still wandered. The urban poor still mingled. But discourse has effect—boundaries are policed, class groupings receive different treatment and are incarcerated in a specialised range of institutions. The consequence is border wars and class struggle. But that is another story.

1 Population and society

In the 1840s social commentators began to voice an alarm, bordering on panic, that complete ignorance about the urban poor was leaving a potential threat to social order quietly simmering at the doorstep of polite, middle class society. The threat posed by these dwellers of the industrial slums was located in the very fact that they were the 'unknown'. Highlighting this fear drew attention to a vital aspect of the bourgeois world-view: it illustrated the importance of the space in which the unknown existed for social commentators articulated the belief that everything *can* be known—that perfect knowledge is possible. Furthermore, it was the confident assertion of the enlightened thinker that there was a very small range of ways in which the observed data could be understood, as 'facts' were perceived to 'speak for themselves'. David Harvey explains this aspect of post-seventeenth century thought as follows:

> The Enlightenment project . . . took it as axiomatic that there was only one possible answer to any question. From this it followed that the world could be controlled and rationally ordered if we could only picture and represent it right. But this presumed that there existed a single correct mode of representation which, if we could uncover it (and this was what scientific and mathematical endeavours were all about) would provide the means to Enlightenment ends.[1]

According to Harvey, this confident style of reasoning began to break down after 1848. It was clearly present in the social

surveys of the 1840s and, furthermore, it continued t
reasoning in social investigation for at least the next forty .
This chapter sets out to contextualise the quest to know the
ranks of the urban poor and to organise information about them
through a key set of categories based upon a particular understanding of morality, within this enlightened pursuit to know
everything in the material world. It begins by looking at a vital
shift in Western philosophy, that of the move from the quest to
understand the will of God, to a concern with the new construct
which was called Man. It then discusses the rise of the human
sciences, and the notion of population within this new movement
in the pursuit of knowledge.

The social surveys organised information about the various
ranks of nineteenth century non-middle class society around a
notion of morality. This begs the question of what middle class
surveyors understood by this term, morality. Late eighteenth and
nineteenth century commentators, while using the term constantly,
rarely, if ever, supplied definitions to assist in understanding what
was being discussed. They relied upon references to observable
behaviour, and the role that that behaviour played in the maintenance of social order. People engaging in forms of behaviour
considered to threaten social order could not be considered moral.
As the family unit was perceived as the basic unit of order, and
the cornerstone to social stability, those who did not marry but
were not chaste either, were immoral. Those who drank, too,
were considered immoral for a different, but related, reason.
Drinking, it was argued, deprived men of the ability to reason,
and women of the ability to control their sexual urges. Enlightened thinkers saw reason as the road to truth and order, and
unreason manifested in forms of behaviour they labelled as
'madness', as well as drunkenness, as the road to disorder. By
contrast, in pre-enlightened thought, morality was understood in
relation to God; within Christianity, how closely an individual
was perceived to be following the teachings of Jesus, determined
how moral they were considered to be.

By the end of the eighteenth century bourgeois promotion of
scientific inquiry resulted in the world-view of that class being
characterised by an unshakable faith that the environment, both
material and social, had no utility independent of the needs of
humans and, secondly, it had no secrets that rational thought
could not unravel. Sponsored by bourgeois monies, European
scientists 'adopted an ideology asserting a utilitarian aim for
science; domination over nature allied to the national interest'.[2]
This simple dogma of modern industrial thought signals a deeper

17

shift in Western epistemology, and is dependent on the emergence of a new construct, Man.

In *The Order of Things*, Foucault identifies the emergence of this construct as the first moment in thought when the inquirer and the object of inquiry merged as the same body. Man was both the known and the knower.[3] The object, Man, is new to Western thought—'no philosophy, no political or moral option, no empirical science of any kind, no observation of the human body, no analysis of sensation, imagination, or the passions, had ever encountered, in the seventeenth or eighteenth century, anything like Man; for Man did not exist'.[4] Man arose as Western philosophy abandoned its central and driving aim of understanding the intention of the external author, God. This, according to the enlightenment historian, Norman Hampson, occurred during the half century from late in the seventeenth century to mid-way through the eighteenth.[5]

In the shift, Man did not simply replace God. The role of this construct was quite different. Whereas God occupied a space outside an already existing world, Man was located inside it and as part of it. Man sought to know the system and to organise it for human utility, oblivious to the requirements of all other components of the system, and certainly to the will of anything external. As Bauman puts it, whereas the 'assumed omnipotence of God drew a borderline over what Man was allowed to do', once 'God was dethroned':

> The world turned into Man's garden that only the vigilance of the gardener may prevent from descending into the chaos of the wilderness. It was now up to Man and to Man alone to see to it that rivers flow in the right direction and that rain forests do not occupy the field where groundnuts should grow.[6]

Concurrently with this epistemological revolution, a new class emerged utilising a mode of capital accumulation which altered the world by converting raw, or natural, material into commodities, or goods produced by humans. The landed aristocracy, by contrast, extracted profit from harnessing the God-given seasons, to produce crops on land given by God.

The conceptualisation of Man in Western thought allowed the possibility of the nineteenth century human sciences of demography, sociology, psychology, phrenology and sexology.[7] Their very possibility lay in the fact that Man, 'whether in isolation or as a group, and for the first time since human beings have existed and have lived together in societies' had become 'the object of science'.[8] Studies of Man 'as a group' included both the late nineteenth century discipline of sociology, where the internal dynamics of 'society' were considered, and the discipline of demography, which began in the seventeenth century, in which the patterns of growth and movement of the 'population' were studied. Demography is based upon a perception that the accumulated numbers of individuals living in a geographical area represent a unified group, or several unified groups, operating with modes of behaviour and mappable patterns of movement. For demographers, the population took on the same machine-like qualities that medical science was attributing to the individual body of Man.

A single individual, the Englishman John Graunts, is credited by demographic historians as being the founder of demography. In 1662, Graunts studied parish data and noted that London was both increasing in size and moving westwards. In seeking to know what was happening to London's population he commenced the process of deploying population as a meaningful category. This significant step located Graunts as 'the first to study historical records of population critically, with a view to deducing entirely new facts from them'.[9] Peter Cox has identified an epistemological break between all previous 'collection[s] of statistics of people and their possessions [which] began many centuries ago', and the form of reasoning exhibited by Graunts' treatment of the data. Crucial to the break was the notion of population:

> . . . the idea of using these statistics for any other purpose than
> the practical matter in hand does not appear, however, to have
> occurred to the collectors. Indeed, the very concept of a
> 'population' does not appear to have been entertained until the
> beginning of the seventeenth century.[10]

The title of Graunts' book reads like a prophetic manifesto of a new discipline, for the list covered most of the concerns that demography adopted from that time until the present. It was, he proclaimed, a study of 'the government, religion, trade, growth, ayre, diseases, and the several changes of the said city [London]'.[11] The text covered such variables of population as fertility, migration, housing, family patterns, numbers of men of military age, and the differences between areas such as town and country.

It was not until the eighteenth century that demography was accepted as a science. In order to chart a population through its physical movements and laws of operation, eighteenth century demographers designed such tools as the life table, which is a table which shows the numbers living and dying at each age, and the fertility index. Thomas Malthus' *An Essay on the Principle of Population*, first published in 1798, was a key text in this quest to explore the laws of operation of this new object of inquiry.[12] From the moment of its birth, demography sought to know in order to manage. It did not simply chart the 'variables' of population, such as rich and poor, weak and strong, healthy and sick, submissive and restive, but was much more actively concerned with knowledge of how the population patterns could be rearranged for greater utility.[13] Demography, like all of the human sciences, set itself the quest of knowing Man (in this case as a group), buoyed by an enlightened faith that perfect knowledge divorced from the need for divine interpretation was possible.

Founded in the late eighteenth century, the Australian convict colonies represented a perfect population for the demographer for they came into being as an enclosed and knowable population—a population which never went home at the end of the day and which had no social reality outside of its structural confines. It is for this reason that the first 'perfect' population surveys—that is, the first surveys of a population which made a serious and committed claim to leave no space unknown, and where every physical and demographic movement was recorded—were the late eighteenth century surveys of the Australian convict colonies.[14] Demographic records were assisted by the fact that individuals, dependent on government stores and afraid of the unfamiliar bush, did not stray far. Yet, the physical constraints on the population do not explain the detailed nature of demographic returns from the colonies. Between 1790 and 1825 the entire population was 'mustered' every year, under the supervision of the governor. Efforts to construct a perfect record of the population were taken so seriously that 'those who failed to attend would "be either confined to the cells, put to hard labor [sic], or corporally punished"'.[15] Thus the first demographic reports from the Australian colonies were filed years before Britain's first census in 1801, and were far more detailed than any census.[16]

Within efforts to understand all that was important about the populations of the convict colonies, certain information about the population was prioritised over other data. From the moment the colonial populations were perceived of as representing a unit—and that was from the moment they were confined on colony-bound ships—it was the duty of colonial administrators to study and know, to report upon and organise the convict populations. As James Watt argues, '[c]onditions on the voyage had an important bearing upon the health of the colonists and their subsequent usefulness in the colony'.[17]

Understandings of social order and social patterns, from the eighteenth century until the twentieth, gave an important role to a particular understanding of bodies. The significance of male bodies rested in their potential to labour, and the significance of female bodies, as will be discussed later in this chapter, relied upon their complex location as the site around which the basic unit of social order, the family, was organised. Thus we find New South Wales' first governor, Captain Arthur Phillip, complaining in July 1790 of being sent convicts whose bodies were untrained to labour:

> I wish, sir, to point out the great difference between a settlement formed as this is and one formed by farmers and emigrants who have been used to labour, and who reap the fruits of their own industry. Among the latter few are idle and useless, and they feel themselves interest in their different employments. On the contrary, amongst the convicts we have few who are inclined to be industrious, or who feel themselves anyways interest in the advantages which are to accrue from their labours, and we have many who are helpless and a deadweight on the settlement.[18]

As well as being untrained, Phillip pointed out that the bodies were in a very poor state of health, that many had died, and most were sick. This report mirrors the same style of reasoning of the British utilitarian investigations discussed by Karl Marx, who sought to calculate the exact amount of food the labouring body needed to be able both to labour, and reproduce labour power. In 1862, the cotton famine led the Privy Council to employ a medical doctor to study starvation in Lancashire and Cheshire. He reported that:

> . . . to avert starvation diseases, the daily food of an average woman ought to contain at least 3,900 grains of carbon with 180 grains of nitrogen; the daily food of an average man, at least 4,300 grains of carbon with 200 grains of nitrogen; for women, about the same quantity of nutritive elements as are contained in 2 lbs. of good wheaten bread, for men 1/9 more; for the weekly average of adult men and women, at least 28,000 grains of carbon and 1,330 grains of nitrogen.[19]

Phillip's opinion was that either the amount of food being received by convicts was below that required to ward off starvation or disease, or the punishment of the body on the ships was greater than that possibly sustainable for life to continue.[20] His detailed report of the state of the potentialities of labour in his colony was as follows:

> Many of those helpless wretches who were sent out in the first ships are dead, and the numbers of those who remained are now considerably increased. I will, sir, insert an extract from the surgeons's report, who I directed to examine these people. 'After a careful examination of the convicts, I find upwards of one

21

hundred who must ever be a burden to the settlement, not being able to do any kind of labour, from old age and chronic diseases of long standing' . . . Of the nine hundred and thirty males sent out by the last ships, two hundred and sixty-one died on board, and fifty have died since landing. The number of sick this day is four hundred and fifty; and many who are not reckoned as sick have barely strength to attend to themselves. Such is our present state; and when the last ships arrived we had not sixty people sick in the colony.[21]

Phillip's determination to record in such detail the state of health of each and every body was, like all eighteenth century population surveys, not simply a quest to map who was sick and who was healthy but, rather, represented the mapping of the population as either useful or not, and was concerned with the management of that population for greater utility. His belief that he should be sent 'healthy young men and breeding women'[22] saw him struggle in vain to alter what Portia Robinson has shown to be a 'haphazard process of selection of convicts for transportation . . . throughout the convict period'.[23] Sending diseased, sick, crippled and old convicts helped alleviate overcrowding in Britain's goals, he acknowledged 'but what of the colony?'.[24] Subsequent governors continued to demand more useful labouring bodies but, as the aims of the British governments and those of the colonies' administrators diverged, the pleas were to no avail.

Information about the population of the colonies was not, however, only organised through grids of potential to labour. The heterogeneous nature of observable data about the people was also organised through meanings based upon moral categories, and it was through this set of categories that the bodies of women played a central role. As all meaning takes form through discourse, the female body was given new meaning during the eighteenth century through the discourses of the human sciences. For the first time the female body was constituted as being nothing but the shell around the womb. Jill Julius Matthews has shown how 'population ideology' played a crucial role in constructing this reading of female bodies.[25] In three interrelated ways medical practice constituted the female body as a pathologically sexual unit—through the social body of the population 'whose regulated fecundity it was supposed to ensure'; through the family space 'of which it had to be a substantial and functional element'; and in relation to children 'which it produced and had to guarantee, by virtue of a biologico-moral responsibility lasting through the entire period of the children's education'.[26]

Most knowledge about the population—its basic unit of order, the family, its very possibility through a viable birthrate, and its

22

health patterns and moral strengths—was given meaning through the central location of the female body. Therefore, descriptions of the population of the convict colonies largely relied upon juxtaposing knowledge about behaviours with perceptions of the threefold role of feminine bodies. Robert Hughes is one author who has highlighted the important rhetorical power of female representation. He substantiates this by arguing that within the convict surveys 'there was rarely a comment on colonial society, scarcely a passage of evidence to the various Select Committees on Transportation, hardly a tract or a diary or a letter home, that missed the chance to describe the degeneracy, incorrigibility and worthlessness of women convicts in Australia'.[27] Robinson, in *The Women of Botany Bay*, disagrees with Hughes' interpretation of the morality of the convict women, claiming that his work is a 'rehash of the old nineteenth century "convict novels"'.[28] On the *rhetorical* significance of female convicts however, she is in complete agreement. 'The women of Botany Bay', she writes, 'were . . . believed to typify the debauchery, depravity and criminality which was Botany Bay'.[29]

Journeys to the colonies served as the source of a large amount of documentation of the social facts of convict and colonial populations. On ships, as in the colonies, differentiation was made between the good or moral, and the bad and immoral, and attendant sets of management accompanied the differentiation. Anne Gratton's 1858 account of her journey to Australia showed a clear example of this:

> There is not half the strictness I expected to find, but the most respectable are soon singled out by the Doctor and the Captain, who are extremely kind and show us many favours. I would here say to anyone coming out—you cannot keep too respectable . . . I am thankful that I chanced to get into such a respectable mess. The doctor said we are a credit to this corner of the ship and anything we want we shall have by going quietly to him.[30]

Both official and private reports of the conditions on board the ships divided the microcosmic population upon moral lines. Mrs King's 1799 diary of her trip to Australia shows a clear distinction between the moral and the immoral, although the criteria she used probably points to a change in notions of respectability from the end of the eighteenth century to the middle of the nineteenth. Her lack of concern with marital status would have been unlikely to have been voiced by her contemporaries of the next century. She wrote that she thought highly of one female convict who was 'a clearly better sort of woman—not withstanding she lived amongst the officers'.[31]

What is common to these reports is that they do not just describe forms of behaviour and the attendant responses elicited from middle class observers. They impose a style of reasoning which equates *behaviour* with *type*; that is, what was being reflected was a belief that observed behaviour can be perfectly represented on a map of human types independent of social circumstances, or a range of other meanings which could be attributed to the behaviour. This view reflects the confidence noted by Harvey in the above quotation, that there is only one answer to each question, and one correct mode of representation of the material and social world. Psychological reasoning, by contrast, with a measuring gauge of sexuality, looked for an inner essence which behaviour could just as easily conceal, as reveal. Therefore, while behaviour revealed a truth about the type of person in the nineteenth century, in the twentieth century it did not.

Efforts to manage the colonies, especially after the first two decades when it was no longer considered reasonable to continue the settlements just for prison purposes, reveals a steady belief that certain types could be introduced into the colonies and a better, more useful, population would be thereby created. This 'farming' of the population, which selected types based upon behaviour displayed before embarkation was experimental but did not claim to be scientific as did the twentieth century field of eugenics.[32] While eugenicists, using psychological reasoning, were 'generally concerned about the transmission of mental defectiveness from generation to generation'[33], eighteenth century population management in the Australian colonies aimed to facilitate the introduction of morality and thus create a better type of population. This led to many arguments between emigration officials and those entrepreneurs who set themselves up in the business of supplying suitable immigrants.[34] The language of these interactions spoke of the 'importation' or 'supply' of suitable emigrants, and noted of these importers of humans that 'colonialists have obtained the benefit of their services'.[35]

The whole scheme was, therefore, very much framed in terms which reflected the farming or management of stock. The trade in female emigrants under the bounty system, in particular, found traders treading a fine line as they sought to show that their supplied females had conducted themselves within the limits of moral behaviour. An example of the level of scrutiny of the morality of females under this scheme can be found in the case of the company Carter and Bonus Ships which, in 1845, complained that it had been falsely deprived of bounty payments for the supply of single females to New South Wales. The

Colonial Land and Emigration Commissioners had refused to pay the bounties for most of the young women the company had delivered because they alleged that they had failed to meet the first general principle laid down for control of the scheme:

> Where no reason appears to doubt that single females were of good character at the time of embarkation and when their conduct was good during the voyage so as to justify the practical efficiency of the protection under which they were placed, the refusal of bounty under the strict letter of the rule on the latter point will, as regards the past be reconsidered.[36]

Therefore, the extremely detailed nature of reports of behaviour and population patterns of the new colonies can be contextualised within the new perception of population. The view that all aspects of this population can be known, and the sense in which population management was being adopted in the colonies, is reflected in the level of detail sought from British emigration authorities about the success or failure of each and every shipment of 'stock'. For example, Governor Bourke's reply to the emigration commissioner in 1833 is telling, not for the information which was forthcoming from him but for the way in which the nature of the request for details about an individual shipment of females is revealed:

> You have requested a particular account of the general character and behaviour of the young women who arrived by the *Bussorah Merchant* and of the manner in which they have been disposed of. Their character and behaviour have proved, as far as I have ascertained, in general satisfactory . . . They were placed on arrival under the charge of a Committee of Ladies and disposed of in the same manner as those who arrived by the *Red Rover* to the various persons who applied for their services. The greater number went off in the course of a few days in the capacity of domestic Servants, and I believe there remain few, if any, who are not now provided for.[37]

The juxtaposition of behaviour and type, and the careful scrutiny of morality, is the key to understanding most demographic details sent from the colonies. For decades, reports contained details which focused upon the birth rate, the legal marriage rates compared with the percentage of the population living in concubinage, illegitimate births compared with legitimate births, prostitution and child welfare. Such social facts filled the depositions from the colonial authorities to their British superiors. The Reverend Samuel Marsden's 1806 report on New South Wales is typical of colonial demographic reports:

> The total number of women in the colony is about one thousand four hundred and thirty, including Officers and free Settlers wives; the number of married among them, is three hundred and ninety-five and unmarried one thousand and thirty-five—these in general are living in open Prostitution. The total number of legitimate children is eight hundred and seven, and the number of natural children, one thousand and twenty-five.[38]

A division based upon economic ranks was of so little importance that the proportion of women who were convicts, officers' wives, and free settlers' wives was hurried over in a single indeterminate phrase, yet the moral base of the society was given great prominence.

The key measuring gauge of morality as a way of understanding the nature of the population under observation, refers back to the central location of the family within social order, around which the bourgeois notion of morality took meaning. The family's social place in social order meant, in turn, that marriage has always occupied a significant space in bourgeois social order. Christopher Hill notes that under the influence of Puritan thought, marriage gained its prominent role as the function through which social order and religious control were exerted.[39] The medieval church, by contrast, had only slowly come to view marriage as important enough to be considered a sacrament.[40] Jon Stratton builds upon Hill's work, pointing out that the significance of marriage within social order was based upon the inherently non-public nature of Puritanism.[41] His point, based upon Weberian theory, rests on the fact that Catholicism was a religion of public example in which one was 'good' in order to influence others to do likewise. Puritanism was a religion in which one lived one's 'goodness'; not in order to influence anyone else, but rather to ensure one's own salvation. To the Puritan ideal, the family was the most important social unit for it was here that the compact group lived its holy quest for a sign of divine favour. Under Catholicism the entire society necessarily had to witness the example of the 'good', a requirement potentially hindered, rather than assisted by, a small compact family.[42]

As the family played a crucial role in Puritan religious and social order, the process through which it was brought into being became increasingly important, and carefully defined. The degree to which Puritan ideals represented a rupture in established order can be seen in the amount of time it took for widespread acceptance of the more formally enacted marriage contracts. It was not until 1753 that Lord Hardwicke's *Marriage Act* significantly altered marriage practices. This Act, which did not apply in Scotland, transferred '[t]he right to set up conditions for valid marriage from Church to State'[43], subsequently bringing what Stone identifies as 'coherence and logic to the laws governing marriage'.[44]

Empirical studies show that the bill's enactment affected primarily the upper and middle classes until the end of the nineteenth century although some working class marriages immediately conformed to Hardwicke's Act.[45] The Australian colonies again provided the arena for a major effort to affect the marital patterns of the ranks of the urban poor. Marsden's report was one of many which spoke of the reticence of the lower orders to marry. Governor King's report the same year made the same point, noting that only one-quarter of all adult women were married, over three-fifths of whom are free women who 'cohabit openly with one man'.[46]

In the interests of social order, and in keeping with the general notion of population management, from the end of the eighteenth century the British Colonial Office commenced a series of orders to Australian governors, that legal marriage was to be promoted among all levels of society.[47] In 1807, for example, Governor Bligh received a very curt letter, which noted that '[y]ou appear to be sensible of the importance of promoting the increase in marriages in the colony'. It then went on to admonish the governor for his failure to pursue seriously any scheme to implement this aim: 'undoubtedly, the very great proportion which appears to exist of illegitimate in comparison with legitimate children, leads to the conclusion that a proper system for advancing this grand object has not been adopted'. The reason behind the apparent failure, according to the Colonial Office, was the ordinarily acceptable application of utilitarian notions of costing the viability of an exercise. So, whereas utilitarian notions of calculating a reasonable wage could be based upon the amount of food the body needed to labour and reproduce labour power, and the amount of punishment exerted on the convict body was calculated by the levels of punishment which the body could accept, and still live; in the case of morality no such logic was to apply. As the governor was informed:

> I have understood that sufficient pains have not been taken with respect to the Disposal of the female convicts on their first arrival in the Colony, and that they have been indented to improper Persons in order to ease, as soon as possible, the Expense of supporting them by Government Rations. The impolicy of this System is so obvious that I trust you will not persevere in it, but in every case endeavour to make the Reformation of the Female Convict and her regular Settlement by marriage a Consideration

superior to the saving, for any short period, the expense of maintaining her.[48]

For the next half century, Australian governors instituted a range of practices designed to increase the incidence of legal marriage in their colonies. In the 1810s, for example, Governor Macquarie withdrew from women the inheritance rights to property owned by *de facto* husbands. During the mid-1820s, Governor Darling initiated a scheme rewarding female convicts who married with free work days, and waived the fee for the marriage bans for all convicts. To other women who married, he granted marriage portions of land, provided they were 'of good character . . . born in wedlock . . . [and were not] the children of actual convicts'.[49] Through the following years, the state of marriage continued to preoccupy middle class administrators, and a series of Select Committees looked into the problem of low marriage rates among the lower orders. In 1857–58, Victoria's *Select Committee into the Laws affecting the Solemnisation of Marriage* proposed a series of steps to assist in promoting the practice. Most witnesses conceded that the most positive steps would be to remove all obstacles from the path of those who did want to marry, such as lowering the age of majority to nineteen, as 'the growth of the human frame and mind is more rapid here than at home'; allowing a married sister or brother to stand in as guardians; allowing marriage without a ring; reducing the amount of notice necessary before marriage could take place; allowing marriage by registrars; and recognising a wider range of religious denominational marriages.[50]

Most of the witnesses were Anglican ministers who argued that impediments to marriage were bad for the morality of the colony but, they noted, it was not legal hindrances but rather a popular reluctance to marry which produced low marriage rates. As the Reverend Hetherington explained:

> I have experienced that there were instances in which marriage might not have been accomplished. I have got persons living in concubinage to marry; and I think, if I had allowed the man to go away, I might not have been able to get hold of him again.

The Reverend Andrew Ramsay pointed out that not only were colonists reluctant to marry, but also 'the violation of the marriage contract in this country, and the desertion of wives by their husbands, and the desertion of husbands by their wives, is truly awful'. As 90 per cent of these marriages had been solemnised in Britain, even the high desertion rate did not reflect a high marriage rate in Australia. This pattern was not unique to the Australian colonies but, rather, was typical of the urban working classes of all industrial societies. In Britain, for example, among the urban poor legal marriage was not the norm until the end of the nineteenth century.[51]

The colonial census reports, unlike private studies, and governors' reports, did include statistics on marital status until the 1840s, probably revealing more about the state of the new practice of census taking than accurately reflecting societal concerns.[52] It was not until 1881, three-quarters of a century after Marsden had detailed evidence of the trend, that the first census included data of the marital status of the population of the colonies.[53]

For the first four decades, at least, of its construction as a British settlement, the white population of the Australian colonies was one of the most observed, mapped and organised populations in the enlightened world. So far, this chapter has shown the types of behaviours which were considered to be meaningful indicators of the population: What type of population was growing in the Australian colonies? What types of morality? What levels of utility? What degrees of geographical mobility? As these questions were posed and answered by quasi-scientific modes of observing and interpreting behaviour, a complete representation of the population was emerging. But for all its detail the social facts were vague by late nineteenth century standards. No attention was given to class, for example, and questions of professions and skills were asked only in order to measure the utility of the population as a unit, not to explore its various distinct levels.

The idea of dissecting the population to know its internal dynamics was essential before clear notions of class divisions could be ascertained. This idea was emerging as British authorities sought, and were supplied with, information regarding where various groups of individuals, particularly females, were living after embarkation, how they were conducting themselves and details of their marital status. Through these questions a form of knowing was emerging. These detailed surveys were the precursors to the discipline of sociology (or at least the empiricist British version of it[54]) which sought to know and record the mechanical structures and relations *inside* the population. The social space existing within the population was, in the process, being reconceptualised as 'society'. It is society which is divided by class, not population.

Commencing with the view that perfect knowledge was possible, and preoccupied with an anxiety that the observed were the unknown, social surveys, the precursors to sociology, became a growth industry in the 1840s. Rhetoric and perceptions once confined to explorations of the globe, such as the term 'terra incognita', during this period, were adopted to refer to the social conditions of the urban slums.[55] An 1842 text by the social commentator James Grant asserted that the 'great mass of the metropolitan community are as ignorant of the destitution and distress which prevail in large districts of London . . . as if the wretched creatures were living in the very centre of Africa'.[56] Henry Mayhew's four-volume *London Labour and the London Poor*, published in 1861, prefaced his search of the social relations and behaviours of the societies of London's urban slums with the same reference to their unknown qualities. His aim in gathering data together as a coherent body of knowledge was:

> . . . supplying information concerning a large body of persons, of whom the public had less knowledge than of the most distant tribes of the earth—the government population returns not even numbering them among the inhabitants of the kingdom; and as adducing facts so extraordinary, that the traveller in the undiscovered country of the poor must, like Bruce, until his stories are corroborated by after investigators, be content to live under the imputation of telling such tales, as travellers are generally supposed to delight in.[57]

Mayhew's preface is particularly interesting for the sideswipe he took at the official census procedures which had failed to supply any information about, or even record the existence of, the non-respectable working class. It was, accordingly, specifically with the intention of casting light on the dark regions of society that the social surveys of British slums commenced, the best known being Mayhew's *London Labour and the London Poor* (1861–62); W.C. Mearns' *The Bitter Cry of Outcast London* (1883)[58]; and Charles Booth's *Life and Labour of the People in London* (1902–3).[59]

The social surveys of Australia also announced their quest as one which would explore a dark continent. This was to be expected for, as Graeme Davison and David Dunstan have shown, the journalists and investigators of the slums in the Australian colonies styled themselves on Mayhew and his contemporaries.[60] William Stanley Jevons' 1858 study, *A Social Survey of Australian Cities*, was the most sociological of the private studies.[61] Jevons had arrived in Australia at the age of nineteen to take up a position as assayer in the newly formed Sydney Royal Mint.[62] While in New South Wales he developed an interest in social sciences. In 1858, when he was twenty-three— one year younger than Engels when he wrote *The Conditions of the Working Class in England*—Jevons completed his study of social classes in Sydney. During the following two years, Henry

Parkes chaired the Select Committee on the Condition of the Working Classes of the Metropolis, a New South Wales government initiative, set up with the stated Fabian aim of ameliorating the conditions revealed by the survey.[63] Of the journalistic slum reporters, Davison and Dunstan detail the roles of Frank Fowler whose *Southern Lights and Shadows* was published in 1859; the novelist B.L. Fargeon's *Grif: a Tale of Australian Life*, an 1866 novel styled on Dickens' studies of the British poor; John Stanley James, better known as Julian Thomas, who from the 1870s to the 1890s investigated the living conditions and morality of the urban and rural poor; and Marcus Clarke.[64] James' reports appeared regularly in first the *Argus*, then the *Age* and finally the *Leader*.[65] Two books appeared under the pen-name J. Thomas: in 1876 *The Vagabond Papers* appeared[66] and, in 1877, *Sketches of Melbourne Life in Light and Shade*[67] continued his commentary on the Australian poor. That same decade Marcus Clarke also began to publish commentaries on colonial society in both the *Argus* and the *Age* and, although he often focused on what he perceived to be the vulgarity of the *nouveau riche*, his *Sketches of Melbourne Low Life*, published in the *Argus* in February 1868, followed the journalistic tradition of James and Mayhew in focusing on the life of the poor and outcast.[68]

The epistemological shift through which the omnipresence of God was replaced by the presence of Man ushered in a whole new economy of understanding. It made possible the view that nature could be tamed, that no secrets were beyond the reasoning power of rational thought, and that only one answer existed to every question. The notion of population, the body of Man as a group, was born in this shift, and understanding of the management practices at work in the Australian colonies can be contextualised within the birth of the discourses of population. The idea of total knowledge, of scrutinising each and every inhabitant of the Australian colonies, reflects the enlightenment view that perfect knowledge was possible. Through the quest to know all data about the population, a new object of inquiry was born. The nineteenth century notions of society, and sociology, reflects a different set of preoccupations from those of demography.

2 Two working classes

Until the middle of the nineteenth century reference to the inhabitants of the urban slums was made by using the term 'the lower orders'. Within this umbrella term were many overlapping substrata. In the middle of the century, during a series of social surveys, the inhabitants of poor non-middle class areas were referred to as 'the working classes'. Inquirers were in agreement that two, or sometimes three, distinct groups made up the working classes. This chapter looks at the way the distinction was made between the groups within 'the working classes'. It argues that the utilitarian style of reasoning which had equated behaviour with type and which had previously dominated demographic surveys was being replaced by the emerging psychological style of reasoning—this brought into play less visible factors than behaviour, such as intelligence and sexuality. It shows that even before psychology was constructed as a legitimate science at the end of the nineteenth century the methods through which it organised knowledge, such as reading faces and eliciting confessions, were being used in mid-century studies of the working classes.

The mid-nineteenth century social surveys which discursively constructed both working classes were conducted in Europe, Britain and the colonies, using a homogeneous range of behaviours as categorising items and the same interpretations of those behaviours. The uniformity is a feature of rational thought. Locked within the confidence of the enlightenment project, these explorers of an unknown which existed within walking distance of their homes, could commence their quest, already knowing the range of questions they would ask and, certain too, that only one answer awaited their every query. While convict surveys had, in distinguishing between types, depended upon the social categories of the moral and the immoral, the social surveys commenced with a reliance upon another related term, respectability, to distinguish between the various ranks of the lower orders. This is a notion which included morality, but also brought into play the observable factor of intemperance.

Organising the lower orders into two distinct separate classes involved identifying patterns of behaviour, and prising out the 'truth' thereby revealed, in a scientific method following set steps. First, the observer noted the behaviour of the observed and then asked the question 'Is the behaviour true or false?', or to put it another way 'Are environmental factors altering the behaviour in such a way that the behaviour is not truly representative of the person's type?'. Making allowances for the environmental distortion, the observer then placed the person, and their family, into their correct class. This was the enlightened, utilitarian style of knowing society.

By using an either respectable or non-respectable dichotomy the first social surveyors forged a path through the unknown morass of the lower orders, dividing them into more accessible, although still large, groupings. Henry Morley's mid-1850s British publication *The Quiet Poor* is a typical example of the manner in which the surveys commenced the representation of the poor into different types. He found in one part of Bethnal Green:

> . . . not the workhouse, criminal, or begging poor, but the 'quiet poor'—a stagnant and politically supine community of some fourteen thousand weavers and hawkers, sunk below the level even of discontent, each family occupying with dreadful respectability its own little room in which people out-numbered all the other objects in it.[1]

Using the scientific method, Morley declared that the impact of the environment upon these people was obscuring their true types. The respectable, he advised, could 'conceivably be raised by degrees, their finer feelings—brutalised though they were—could be aroused', and something could be done to 'raise them a rung in life'.[2]

The work of Frederick Engels and Karl Marx did not refer to the rungs of life, nor represent the urban slums as a foreign place, but rather focused upon pointing to and noting the role of the players in the capitalist system. It was their joint concern to name and illustrate the political origins of the range of types who could be grouped into either side of the dichotomy among the proletariat, which in their work, as in other social theorists' texts, was based upon a range of behaviours. While Engels described the ideal of respectability as 'a most repulsive thing' and a false consciousness 'bred into the bones of the [British] workers',[3] nonetheless he, too, divided the working classes along similar lines.

Undoubtedly, for both Engels and Marx, there were two types of proletarian, the labourers who sold their labour in the market and the *lumpenproletariat*—'the "dangerous class", the social scum, that passively rotting mass thrown off by the lowest layers of old society'.[4] In the *Eighteenth Brumaire of Louis Bonaparte* Marx explained just who the 'dangerous class' were and where they had come from. They comprised:

> . . . vagabonds, discharged soldiers, discharged jailbirds, escaped galley slaves, swindlers, mountebanks, *lazzaroni*, pickpockets, tricksters, gamblers, maquereaus, brothel keepers, porters, *literati*, organ-grinders, rag-pickers, knife grinders, tinkers, beggars.[5]

In Australia, Henry Parkes' Select Committee report of 1860 also subscribed to the orthodoxy that there were two distinct classes within the society of the urban slums.[6] There were the bottom group of squalidly housed intemperate paupers whose neglected children roamed the streets and who were perceived to be the major cause of their own distress, and another group whose plight was the product, not of their own immorality, but of the economic climate, extremely high rent and poorly constructed houses. Sydney's accommodation was, according to the Health Officer, 'worse than in any part of the world that I have seen—worse than in London'.[7] These latter people, it was thought, would have had a tendency to self-betterment were it not for external factors.

Evidence from one witness, Dr Isaac Aaron, who had been 'in direct contact' with the poor for 'upwards of twenty years', categorised the poor into three groups: the respectable, a middle group who could go up or down depending upon environmental conditions, and the hopeless non-respectables. This lowest group lived 'in all manner of holes and corners in the most dilapidated places, paying little or no rent, and existing no-one knows how'. They lived, he believed, 'more like beasts of the field or pigs'. This group was 'a rather numerous class in Sydney', and many of them were either 'in their own persons' or 'the descendants of, those who have been prisoners of the Crown'. The beast-like existence of these people was a theme returned to by many commentators, who saw among them evidence of unreason which was threatening to social order and which undermined that cornerstone of social stability, the family. This theme will be returned to in the next chapter, which focuses on the modern family.

The central ground between the bestial non-respectables and the reasoning poverty of the respectables was occupied in Aaron's scenario by a middle group who 'generally get their living more or less by labour, sometimes employed, sometimes not, according to circumstances'. His third group were the respectable working class, a group which:

> . . . consists of those who, by industry and frugality, have been able to save sufficient either to rent a decent house or to build one for themselves. This I am happy to say, is a tolerably numerous class in Sydney; but even here there is something wanting in the mode in which houses are constructed, even when building for themselves. They want the knowledge to construct them with the best regard to bodily health and for decency.

That there were two distinct working classes, albeit with a potential middle group which hovered between the two, was widely, and indeed probably universally, accepted among social surveys of the mid-nineteenth century. Similar congruency of opinion can be found in the discussions of the environmental factors which obscured the truth of the observed groupings' rightful categorisation. Aaron's evidence, for example, typified the trends identified within Benthamite logic:

> The want of proper accommodation has a direct effect on the moral sense of the occupants, because they are obliged to do everything in public you may say, and the state of bodily feeling which is induced by the absence of sanitary conditions no doubt induces many of these people to resort to intemperance. They sleep in ill-ventilated and over-crowded apartments—get up in the morning, especially in the summer time, unrefreshed, and want something to rouse them. It is not, therefore, to be wondered at that they should go to the public house for a morning dram. [They would] if they had the opportunity, live in a better condition.[8]

The factors identified here were the inability, not the desire, to demarcate some human functions as private, to be confined away from public gaze, in rooms designed especially for that purpose. Due to environmental conditions, the social surveyors argued, these people were 'obliged' to carry out all aspects of their lives in public—although it was other inhabitants of the living space, usually their family, who made up this 'public'. The implication of Aaron's reference to intemperance was that the indignity of their forced public existence led them to drink to both blunt the shame of their lack of privacy and also as a stimulant in the absence of proper sleeping arrangements. While Aaron focused upon the forced public nature of the lives of the impoverished respectables, other witnesses noted that cleanliness was also being kept out of their reach by unfavourable environmental conditions. This was, for example, an opinion offered by the surgeon, Mr Roberts, whose position as a medico seemed to qualify him to speculate that:

> . . . it would be utterly impossible for a housewife to keep a bad house tidy. When she is placed in such a house, she soon ceases to strive to preserve order and cleanliness in her house; the husband does not care about coming home to his wife; she becomes careless and neglects her children.[9]

At the other extreme of publicness were the street-dwelling, beast-like non-respectables, who carried out all aspects of their lives, not just in the public gaze of their families, but in the true public gaze of all other inhabitants of the street. These people were represented as having no family ties or familial (meaning motherly) emotions, nor any sense of shame. They left their children to raise themselves in the streets:

> The evidence abundantly shows that a large class exist to whom the possession of parents is of no value in giving direction to their lives, and who are growing up to be an encumbrance and a curse to society.[10]

The report noted that 'the streets of Sydney are infested by a large number of vagrant children, or children entirely neglected by their parents; and some of the revelations of juvenile depravity are appalling and almost incredible'.[11] While little detail was supplied of this 'incredible juvenile depravity', other contemporary reports were prepared to be more specific. In 1859, for example, the Australian *Medical and Surgical Review* published an article which stated that the children of 'the lower orders' were educated 'not in knowledge but in vice and crime'. So horrified was this author, like many early nineteenth century commentators of the urban poor, that he described these children as 'born whores'. 'Their parents', he wrote:

> . . . are the offscourings of the earth—the first words a daughter hears are those of cursing and blasphemy; the only example her childhood sees is that of obscenity and vice, such youth is an apt learner; and, at the age of ten or twelve, she may be both a prostitute and a thief—her lapsed state having proved rather a simple progress than a fall. [12]

Alongside the observation that the non-respectables were identifiable by the absence of the family unit was the overriding
assumption that they also displayed an active desire to continue
with their present type of life. In the case of women, the surveyors
repeatedly gave examples where they claimed to enjoy their lives.
A typical case study was presented by one witness who:

> . . . met a girl, now about sixteen, far advanced in pregnancy,
> with her second child, and who must have commenced her career
> of profligacy as early as thirteen years of age . . . She . . . was
> longing, to use her own expression, to be 'upon the batter,' and
> lamented, in the most revolting terms, that her conditions at
> present prevented her plying her disgusting trade.[13]

For both men and women, the public nature of their existence
was read as deliberate, a display both of animal-like unreasoning
natures and also, paradoxically, of reasoned political intent to
disrupt ordered society. They were, the social theorists agreed,
dirty, loud, unmotherly and intemperate through choice, and it
was this choice, this exercise of will, which determined that they
were truly non-respectable and, as historians of charity have
noted, undeserving of either Christian pity or help.[14]

At this stage it is useful to point out the patterns in differentiation which were being presented. It is possible to see the
distinction presented here as merely one of degree. The entire
category of the working classes could be mapped on a scale in
which at one end is the private, sober, clean, industrious and
motherly, while at the other is the inebriated, public, dirty,
unmotherly and lazy and, in between, the various different levels
would be positioned. This would simply be a scale of behaviours,
according to utilitarian logic. It would be an accurate representation of the social theorists' distinctions between one type and
the other, were it not for their assertion that a clear break existed,
at some point on the continuum, which clearly placed the
observed in one class or the other. On what grounds was such
a break decided? It was on the element of choice. One group,
the argument went, chose to be dirty, lazy, etcetera, and the
other would rather not be. Along with this perception, that it
was free will which distinguished between the types, was the
assumption that the choice was the product of *natural* predispo-
sition. The non-respectable are naturally antisocial and immoral.
Yet, the idea of 'the natural' played no role in utilitarian
reasoning, for it requires a notion of invisible forces, such as
intelligence, at work within the individual body of Man. In fact,
the dichotomy of the natural and the unnatural is the bedrock
upon which psychological reasoning rests.

The natural and the unnatural were the main characters in the social sciences of the twentieth century. The idea that each and every person is subject to natural forces plays a central role in the application of the notion of sexuality, and it is appropriate at this point to leave the social surveys and explain the emergence of the notion of sexuality, before returning to show how such ideas can be found in the separation of the two working classes.

Before the intervention of Michel Foucault, sexuality was widely assumed to have been a meaningful category across time and cultures. Foucault's multivolume *History of Sexuality* has, at the very least, problematised that assumption.[15] Both the word, and the notion, are, he points out, nineteenth century constructions. The difference between sexuality and earlier understandings of the range of subjects related to sexual activity and urges, is dependent upon a move away from the central location of anatomy, or genitalia, in understandings of the sexual. The *Oxford English Dictionary* locates the first use of the modern meaning of sexuality in J.M. Duncan's *Diseases of Women* of 1879, in which he noted, 'In removing the ovaries, you do not necessarily destroy sexuality in a woman'. Duncan articulated a completely new idea, that sexuality was not dependent upon anatomy, and that removing the organs of sex did not strip a person of the hidden essence that was sexuality.[16] The idea of gender identity disorders began to appear in medical texts late in the nineteenth century, only when a separation of genital sex from sexuality was occurring, and only when utilitarian styles of reasoning were being joined by psychiatric styles.[17] Whereas sexual identity was based only on observable sexual anatomy, sexuality brought into play the non-observable phenomena of feelings, sensations, urges, and a whole economy of the psychic .

Sexuality was, and is still, a 'thing'—an aspect of Man. From late in the nineteenth century it became possible to talk about sexuality, as a concept independent of the body, and the individual. At the same time, the individual became identified by her or his particular type of sexuality or, in Foucault's words, became sexualised. This priorisation of sexuality, as a locating or fixing tool, meant concurrently that sexuality was constructed as a thing with a presence of its own. The homosexual, for example, was identified as being the bearer of, or driven by, a particular type of sexuality.[18] The prostitute was the victim of another family of types.[19] Black women were the bearers of yet another pattern, or family, of sexuality's many varied deviations[20] while childhood sexuality occupied a particularly complex place in these discourses.[21] Before sexuality, sexual acts and activities were perceived in a variety of historically specific ways. For example, the

Christian notion of 'the flesh' holds sexual urges to be driving forces. Humans could only battle to control these urges of the flesh. But there was nothing specific or individualistic about them—a particular person did not have a specific urge which identified him or her as a person subject to X-urge, while another might be subject to Y-urge. During the eighteenth century, sexual activity had been exactly that—an act. For example, although sodomy had long been a sin and a crime, up until the end of the eighteenth century its perpetrator had simply been a man who had committed a criminal act. In the nineteenth century, however, a man who engaged in sodomy with another man was reconceptualised as a 'homosexual', a person identified by a particular type of sexuality, indeed a 'species' of sexuality.

Within the new concerns of sexuality there appeared an attendant economy of punishment. Previous notions of sexual urges, such as the flesh, had been policed by a dichotomous understanding of the lawful and the unlawful. Certain sexual acts, within the eyes of the policing agency of the church, fell within the range of lawful behaviour while others were outside, such as the earlier example of sodomy. As the next chapter will examine, from the middle ages, the church produced increasingly minute lists of that which was lawful and that which was not, focusing upon marital relations rather than sexual relations outside of the marital contract. Within a history of the flesh a whole pharmacopoeia of virility or pleasure enhancing substances had existed but the use of these compounds was unlawful.[22]

But within a history of sexuality, what is important is not the lawful and unlawful, but rather the natural and unnatural. Any departure from normality involves a deviation from the unchallengeable laws of the natural functioning of Man. Within the discourse of sexuality, deviation requires 'treatment', not punishment, for the person is secondary to the sexuality. The sexuality, the particular perversion, has a presence, a space or reality of its own. Although it is the person, the pervert, who must be treated, it is the sexuality, the perversion, which is the real subject of medical attention.

The idea of natural predispositions was the unwritten agenda behind the suggested solutions to the problems facing the respectable poor, in Parkes' inquiry. Solutions were on two levels—those designed to allow the respectable poor to rise above their distressed condition and those designed to attack institutional poverty. The first set were 'increased means of public education, greater sanitary provisions for the regulation of buildings, more rational modes of popular recreation, and more active sympathy in the intercourse of classes'. The macro-solutions called for an end to 'mal-administration of the public lands'; a revision of the taxation system to direct taxation with 'the burden [to be] borne in just proportion to the ability to bear it, and the advantages enjoyed for which it is imposed'. These were solutions designed to provide the political and infrastructural environment through which the respectables would be enabled to modify their behaviour, so that it would fall within the bounds of respectability, with its attendant requirements of privacy, affective familial ties, motherly guardianship of children, and cleanliness within that middle class shrine, the home.

The solutions for the non-respectables, however, assumed a completely different set of priorities. In general, any action directed towards them was aimed at eradicating their public displays on the streets, in the public houses and brothels. Parkes devoted very little space to solutions of the problem of the non-respectables, advising only briefly that the government should hasten 'the establishment of a reformatory for juvenile delinquents [and] . . . an Asylum for destitute children along with the establishment of a Nautical school'. Beyond these practical suggestions, he could add only the vague assertion that 'some more effective means should be devised for the suppression of the odious traffic in vice'.[23]

The shift from moral divisions to divisions based upon inner essences, such as sexuality and intelligence, brought with it a different way of reacting to the observed. There was, in short, a complete realignment from the restrictive management of deviation to an entire economy of regulation. During the history of the flesh, the law and the church could punish the individual who deviated, and lock up the perpetual offender, without the action reflecting upon any other person. The person who committed a crime was punished and no-one else bore any of the guilt of that person's act. However, through the deployment of sexuality, deviant sexuality has repercussions for others also. Once the behaviour of a pervert reveals that a type of perversion exists, the search must be carried out for other bearers or victims of the perversion. Each and every individual who shares that perversion is capable of that same behaviour—thus each and every one of them constitutes a danger.

Detention and incarceration, as suggested here, were posited as the strategies for dealing with the non-respectable working class, from the first moment of their articulation. Raymond Evans, using the example of the colony of Queensland, identifies the *Contagious Diseases Act* (1868), and the *Inebriate Institutions Act* (1896) as key pieces of legislation in effecting this purpose.[24] Similarly, it can be seen that the 'solutions' offered by Parkes for dealing with the problem of the non-respectable working class, with its attendant range of unnatural feelings and urges, were aimed, not at eradicating their behaviours through alteration, but at removing from the agenda of social theory any discursive articulation of the class. Through a policy of what Evans has termed an 'out of sight, out of mind' approach, these people, he points out, were the inmates of the destitute and benevolent asylums, the lunatic asylums, the Lock Hospitals, the prisons, the children's homes, and the Lying-in Hospitals. They disappeared from the 'sight' of one group of social theorists, the sociologists, but were very much in the 'minds' of another. Indeed the practitioners of the mind, through those sciences which were created through psychological reasoning, took over this discursive grouping as their exclusive subjects. As Evans points out, however, these patients were given very little psychological or medical attention or treatment and the conditions of their incarceration conformed more to styles of punishment than to styles of 'caring'.[25]

Sexuality, and the style of reasoning which made its emergence possible, played a key role in the articulation of the respectable working class as the only working class. The deployment of the notion also shaped the range of suitable treatments of the problem of the non-respectables. For, while the patterns of privacy and cleanliness described by witnesses relied solely upon utilitarian notions of observation and equating behaviour and type, it is possible to distinguish another style of knowing running through these same surveys. The psychological style of reasoning also brought into play the possibility of reading the psyche of an individual though the face. For the first time, during the nineteenth century, the face was perceived to be a window to the inner essences of Man, sexuality and intelligence being those with which the twentieth century was most preoccupied.

Arnold Davidson's work draws attention to one of the earliest medico-sexual texts to make use of the psychiatric style of reasoning, D.M. Rozier's 1825 tract on female masturbation. Whereas earlier medical treatments of the subject of ambiguous or abnormal sexuality had drawn attention, and illustrated the genital area, Rozier's frontispiece features:

> . . . a drawing of a young woman. Her head is stiffly tilted toward her left, and her eyes are rolled back, unfocused, the pupils barely visible. She is a habitual masturbator. The depicted portion of her body looks normal, but we can see her psyche, her personality, disintegrating before our eyes. She stands as an emblem of psychiatric disorders, so distinct from her anatomically represented predecessors.[26]

The face became a crucial site through which the invisible presences within the body showed themselves. By the late nineteenth century, Doctor James Shaw entitled one of his articles 'Facial Expression as One of the Means of Diagnosis and Prognosis in Mental Disease'. The face, he explained in this text, should be examined in repose and in animation during conversation. The practitioner should:

> . . . watch the changes of facial expression carefully, or to note their absence . . . Attention to these simple directions, together with a general knowledge of the facial signs given below, will enable any practitioner to refer most cases to one of the ten great symptomatic groups into which I have divided mental cases.[27]

Victorian psychiatrists often analysed patients using only asylum photographs. Without ever meeting or speaking with the subjects of the photographs, they constructed entire case histories and surmised the type of moral lives they had led. It was, according to Elaine Showalter, mostly women who were studied in this manner.[28]

In 1858 William Stanley Jevons' study, *A Social Survey of Australian Cities*, called upon this methodology of reading faces in his description of the extreme depravity of the people of Sydney's urban slums.[29] His description of the non-respectable elements of the working classes was based almost exclusively upon female sexual behaviour. They were a people for whom he felt no sympathy, being, in his scenario, totally to blame for their own distress. They were a vicious and unnatural class, among whom:

> . . . some female inhabitant . . . is punished almost everyday at the Police Court for offences chiefly connected with prostitution. I walked through these miserable alleys which are quite shut out from common view and almost form blind alleys. No more secure and private retreat for vice is offered.[30]

Jevons' horror at these 'slovenly' and 'repulsive' people is nowhere more obvious than in his descriptions of the young women, whose immorality and depravity he measured by references to a reading of their faces:

> One young but intoxicated woman, whose wicked dissipated face was further swollen by a black eye and a bruised swollen forehead, presented as striking a picture of the depths of vice as ever I saw.[31]

Just as Oscar Wilde was later to do in *Portrait of Dorian Gray*, Jevons presented the idea that dissipation can be worn on faces, and that the face represents a lasting map of immoral acts and behaviours.

Peter Botsman's study of the conceptualisation of venereal disease during the nineteenth and early twentieth centuries has also illustrated this perception that faces act as maps of hidden perversions. Botsman notes a letter from the Comptroller General's Office explaining the reason for the detention of Alice O in the Biloela Reformatory:

> . . . some time ago this woman was seen by an officer of Darlinghurst Gaol washing herself and drinking from a fountain in one of the Public Parks.

Although a remarkable reason for incarceration, the factor which condemned Alice as an outcast, and a pervert, was her face. Hand-written on the bottom of the letter was the explanation: 'This woman is of the prostitute class and she has cancer of the face'.[32] Botsman notes of this damning letter:

> She had no need of an elaborate record. There was not even any need to know her age, her name, the number of convictions. Neitenstein's note sufficed. She was a prostitute. Her record was her face.[33]

This reading of faces can be seen in the context of the cross-over from purely utilitarian methods of observation, which permit only observable data, to that of psychological methods, which measure non-observable phenomena. The face, in the changing methodologies and styles of reasoning, remained as a visible representation, an observable and readable object, which allowed visibility of the newly conceptualised non-visible essences which had begun to assume importance.

Apart from the reading of faces which is present in the social surveys, suspicion of sexuality, particularly female sexuality, combined with anxiety about male unreason, lies at the core of the late nineteenth century incorporation of patterns of alcohol consumption into social theorists' separation of the two working classes. While patterns of cleanliness, notions of privacy, and evidence of familial ties were used to divide the respectable from the non-respectable, the role of alcohol consumption was also frequently mentioned, especially in relation to forms of action appropriate to ameliorate the situation of the observed. Charitable organisations, for example, would not assist the distressed and pauperised if there was evidence that their condition had been caused by intemperance. For example, the Brisbane Charity Organisation Society reported that out of ninety cases who had applied for help, seventy-two had been refused due to a combination of drunkenness, laziness, roving dispositions and dishonesty.[34]

Nineteenth century surveys interlinked the twin evils of non-respectability and intemperance. Consequently, inquiries into the sale of alcohol were inevitably arenas for comment upon the sexual behaviour of the urban poor, simultaneously contributing to the discursive process of categorising them into two distinct groups. The 1867 Report of the Royal Commission into the Wine and Spirits Sale Statute in the colony of Victoria was ostensibly appointed to inquire and report upon 'the operation and effect of the Wine and Spirit Sale Statute, No. 227' in order to determine 'its effects upon the quality of the wine, beer, and spirits supplied to the public'.[35] Publicans had been complaining about what they saw as unfair competition from 'low houses' and other proprietors, such as grocers, who were also allowed to sell beer. While the commissioners did find that the respectable houses had a legitimate grievance, their findings had little to do with restrictive trade practices. The report devoted several pages to explaining that the two different types of venues attracted two different types of clientele. The low and vicious were being allowed to gather and display their offensive behaviour in the cheap houses, and this, rather than any economic considerations, was the central concern of the report.

The central nature of the concern with morals, rather than economics, was apparent in the type of witnesses sought, and also with the priority given to particular evidence. Evidence had been sought from publicans and the variety of other proprietors then authorised to sell liquor under the existing statute, as well as from 'those who might be presumed to be concerned about the laws relating to the sale of intoxicating drinks from a moral and religious point of view'. The evidence of the former was effectively dismissed in two sentences:

> The publicans condemned the license to grocers, who, in turn, maintained that the privilege of selling a single bottle had had a salutary effect. The wholesale dealers again were divided, just as their trade lay among grocers or publicans.[36]

The effect the relaxed laws were having upon the quality of the liquor was discussed in a half-page paragraph, which detailed that skimping on hops, combined with the warm temperatures, was producing a particularly powerful and debilitating beer in the colonies.

The rest of the report was devoted to the effect the liberal laws were having upon morals of the working classes. Indeed, the sole conclusion reached was summed up in one sentence,

'[w]e regret to inform Your Excellency that the universal conclusion arrived at, after two years' experience, is, that the existing
Act has operated most perniciously'.[37] The statute had greatly
exacerbated 'the tendency of the lower classes to congregate at
night in tap-rooms and public-house bars—which, in itself, is a
prolific source of dissipation and crime', and the commissioners
concluded that 'the closing of the smaller public-houses at ten
o'clock p.m. would have a salutary effect on the morals of the
population'.[38]

In the report's entirety only one example of the deleterious
effect the statute was having upon 'the morals of the population'
referred to men:

> Probably you have seen a respectable man suddenly vanish for a
> short time . . . about a month you see him again. The man has
> fallen, and you see what a state he has come to. He goes into a
> lower house than he has been accustomed to drink at; he cannot
> work, nor does he care what becomes of him, and the liquor he
> has been drinking, perhaps for not more than a fortnight, has had
> a worse effect upon him than what he has drunk for many years.
> The police have no power to have the liquor analysed.[39]

Even this single example of the 'fallen' respectable man bears a
striking similarity to examples of the 'fallen' respectable girl. A
man's fall away from reason could be brought about by both
female lasciviousness and alcoholic stupor. A girl's fall away from
chastity could result from whatever avenue was required to
weaken her hold on her sexual urges. This could be either
seduction or alcohol. Thus, to the Victorian social theorist, once
a woman had experienced sexual gratification she would be
insatiable. The chaste girl fell into prostitution. Giving evidence
to an 1887 Commission into Prisons, witness Dr Jackson testified
that 'single women who drink are most likely to gravitate
unchecked to the ranks of prostitution'. Examples of this view
can be found in most nineteenth century, and early twentieth
century, reports which discussed social order, punishment, crime,
or alcohol consumption.[40] The respectable man fell into inebriation, crime and eventually insanity. Both took their places among
the non-respectable, and unnatural, in the process.

The rest of the case studies were about women. Competition
among the grocers had resulted in inexpensive beer being avail-
able to working class women, the commissioners argued. This
meant that although mothers of poor families were reluctant to
be seen drinking in a public house, they could now indulge in
'secret drinking'. As a result 'the vice of intemperance [was]

extending among women'.[41] Giving evidence to support this finding, a police witness, Sergeant O'Reilly, stated that:

> I find more women half drunk during the day, when I go round to collect moneys and rates from the houses. I collect rates by warrant when they do not pay, and I generally go to the very poorest people, and I find that the women drink so much beer because there is so much competition among the beer houses that they sell it very cheap. If I go to those low places, I generally go as early as I can to get them sober, for in the after part of the day it is impossible to find them in a state of perfect sobriety . . . The women do not care what it is so long as it keeps their spirits up when they are washing and working, and so long as it intoxicates them.[42]

For the commissioners of the Wine and Spirit Sale Statute, female inebriation was problematical because, due to the ready availability of cheap beer, potentially chaste wives were enticed into immoral ways. The biggest problem, the commissioners found, was the dancing houses and saloons associated with the public houses. Here, young women were induced into a life of prostitution and crime. These places, the commissioners asserted, 'do not only harbour vicious persons but create them'.[43] The Police Magistrate of Sandhurst, Mr McLachlan, was one of a series of witnesses whose experiential opinion supported this view:

> Young girls are got in there, and children twelve and thirteen years of age, and they are led to prostitution, and every vice and crime. They are the nest and haunt of vice, a perfect pandemonium. Here they are a crying evil . . . I would prohibit them altogether if I could but I do not see my way to do that. They are a rendezvous for thieves, prostitutes, and every bad character, horse-stealers, burglars, and all those young rips.[44]

From the juridical view of the magistrate, to the medical view of the Chief Medical Officer, there was complete agreement that:

> A great number of young girls have come under my notice in the gaol, who state that the dancing saloons and night-licensed public-houses were the ruin of nearly all the young women about Melbourne who go astray.[45]

The final 'proof' of this came from the clergy, as the Reverend Mr Machie was called upon, and declared that he too had witnessed the ruin of young girls in just this manner:

> I found, in almost every case of young men and young women, that their course of crime began in those low public houses where there were casinos, dancing saloons, free-and-easies, and amusements of that sort. It was there chiefly that their career of

downward progress began. Multitudes of them have said that, but for these they never would been tempted to go aside from the paths of rectitude and virtue.[46]

The study concluded that the effect of what were perceived to be casual drinking laws was to exacerbate the behaviour of the non-respectable working class by providing them with a place to congregate, and to encourage the potentially respectable on a downward path. The overlaying of space with type was a characteristic of bourgeois ideology which will be returned to in chapter five. It can be seen here that various types were seen to congregate in various places and that the level of depravity of the place determined the level of depravity of the people. In seeking to rectify this, chapter five shows, bourgeois reformers constructed their own network of spaces, with distinct types of reformatories and rooms for distinct types of people. In identifying the dancing saloons as 'a rendezvous for thieves, prostitutes, and every bad character, horse-stealers, burglars, and all those young rips' the report identified and categorised a subgroup—an undesirable, criminal and lazy class among the urban poor. This description of them furthermore closely resembled Marx's and Engels' description of the *lumpenproletariat*.

Utilitarian reasoning and the scientific method provided the base from which two distinct working classes emerged. It is also possible to see, within the social surveys, the new psychological style of reasoning beginning to permeate ways of interpreting the observed. It is clearest when witnesses struggled to describe the non-respectables, for it was not their behaviour which identified them—rather than their being represented as *behaving* in a certain way, they were identified as *being* a certain way. It can be seen, therefore, that the singling out of this grouping for special attention commenced with their very articulation. They were discursively constructed through reasoning that required the new psychological preoccupations to emerge, for their difference was, in the first place, a depravity which pervaded their total being, irretrievably damning them.

Just as they were articulated through psychological reasoning, albeit in a very early form, they became the natural objects for psychological treatment. When the habits of the non-respectable working class came under the gaze of psychological sciences, it led to a reclassification of their behaviours, not as symptomatic of immorality but of sickness. They became the feeble-minded of eugenics[47], the criminally insane of psychology[48], the sexually psychotic of psychoanalysis, the sex-killers of the popular press, and the bludgers of the labour movement[49]—and, in all cases, the abnormal, against which the normal could be identified.

By the second decade of the twentieth century sociological texts had stopped discussing or even referring to the non-respectables, and for all but medical and juridical experts they no longer seemed to exist. From this time sociologists were concerned with a working class that was clearly the respectables, despite the fact that no social theory existed to explain how, within a period which covers no more than twenty years, sociologists who had been in complete agreement that two distinct classes existed, could now refer to only one. The non-respectable had become the objects of medicine, and had disappeared from the discourses of sociology and social theory. By contrast, fiction writers continued to represent characters who were clearly the non-respectable working class. They, and their subjects, were in no doubt that this fundamentally nineteenth century grouping still lived their lives in urban slums. For example, William Dick's *A Bunch of Ratbags* has a central figure whose family and friends are clearly representatives of a non-respectable working class community. Living in overcrowded slums, with chickens and rabbits crowded into tiny inner-city backyards, their post-World War II existence was remarkably similar to Henry Parkes' mid-century subjects of the previous century.[50]

In the late 1970s, when social history began to pry into the lives of the poor and powerless, the spotlight again fell on people who were clearly non-respectables. Janet McCalman's study of Richmond contrasts the attitudes and behaviours of the respectable and non-respectable who were living within close proximity of each other in the inner city. The study is primarily about the respectable working class, among whom morality 'was worked out on a very public stage. The rich community life of Richmond inevitably limited privacy—just one slip from respectability and everyone knew about it'.[51]

By contrast, the non-respectables make a brief appearance in McCalman's book, in the form of the 'famous Richmond family, the Eddys':

> Billy Eddy, however, spent a lifetime at war with the police. In May 1938 he was sentenced to eight months' gaol after a fight outside St James' Hall . . . Seven others were convicted with Billy that time. Two months later his father was again in Court and was convicted of assault with a beer bottle.[52]

In the 1990s, spectacularly violent crimes, such as the tragic Anita Cobby case, were clearly presenting not just a few depraved individuals but an entire strata. The attitudes and standards of behaviour deemed acceptable by the men who had committed the murder and their friends (including females) was outlined in the press and in a subsequent book about the case. It presented a picture of violence, public sexual acts and recreational assaults which mirrored nineteenth century surveys of the non-respectables.[53]

Whereas, as the last chapter discussed, utilitarian notions relied exclusively upon juxtaposing behaviour with type, the style of reasoning which identified a species of sexuality, a perversion, and then characterises the bearer, the pervert, as a type of person, also brought into play a whole other range of ways of identifying types. The human sciences which developed as a result of this new epistemological tradition focused upon the individual far more clearly than those which relied upon utilitarian notions. The truth about type could be found through prising out the secrets of the mind, and the body, and not, as the social surveyors asserted, in considering the environmental or social factors through which the person existed. The sciences of the individual included eugenics, psychology, psychiatry, sexology and criminology, and from the end of the nineteenth century, that is from the time that the working class was articulated as a single, knowable entity, discussion and intervention into the class was framed within the reasoning of some or all of these sciences.

It can be seen, therefore, that during the nineteenth century the exploration of society became a quest of the human sciences and, in the process, the unmapped, unknown regions of the urban poor were singled out for particularly detailed scrutiny. From the urban poor emerged the working classes, to then be divided into two distinct groupings, based upon a combination of observable behaviours according to the utilitarian styles of knowing of sociology, and the more obtuse patterns of sexual deviance and weak intellect of the psychological sciences. By the end of the century the respectable working class alone were left in the public gaze of sociologists, to be discussed and analysed, and of charity groups, to be assisted; the other working class had disappeared from the discussions and concerns of these groupings. In a process which sociologists do not discuss, they simply seemed to become un-history, for no theorists detailed the stages through which two working classes became one. The non-respectable working classes emerged briefly from this time, as later chapters will show, but only as the sick and unnatural, and public reference to their behaviours and pathologies became relevant only by way of illustrating how their deviance contrasted with natural and desirable behaviour.

3 Sexuality and the modern family

Of the social indicators which separated the two working classes it was the new construct, sexuality, more than that of intelligence, which relegated people to the ranks of the unnatural and which made them suitable cases for treatment rather than punishment. This chapter points to the indicators, within middle class reports, which show that sexuality was the principal concept around which information about the dichotomy was organised. The period of time covered is 1850 to 1920 as this was when the first wave of modern reports were written about working class families giving heavy emphasis to sexual behaviour in general, and incest in particular. During this period most major reports into the lives of the urban poor included direct or implied reference to incest. These surveys were, furthermore, specifically referring to a particular form of incest—sexual intercourse between father, or father substitute, and daughter (brother–sister sexual relations were also considered but to a far less extent). This was not the form of incest which, in early modern times, had been considered of primary importance. The canonical courts very rarely heard cases of father–daughter incest.[1] Their concern lay in incestuous marriage, such as between cousins, or uncles and nieces.[2]

This chapter aims to show that the reason for this sudden upsurge in reports about father–daughter incestuous sexual relations, is that incest was neither being discussed for its own sake, nor to identify victims. The scores of little girls who were discussed in the reports were neither represented as pitiable nor even recommended for treatment in the text of the reports. This is, of course, not to say that the authors did not feel pity for them, merely that any such feelings were not included in the texts. Rather the mention of incest signalled an attendant problem—the problem of the unnatural. *This* is how depraved these people are, the reports were designed to show. *This* is the level of sickness and irredeemability that is present among this class.

Incest became a powerful rhetorical device for separating the two working classes but the division between the two was concreted only under the influence of psychological reasoning. Utilitarian ways of seeing which dominated to the 1880s blamed overcrowding, that is, environmental conditions, for behaviour. Utilitarian incest reports, therefore, used the same explanation for incest as had been posited in early modern times. Lawrence Stone notes that:

> . . . the punishments meted out by Church courts in cases of incest in Elizabethan England were surprisingly lenient, and there is reason to think that sodomy and bestiality were more repugnant to popular standards of morality than breaking of the laws of incest, which must have been common in those overcrowded houses where the adolescent children were still at home.[3]

Presumably Stone is referring to incestuous sexual relations here, rather than the problem of unlawful incestuous marriages.

Psychological reasoning brought about a radical shift in understandings of incest. Such reasoning was not concerned with unlawful acts, but rather with unnatural sexuality. So, in brief, to locate incest among the ranks of the urban poor, within utilitarian reasoning, was merely to illustrate that unacceptable behaviour was present there. Within psychological reasoning, to point to incest was to locate an entire stratum of people who were the bearers of unnatural psychic traits. It identified and branded, isolated and damned, and irretrievably separated them from their respectable peers. Through both styles of reasoning it was implied (through the absence of discussion) that incest occurred only among the working classes. Accordingly, the symbolic significance of incest was two-fold—it separated the two working classes and it pointed to the vast moral superiority of the modern middle class family without this unit having to expose itself to wider public scrutiny.

The modern middle class family has been labelled by Lawrence Stone as 'the closed domesticated nuclear family'[4] precisely because it was the first family unit which attempted to close its doors to public scrutiny and stricture. In Britain, it emerged historically in the second half of the seventeenth century as the power of the ecclesiastical courts began to decline, except in Scotland.[5] These travelling courts relied upon public gossip of villagers providing evidence of the moral and sexual transgressions of neighbours. Punishment by public shaming attended this form of moral control.[6] By contrast, the modern middle class family, relying on the Protestant doctrine of personal salvation as discussed in chapter one, was a very private unit. This privacy was made a moral virtue. Stone defines the key features of the modern family as a 'walling-off of the nuclear family from either interference or support from the kin, and a further withdrawal from the community . . . [and] affective relations between husband and wife and between parents and children'.[7] As well, there 'was the identification of children as a special status group distinct from adults'[8] which will be returned to in chapter four.

Before the notion of sexuality governed human understandings of sexual activities, all sexual acts were represented on a scale of permissibility. They were defined and identified in relation to their departure from, or adherence to, lawful marital sex. Thus courts, and regulatory texts, grouped all acts which departed from this centre of conjugal acts as similarly unlawful. For example, debauchery (extramarital relations), adultery, rape, spiritual or carnal incest, infidelity, marriage without parental consent, or bestiality were all considered similar crimes because they all departed from marital sex.[9] However, from the end of the eighteenth century, debauchery, which had been the sexual crime which had most commonly brought about incarceration, was rarely prosecuted.[10] The emergence of the notion of sexuality swept away the relevance of such a concept, with its connotations of illegal acts, to be replaced by a concern with the natural.

The history of psychological reasoning and sexuality has the married couple at its centre also, but it employs a different way of determining departures and deviations. Whereas the early texts had asked the question 'is it lawful?', sexuality required the question 'is it natural?'. As the 'unlawful' was replaced by the 'unnatural', the nature of policing changed from the courts, whether canonical or juridical, to the medical practitioner. The subject of attention changed from the perpetrator of the act to the sexuality that was revealed by the act and, thus, from the individual to the pathology.

Until the end of the seventeenth century in Britain, and the eighteenth in France, sexual activity was subject to two types of restrictions: custom and popular belief, and juridical which was split into three areas—canon law, Christian pastoral teaching and civil law. All three centred on the distinction between the lawful and the unlawful and were specifically concerned with marital relations. The domain of the conjugal couple was 'besieged by prohibitions and recommendations'.[11] The sexual relations of husband and wife were beset by rules and, in fact, it was the marriage relation which was subject to the most intense focus of constraints. Christian conjugal regulators set out various codes, all relating specifically to various acts and their permissible frequency.

From the middle of the sixteenth century, the church's gaze into the marriage relation increased in intensity. Accordingly, the administrative procedures for policing the laws were also increased, so that, for example, Stone estimates that:

> . . . in the one county of Essex, with a population of about forty thousand adults, some fifteen thousand persons were summoned to court for sex offences over the forty-five years between 1558 and 1603 . . . In an adult life span of thirty years, an Elizabethan inhabitant of Essex, therefore, had more than a one-in-four chance of being accused of fornication, adultery, buggery, incest, bestiality, or bigamy.[12]

Accompanying this statistical increase in charges heard in the church courts was an increase in the types of proscriptions subject to church attention. For example, in his meticulous sixteenth century study *De Matrimonio*, Father Sanchez constructed a network of questions, each one leading to its own branch of even finer points, until thousands of inquiries confronted the married couple. Is it lawful, Father Sanchez, asked:

> . . . to think of another woman while in the act of fulfilling the conjugal duty? . . . for each partner to ejaculate independently of the other . . . to practise intromission elsewhere than in the appropriate orifice.[13]

Any medical texts which did comment on sexual activity bowed completely to the church's authority, in a manner illustrated by the early eighteenth century work of Nicholas De Venette, the professor of Anatomy and Surgery at the Royal College of Physicians at Rochelle. In *The Mysteries of Conjugal Love Reveal'd* the primary concern with marital relations is obvious in the title.[14] This French text was translated into English in 1703 and was so popularly read that its 'prolonged success stirred up the moralistic wrath of the "censores morum" especially in the nineteenth century'.[15] The text defends the intervention of a medical man into an area which is clearly not acceptable terrain for a doctor, on the grounds that it makes more accessible to young men and women the medical rationale behind 'the Opinion of the Holy Church'. Written at the end of this phase of the church's detailed intervention and regulation into marital relations, like Sanchez's study of minute possibilities, it ponders over and declares permissible various types of acts and considers the times of the day, month, or year when they may, or may not be carried out. The subtitles are broken into particularly important regulations, such as 'What hours of the Day one ought to kiss one's Wife'; 'How many times one may amorously caress one's Wife in a night'; 'Whether it is lawful to take Physick to overcome an amorous disposition, or to raise one's appetite'; 'after what manner married People ought to caress'; and 'Of the Coitus, or Copulation before a Magistrate'. Copulation before a magistrate had been perceived to be necessary in pre-revolutionary France as impotence had been the only permissible grounds on which the church would agree to dissolve a marriage.[16]

The intense detail of sexual conjugal regulation supplied by learned theologians does not appear to have been out of touch with village opinion. Except in the case of the pre-revolutionary French magisterial witnessing of the sexual act, these detailed conjugal constraints could not have been policed without public help, and indeed, in early modern time it seems that:

> . . . [n]eighbours gossiped about the most intimate details of
> family relationships, and were quick to complain to the
> ecclesiastical courts of anything that violated local mores . . .
> They even knew about, and complained of, unusually enthusiastic
> or deviant sexual behaviour between man and wife.[17]

Starting in England, during the seventeenth century, this pattern of intense scrutiny of conjugal relations began to decline and attention turned instead to 'the rest'. During the nineteenth century, marital relations were increasingly awarded privacy, until they were positioned as occupying an unseen normality which was not subject to the public gaze. Instead, those who would study sexual relations within the discourses of sexuality, the sexologists, and psychoanalysts turned their gaze onto the perversions and pathologies which existed outside the normal family.

Frederick Engels' work on the family, *Origin of the Family, Private Property and the State*, illustrates that the axis around which the family rotates changed when the industrialist class emerged from the dynamic upheaval of social order during industrialisation. The determining axis of the aristocratic family had been parent–parent. The marriage of two people represented a kinship system, or a mechanism for the transmission of property. This family type came into being, therefore, as 'a matter of convenience arranged by the parents'.[18] Within the bourgeois family, by contrast, the determining axis is parent–child. This social unit's primary role is to provide the best possible environment to raise each and every child. In this family, the mother plays a crucial role, both as the key nurturer of her children and, also, as Jacques Donzelot has explored, as the link between the basic unit of society and the state.[19] In the change of axis from one family type to another, a new tension was brought into existence. While the new family placed stress on the link between parent and child, the types of behaviour permissible between these two agents was strictly defined. Sexual contact within this axis was specifically excluded. Yet, there is an *enhanced* sexual presence between parent and child in the modern family. Its role, Foucault points out, is not to exclude or restrict sexuality, but rather to 'anchor' it and 'provide it with permanent support'.[20]

This regulation, or permanent support of sexuality within the family, led to a new role for the mother who was now expected to be always on guard against sexual behaviour displayed by the child. This was a particular obsession of Victorian child-raising manuals which told mothers how to watch out for infant masturbation and advised physically restraining little hands in specially designed gloves if the 'problem' continued.[21] Other advice was 'to provide pants for the little boy without pockets'.[22] It was advice which reached well into the twentieth century. Marion Piddington's 1925 manual *Tell Them! or the Second Stage of Mothercraft* advised that '[i]f the mother should see the child touching himself, it is quite easy to divert the child's mind without tapping his hand or scolding him'.[23] It was, like earlier manuals, quite clear about which parent was the sexual guardian. The role of the father in the sexual economy of the parent–child axis remains a tense presence in the shadows.

The rise of the closed domesticated modern family resulted in the unit being closed to external prying and also in privacy being promoted as necessary within the unit. This process began from the late seventeenth century when church leaders began to voice concern at the practice of many people sleeping within the same bed. In response, ecclesiastical courts began to hear cases brought by villagers against their neighbours who:

> . . . thought it wrong that a boy over seventeen should continue to sleep in the same bed as his mother. They were very suspicious about the household of husband and wife, one manservant and one maid, which only contained two beds, so that the husband slept in a bed with both his wife and the maid.[24]

The demarcation of a particular room for a particular purpose, such as the bedroom, took place slowly over several centuries.

A description by Origo of the daily lives of the Datinis in Prato in the fourteenth century notes that there was neither delineation of functionality nor any notion of privacy within the pre-bourgeois household:

> It will be observed that, though there were many servants, there were no servants' rooms—the explanation being that they slept wherever was most convenient—in the kitchen, on the landing, or on truckle beds in the room of their masters or mistress.[25]

The Italian upper classes, by the fifteenth century, had demarcated certain rooms as both specific to sleeping and private. In France this process occurred in upper class households in the seventeenth century.[26] The privatisation of the conjugal bedroom—'the little capital of the peaceable kingdom of the household'[27]— was an essential element of bourgeois social mores. By the nineteenth century 'the classic bourgeois house [placed] . . . the bedroom upstairs, hidden well away from the parts of the house most likely to be seen by visitors'.[28]

So by the time the social surveys of the mid-nineteenth century began, several key components of bourgeois order were of extreme importance. Conjugal privacy was crucial. So too was identification of particular rooms with particular functions, separate beds for each member of the family, and the overall privacy of the unit from outside viewers. With such things being of vital importance, the middle class surveyors of the lives and behaviours of the urban poor already had a predetermined set of questions ready. In the first round, from 1840 to 1880, they started with a utilitarian preoccupation with living space—noting the amount of space allotted to each person in the family and the use of the space.

The detailed scrutiny by middle class reformers of working class domestic geography was an international phenomenon. Donzelot outlines the following debate from the 1851 Congress of Public Hygiene in Brussels as evidence of how important the issue was considered to be for bourgeois order:

> Ebrington: . . . A minister said to me: 'I have done all that I could, but the common bedroom has gotten [sic] the better of me.' Ducpetiaux: 'In cases where this separation is not possible, can't we achieve the same effect by suspending bedding from the ceiling for the children?' Gourlier: 'One would have to separate the hammocks from the rest of the room by a kind of curtain: but it would be there one day and be taken down the next.' Ramon de la Sagra: 'Would you prefer hammocks, or a bed where parents and children are all brought together?' Gourlier: 'Supposing that this separation were not achieved, then our efforts

would come to nothing. The children would see the parents from their hammocks, and thus the requirements of decency would not be satisfied.' [29]

The insolubility of the problem, and its obvious import, resulted in evidence of overcrowding and the impact this had upon morality, filling the pages of mid-century reports all over the Western world.

In 1859–60, Henry Parkes' Select Committee on the Condition of the Working Classes of the Metropolis played a vital role in Australia in identifying and distinguishing between the two working classes. It was primarily a utilitarian document, although, as the last chapter has shown, elements of psychological reasoning were beginning to permeate its evidence. The report stressed the important, deleterious effect of the inability to privatise the conjugal bed. In giving evidence, the New South Wales Inspector General of Police, John McLerie, was adamant that high rents and inadequate accommodations were forcing even the families of 'men engaged in honest occupations', into dangerously immoral cramped conditions. Several families were forced to cram into one house, he stated, and, like his contemporaries, he expressed his concern that 'the consequence is that children of mature years are compelled to sleep in the same room with their parents; children of fourteen or fifteen years in some instances sleeping in the same bed with their parents'.[30]

Building upon this same theme, Isaac Aaron, Health Officer of the Sydney Municipal Council, stated that it was normal for houses to be sublet by the room. His evidence left a vivid picture of the living conditions of labourers' families in the developing inner section of early Sydney. It was 'a common thing', he stated:

. . . for a labouring man of some sort or other to take from the original landlord the whole house, live in one room himself with his family—perhaps carrying on a trade as shoemaker or greengrocer—and underlet the other three rooms to separate families. In one instance I remember I had occasion professionally to visit an old woman in one of these rooms upstairs, and I found that the room was occupied by herself, an adult son working at his trade as a shoemaker, and his daughter, a child of about eleven or twelve years of age. The room was filthy in the extreme, everything being carried on there—cooking, sleeping, and everything else. This, I may mention, is one instance of very many of a similar kind which have come under my notice.[31]

The rooms in these usually wooden tenements were 'about twelve feet by ten on the average'. In these tiny spaces, Aaron was at pains to stress, were often, not only an entire family of (on average) five or six children, but also, sometimes a grandparent and 'very often a lodger or two, probably a servant girl out of place'.[32] Parkes' report stressed that the moral effect this had upon the children of the working classes was extremely detrimental.

Along with social surveys which had concentrated upon life in the urban slums, other commentators turned their attention to social and moral conditions within the geographically unknown space of 'the interior'. People living in remote sections of the country also became the subject of social inquiry and here, too, despite the vast expanses which did not lend themselves well to accusations of overcrowding, it was thought to be environmental conditions which brought about illicit sexual relations. In 1875, during a debate about education in the colony of Queensland, Legislative Assembly member, A.H. Groom, challenged members to go out and see for themselves:

> . . . what might be termed the dark side of this colony—and in which they would see the gross ignorance and immorality that prevailed in the interior of the colony . . . he might say they would have revelations of mother and father, daughters grown up to years of discretion and maturity, and sons in the same position, all huddled in one room, eating and sleeping together.[33]

Social surveyors' documentation of incest began, in the first instance, as a way of illustrating how important privacy within the family was to social order. Even in respectable working class families, they pointed out, incest could occur if they were not given adequate living space to privatise the bedroom of the conjugal couple, and the sleeping spaces of all other members of the family from one another. William Booth's social survey of working class living conditions occurred late in the century for an environmentalist survey, but his analysis in 1890 was that it was overcrowding which caused the very common incidence of incest. In *In Darkest England and the Way Out* he reported that 'incest is so familiar as hardly to call for remark'.[34]

The 1881 House of Lords Select Committee on Law Relating to the Protection of Young Girls heard evidence that, among some levels of the working class, the pattern of incest was deeply entrenched in social behaviour, and crossed several generations. William Hardman, Chairman of Quarter Sessions for the division of Surrey, for example, was quite sure that the 'demoralisation' of young girls was due to 'sleeping in the same room, and performing the offices of nature in the presence of each other'. Hardman could recall a case 'only the other day' in which:

. . . a man who assaulted a little child, who was his own granddaughter, and he was convicted. He did not try to have connection with her, but wished to gratify his passions in some other way; and it turned out that this child was his own child by his own daughter.[35]

Hardman concluded that 'cases of that kind open out to me, from time to time, the horrible scenes of vice, and the terrible state of demoralisation which these people must be in'.[36] In giving evidence to the 1882 House of Lords report on the same topic, the Reverend John Horsley, Chaplain of Clerkenwell Prison, stated quite unequivocally: 'Whenever I have had a case of incest in the prison I have inquired into it, and I almost invariably find that it has been due to overcrowding'. He cited several examples to illustrate the point:

There was a case of a man who was charged with an offence upon his daughter; she and he and two other children slept in the same bed. Another man charged with an assault upon his daughter, thirteen years of age; she and another child, and the wife, slept in the same bed. Another man was charged with an assault upon his daughter, aged thirteen; he and his wife, and two children of two and six years of age, slept in one bed; and there was another bed in the same room with a boy of sixteen, a girl of thirteen, and a boy of eleven, sleeping in it . . . It is almost invariably the case that it is due to overcrowding.[37]

In England and Australia, surveys gathered evidence that incest was common among the working classes; that this was a behavioural problem which truly marked one group rather than the other (as the respectable would only behave this way in certain circumstances); and that it was caused by overcrowding. Furthermore, overcrowding had a very specific meaning—the inability or refusal to demarcate some rooms for sleeping, to privatise the conjugal bed, and to give each member of the family an individual bed. Without these key bourgeois components inside the family, utilitarian reasoning stated, even the respectable working class might commit acts of immorality. What, therefore, was the key difference between the two classes, if both might behave the same way in the same circumstances? The element of choice, the last chapter suggested, was brought into play to explain that one group would rather not live in immorality, while for the other group it was exactly the way they would always behave irrespective of choice. There is, for example, quite a strong suggestion that the examples given above by Reverend John Horsley were drawn from this latter group. But, in essence, utilitarian logic, with its notions of morality and environmental conditions, did not concretely separate the two classes despite its insistence that two distinct classes did exist among the working classes. That function was performed by psychological reasoning.

Environmentalist surveyors did the ground work to identify the problem of incest as being common among some levels of the working classes. From the 1890s onwards, parliamentarians began to feel the need to do something about both incest and other forms of unacceptable sexual behaviour. Throughout these debates it is not utilitarian logic which dominates, but a form of psychological reasoning. As well, evidence of psychological rationales began to be introduced into social surveys which discussed incest. For example, in England, Beatrice Webb's early twentieth century publication of research carried out in her youth also indicated that incest was not just common, it also seemed to be accepted as unproblematical by working class women, so that:

> . . . some of my workmates—young girls, who were in no way mentally defective, who were, on the contrary, just as keen-witted and generous-hearted as my own circle of friends—could chaff each other about having babies by their fathers and brothers.[38]

Webb's reference here to the absence of mental defection is an indication of the deep permeation of psychological reasoning into social theory. Webb positioned herself clearly within the environmentalist camp, maintaining that there was no inherent aspect of her 'workmates' which brought about the common incidence of incest but, rather, it was a 'gruesome example of the effect of debased *social environment* on personal character and family life'.[39]

The processes through which incest came to be identified as, first, an indicator of difference among the working classes and, second, as symptomatic of the unnaturalness of the feeble-minded and depraved, can be witnessed within parliamentary debates. Anti-incest legislation was first enacted in Australia in the colony of Victoria in 1891. Although incest was, at the time, illegal under Scottish law[40] and in some American states, in England it was still only covered by ecclesiastical law.[41] As well, incest did not primarily fall within the legal ambit of the ecclesiastical courts for its own sake, but rather because it brought into fruition an unlawful form of marriage. Therefore, when the Victorian *Crimes Act* 1891 was passed, it was the first modern—that is bourgeois— piece of legislation regulating against the practice within the British Empire. It provided the blueprint in England for the Punishment of Incest Bill, presented to the House of Commons in 1896 and 1903, and finally enacted into British law in 1908.[42] The Victorian Act also inspired other Australian parliaments, the last of these being in New South Wales, which passed a similar Bill in 1924.

The clause in the Victorian Act which commenced this process of criminalising incest was a postscript, an after-thought, to another major piece of legislation. The inclusion of the incest clause in the Criminal Law Amendment Bill was not due to the type of determined lobbying which tended to accompany late nineteenth century legislation about sexual practices. The papers showed no heightened awareness of its prevalence, and the parliamentary papers recorded no petitions calling for it. The same cannot be said for the main body of the Criminal Law Amendment Bill. The bill was divided into five sections, with the first part relating to offences against the person; the second to offences against property; the third covering perjury; the fourth altered punishment, such as the death sentence for rape; and the fifth was procedural. A *major* component of the first section was the quest to raise the age of consent from twelve. This aspect of the bill, which is the topic of chapter five, was the subject of enormous public interest with petitions being signed by thousands of Victorian citizens, frequent newspaper correspondence, and heated debate accompanying its introduction to parliament.

In 1890 the Criminal Law Amendment Bill was debated, but lapsed, to reappear the following year. Both times, in introducing clauses seven and eight, designed to have incest demarcated as a specific crime covered by Australian criminal law, the Honourable H. Cuthbert informed the Victorian parliament that 'there is a new crime, which formerly was not known in this colony or the adjoining colony of New South Wales, but which, I am sorry to say, is not uncommon now that is incest'.[43] After almost half a century of social surveys which had worked at illustrating that incest was common, Cuthbert did not need to prove this and, indeed, he supplied no evidence of this claim. Neither did he attempt to define what he meant by the term, although the relationships covered by clause seven were those between a man and 'a woman or girl who is his daughter, or other lineal descendant'. Rather, Cuthbert relied upon the irrefutable horror of the McCarron case, in which a father and daughter had been imprisoned after being found guilty of 'the destruction of the offspring of their incestuous intercourse'[44] to carry his argument for him. Although this case was not the first incest case to become something of a *cause célèbre* in Victoria[45], Cuthbert was able to convince parliamentarians that the McCarrons' crime was of such hideous proportions that immediate action should be taken and they mounted very little opposition to the bid to criminalise it.

All of the debates carried out under the umbrella of the Criminal Law Amendment Bill, especially those concerned with offences to the person, were framed within psychological, not environmental reasoning. Thus the debate on rape, for example, heard submissions informed by medical and psychological theories. 'Offences of this kind', the Honourable J. Buchanan stated were:

> . . . the deeds of men who were unable to control their natural inclinations, semi-lunatics in fact. In many instances these offenders were no sooner out of prison than they committed similar offences again, and were sent back to prison.

Buchanan accordingly moved an amendment that punishment for rape should be medicalised, and that doctors should be authorised by the court to 'sterilise' convicted offenders, 'seeing that medical science had devised a safe and certain remedy'.[46]

The brief debate on the incest clauses was informed by the same theoretical position. Although all members were in agreement that incest was objectionable, they were divided about the effect that criminalisation would have upon the type of person who committed it. Already the view that these people were suitable cases for treatment by the psychological sciences, not for punishment by the law, had deeply permeated the parliamentary debate. As well, one member thought that the effective separation of the various types, of the respectable and the non-respectable, was the only form of policing at the disposal of juridical proscription. The Honourable G. Davis thought that the act was not the concern of the law, but rather, that 'parliament might leave persons who were so brutalised as to commit the crime referred to, to the contempt of the community, which was a punishment that would come home to them more than the punishment provided in this clause'. The opposite view, still completely within psychological reasoning, was presented by J. Balfour, who stated that:

> . . . persons who practised incest were so degraded and brutalised that they had no regard whatever for public sentiment, and therefore, if such crimes existed, it was absolutely necessary that some punishment should be provided for them.[47]

The law that the legislative members debated covered only that aspect of incest which so worried middle class commentators— father–daughter incest. It was sexual relations between this axis which represented a threat to the middle class unit, due to the unbalanced sexual economy, and the ambiguous sexual role of the father in controlling sexuality within the unit. An attempt by one member, Cooke, to have brother–sister incest covered by the clauses was opposed and indeed did not gain inclusion in the law. It was, however, included in later amendments, and sibling incest was included in anti-incest provisions in other states. Opposition to its original inclusion was expressed in a variety of ways, an example of which was voiced by one member, Davis, whose concern was that 'publication of crimes often led to the committal rather than the prevention of them'. Although in agreement that cases involving brother and sister were 'likely to be the most general', he pointed out that 'it would be very difficult to prove an offence under this clause, and 99 offenders out of every 100 would escape'. But his greatest fear was that 'the effect of multiplying crimes of a social and domestic character would be to excite a morbid feeling in the community detrimental to morality'.[48] This reluctance to legislate signals that it was not sibling sexual relationships which threatened social order, despite the fact that it was probably the most common form of incest; rather the danger lay in sexual activity which problematised the role of the father in managing the sexual economy of the family.

Modern incest laws were based primarily upon psychological reasoning and not utilitarian logic. So, overcrowding, rather than being presented as an extenuating circumstance, which might in some way lessen if not the crime then the punishment, in fact actually further damned the accused. Sleeping arrangements and overcrowding were presented as evidence in court, but not as extenuating evidence which might explain or excuse the offence. Overcrowding was presented, rather, as evidence of personal failure—the failure to privatise the bedroom or to provide an individual bed for each member of the family. For example, in 1895, when Charles Neumann appeared before the South Brisbane police court charged with committing incest on his fourteen-year-old daughter Christina, the depositions show exactly the pattern that the magistrates and gaolers had outlined in the earlier parliamentary inquiries. The family lived in extremely crowded conditions, in a wooden two-room house. Charles Neumann was out of work, the children's mother had left, and Christina washed, cooked, and minded her three brothers, two sisters and two nieces. The oldest boy was nine, the youngest child, a niece, was three years old. The deposition recorded Christina's description of the living conditions in the house that eight people lived in, as follows:

> . . . two rooms in the house one a dining room and the other a bedroom. We all occupy the same bedroom—father and all. There

is an opening for a door leading from the dining room to the
bedroom and anyone could see into the bedroom from the dining
room.

The way in which Christina's evidence has been recorded
indicates the interpretation placed upon Neumann's character. It
was not poverty nor, in any traditional sense, environmental
conditions which were being recorded here, but rather the fact
that he, as head of the family, had made no efforts to privatise
the bedroom. The key phrase here, is 'anyone could see into the
bedroom' from another room demarcated for another purpose,
'the dining room'. One could speculate about whose title for the
rooms was being recorded here—Christina's or the unknown,
middle class clerk who sanitised the evidence into neat articulate
depositions—but very little speculation is necessary in noting that
it was recorded that anyone could see into the bedroom, as the
phrase reappears in the evidence. After establishing the lack of
privacy between the bedroom, and the rest, Christina's evidence
then recorded that privacy *within* the bedroom was also lacking:

> There are two beds in the room. All the girls slept in one bed
> and my father and the boys in the other. There is a distance of
> about five feet between the two beds.

The charge was that, over a period of about five months, from
the time she turned fourteen years of age, Christina had been
the victim of incest. The depositions recorded that while 'both
sober and drunk' her father had raped her several times. Neumann was condemned here both as an intemperate but, more
importantly, as having committed the incestuous act while sober,
thus showing clearly that alcohol was not a material factor in his
unnatural behaviour towards his daughter. The occasion which
led her to have her father charged she described in court as
follows:

> On Wednesday afternoon 16th January instant I was at home and
> my three brothers and two sisters were also at home playing in
> the dining room. My father was lying on my bed that is the bed
> on the right hand side as you go in reading a book . . . I went
> into the room to pick up some dirty clothes that were lying on
> the floor. There was no one else in the room but my father.
> When I stooped down to pick up the clothes my father caught me
> round the waist and threw me on his bed opposite the one he
> had been lying on. He held me down on my right side and then
> lay down alongside of me at the back of me . . . When he threw
> me on the bed I said 'leave me go' He said 'I will not leave you
> go you will have to wait until I finish' He then put his left leg
> between my two legs from behind and pulled up my clothes over

my waist. He then pulled out his person and put it between my legs.

Neumann's fate was sealed in this case, not when his daughter presented a clear description of an act which clearly fell inside the definition of incest, but with the addition, carefully recorded in the depositions, and in fact, probably prised out of the witness by the prosecuting attorney, that the other children were in the house at the time. Indeed, as the deposition spelt out in detail:

> I could see my brothers and sisters then in the dining room and they could see me . . .

The rest of Christina's evidence established her non-complicity in the unnatural act:

> When defendant let me go I picked up the remainder of the clothes I was picking up before this occurred. I said to him you are a 'cruel devil'. He said it is not cruel every woman likes it. He then went back to the bed he was lying on and commenced reading his book.[49]

Neumann stood condemned at a time when incest was increasingly repositioned as evidence of mental deficiency, of unnatural depravity, and not the understandable product of environmental conditions.

Modern incest laws were not framed in environmentalist terms. The evidence sought was that which could establish complicity on the part of the female who could also be charged if she were over eighteen years of age, and also that which would illustrate whether the male had actually committed the crime. Prosecutors constantly returned to the theme of sleeping arrangements insisting that they signalled long-term premeditated guilt. A father who failed to provide separate sleeping places and beds for his children would be quickly damned, but could escape indictment if he had made some effort to do this. An example of this latter point seems to be present in the case of John Richard, who was charged in 1900 with having incestuous intercourse with his daughter Edith Maud. Sleeping arrangements were again returned to by witnesses. Although being twenty-eight years old, Edith was not charged. As was a common pattern in incest cases she, as victim, gave the most detailed account of the location of beds in the four room wooden house:

> My father slept in the sitting room. I generally slept in a room off the sitting room with my daughter who is nearly four years old. My two sisters slept in a bedroom off the sitting room and my brother in a back bedroom.[50]

In order to coerce his daughter into having sex with him, Richard had threatened to report her mother, and his estranged wife, Priscilla, under the auspices of the *Contagious Diseases Act*. Edith Maud's evidence was framed as follows:

> I said 'Don't do that she is earning an honest living and not in the way you say.' He said 'There's one way it can be put a stop to and you can do it.' I said 'In what way can I stop it.' He said 'By being the same to me as your mother has been a wife'. I said 'Anything but that'. He said 'nothing but that will satisfy me' . . . He then took hold of me and tried to put me on the bed. He caught hold of me by the arms. He pushed me onto the bed . . . He then had sexual intercourse with me . . . He said 'I will do what I threatened I will write the letters, nothing will come of it unless you tell.' I did not leave home then because I was afraid.

Despite the evidence that Edith Maud was not a willing participant in this incestuous union, that she was now pregnant as a result, and that children in the family had witnessed this act, the case was dismissed. There is little in the depositions to indicate why this was so, but it is perhaps significant that in this case the accused had made efforts to privatise every bed, and had himself taken to sleeping in the living room after his wife left.

This result contrasts with the case of Robert Walsh, and his daughter Fanny, who were charged with incest in 1898 and were both sentenced to terms of imprisonment in Brisbane gaol.[51] They were the only occupants of their living quarters over a shop. Robert Walsh had little chance of acquittal since John Graham, a horse dealer, gave evidence that:

> . . . on 23rd December last about ten minutes to ten on that night I was underneath the verandah of the Railway Hotel in Makeston Street opposite Walsh's place . . . I went into the backyard and got under Walsh's bedroom window on a fruit case I could see into the bedroom. The light in the kitchen was shining into the bedroom through the door which was left half open or perhaps a little more. I saw the two defendants in the bedroom, no-one else . . . Fanny Walsh then went and lay on the bed which was on the bedstead. Robert Walsh undid the fly of his trousers and had connection with her. The female defendant was dressed bar her skirt. She took her skirt off. They had connection in the bed.

But was Fanny a free agent? Being over eighteen years of age it was alleged by the crown that she had 'consented to one Robert Walsh who was her father having carnal knowledge of her and permitted him so to do'. It was neighbour Alfred Dougteson's testimonial which supplied evidence of her guilt. Dougteson reported that:

> The male defendant carried on business next door to me. His shop was divided from mine by a single wooden partition . . . They have a partition six feet high. I have seen into the rooms. I looked in from my own shop. There is a lot of holes bored through the wood, so you can see all over the rooms. I only saw one bed in the bedroom. He had lots in the shop but not fixed up so that anyone could sleep on them. The bedroom is nearest my partition . . . I have seen both defendants on that bed but not together.

Reminiscent of evidence given to ecclesiastical courts, this single bed, ironically located above a shop full of beds, was the damning factor for the pair, and they were condemned for their unnatural sexuality.

While Robert and Fanny Walsh were not, using economic measures, members of the non-respectable working class, they were brought to trial under a law which had equated their behaviour with that particular class. The juxtaposition of incest patterns with the non-respectable was all but unanimously accepted in reports from the turn of the century. The 1915 New South Wales Select Committee on Prevalence of Venereal Diseases used the same set of assumptions in its discussion of the prevalence of venereal disease among young girls in some working class families. Just as earlier reports had done, the families described in this report were not represented as being forced to endure poverty, but rather as being a different type of people who simply lived that way. One witness described a case of:

> One child we have [who] was adopted by an elderly lady, who is living with her son and daughter-in-law, but they will not allow this child to play with their children; so it is locked in a room, and food is thrown into it. It has been living like that for two months. I could quote dozens of such cases.[52]

The child, caged in a room, was being both treated and conceptualised as a dangerous animal rather than a human, both by the family, but also by the medical witness who accordingly identified her only as 'it'.

Clearly influenced by the assumptions of eugenics, as were the laws which criminalised incest, the report mapped out, in an imprecise and non-detailed manner, the sexual dynamics of a different type of people. Dr Gordon Wolseley Bray, founder of the venereal clinic at the Prince Alfred Hospital, informed a panel of doctors on the committee that 'the great majority of our women patients are children'. 'We have a lot of infants under ten years old', he stated, '[w]e are getting twenty to twenty five a day'. [53] One example was the case of a four, or five-year-old girl:

> Last Wednesday a child, who have been in the hospital, was sent out. She had been suffering from gonorrhoeal proctitis, that is, the back passage was infected as well as the other. . . I sent her to the Board of Health, to the Coast Hospital, and to the Children's Hospital, but they could not take her in anywhere. There were other children at home, and the mother was very much worried and upset. So we agreed to irrigate the child three times a day at the hospital. The mother had to bring her there. She went to the Board of Health, and they promised to get the child into the Strickland Home at Rose Bay. She was to go on the Thursday. The next thing we heard was that the mother committed suicide on the Thursday night. She was brought into the hospital late on Thursday night. She had been worried over the child, but we could not admit the child, and she could not get in anywhere else. In the afternoon the mother had asked to be examined, and it appeared that, as a matter of fact, she had the disease.[54]

By the first decade of the twentieth century, these reports, heavily influenced by the new psychological sciences, began to show a strong reluctance to discuss either the non-respectable working class, or any unnatural practices, such as incest, associated with them. Both the discursive grouping, and their represented and identifying practices, had become the subjects of psychology. So, unlike the earlier social surveys which discussed incest frankly and unambiguously, witnesses to this twentieth century report were extremely reluctant to do so. Bray, although being a medical practitioner was primarily called upon to give evidence in his capacity as the administrator of the hospital, and he adamantly refused to be drawn into mentioning unnatural sexual practices. The cases he dealt with, he insisted, had contracted the sexually transmitted disease, not from sexual abuse, but rather from toilet seats, bedclothes and towels. Bray's linguistic reticence was echoed, in practice, in the way this flood of diseased children, all but one of whom were female, were catered for. The hospital reserved only three beds for children, and children's hospitals were reluctant to take them.

The children occupied a particularly problematical place in social theory. Their presence was an indication of an unnatural group of people who had ceased to be discussed except in relation to pathology. The disease which blighted their small bodies was that which had come to assume meaning as an indicator of a particular range of sexual perversions associated with the prostitute.[55] Despite Bray's efforts to indicate otherwise, medical opinion about venereal diseases did not support the theory that contagion was possible other than through sexual contact. As sexually aware children they occupied disputed territory within psychoanalysis which was, at that time, debating whether sexual urges in children were deviant. This is the subject of chapter four. But mostly, they presented themselves for treatment at a time when, after decades of legal discussion, it was generally agreed that incest occurred only among the sick and feeble-minded, who were increasingly being seen as the territory of a different group of medico-psychological experts.

The long silence in social commentaries about incest from this time until the 1970s, when feminists put it back upon the agenda, mirrors the long silence about the non-respectable working class. Both utilitarian and psychological surveys from the 1850s to the first two decades of the twentieth century acknowledged that a subgroup or, rather, an out-group were the main perpetrators of this unnatural behaviour; in so doing, they kept this class on the agenda. There were no other ways of keeping this class within the gaze of middle class reporting. They were relevant to Marx because they were class traitors, and he warned other sections of the proletariat to keep them out of any class struggle. They were relevant to environmentalist social surveyors like Henry Parkes because they had the power to shock, to illustrate the effect that urban slums had upon people, even in the new countries. But after the turn of the century they lost their relevance within non-psychological discourses, and they and their unnatural behaviour dropped out of social commentary.

4   The innocence of children

The rhetorical power of incest as an indicator of the type of subject under observation and, therefore, of the class into which that family unit was placed, necessarily locates the child in a very central position within the classing process. The nineteenth century saw the divisions between the two working classes solidified and saw, too, an unprecedented interest in the welfare and sexuality of children. As the last chapter explored, the moral superiority of the middle class family was indivisible from its tightly regulated sexual axis. The role of the mother as sexual guardian of her children and the unspecified role of the father within the sexual economy of the unit was also a feature of this closed private unit. The tension was manageable so long as utilitarian reasoning continued to provide the rationale to exclude all intervention and allowed an external policing gaze to fall only on the families of the working classes. It was manageable, too, if the sexuality of children was positioned unproblematically as being absent or, to put this another way, the sexual innocence of children was a crucial factor in the claims to moral superiority of the middle class family and, therefore, to its role as the basic unit of order of society. This chapter is about the child, and specifically looks at the processes through which childhood was discursively articulated. It considers, also, the way in which the very tools used to designate childhood were utilised to intervene into, and control, the working class family.

By the end of the nineteenth century the child occupied a large proportion of the debating time of all Western parliaments. The child was conceptualised as having identifiable utilities, potentialities, health and mortality patterns and sexuality. From the 1840s it was apparent that there was a groundswell of opinion, among the middle class at least, that the child was a distinct type of human which should be isolated in specific children's realms and kept out of adult factories and prisons. The essential element which defined the child in these nineteenth century reports was not their appearance, size, shape, potential for violence, ability to disrupt ordered society, mental capacity or strength, but rather an ambiguously referenced innocence. It was not specifically articulated as sexual innocence but, nevertheless, terms such as seduction, corruption and immorality, which were commonly called upon while explaining the circumstances which necessitated a particular bill, located this innocence as meaningless outside the realm of the sexual.

Childhood innocence has its origins in the early seventeenth century.[1] As both Philippe Aries and J.H. Plumb have illustrated, until at least the fifteenth century, six and seven-year-old children were given the status and responsibility of adults.[2] The word 'child' itself referred to kinship and status, not to age, while the word infant simply meant speechless.[3] Being without speech the infant was not considered to be truly human and the death of an infant was often not considered to be an event of great importance.[4] Once a person emerged from this subhuman category of infancy, she or he was then accorded human importance. By the eighteenth century the infant emerged into 'childhood', a category which gained acceptance through the middle and upper classes during the late seventeenth century. Children of the lower orders, however, mixed freely with, and worked alongside, adults until the late nineteenth century.[5] Ironically, the bourgeoisie, the very class which exploited their labour, developed the determining category of the child, which supposedly accorded a young person different responsibilities, rights and social functions.

Until the seventeenth century the sexual nature of 'children', defined roughly as people under seven, was subject to only amused interest. Children were perceived to be capable of sexual acts just like everyone else. The amusement rested on the undeveloped nature of their sexual organs and on the perception that their sexual activity caricatured adult activity. Aries, and another historian, Elizabeth W. Marwick, utilising the diary of Jean Heroard, physician to the French king Henri IV, have illustrated how early seventeenth century childhood incorporated a sexual component that is missing from modern childhood.[6] Aries has shown that Louis' upbringing was typical certainly of nobles and, probably, also of commoners. For Louis, and most early seventeenth century children, overt sexual references, both humorous and serious, were a part of daily life.

Yet, while Louis' childhood progressed in this atmosphere of what would now be perceived to be coarse ribaldry, a movement had already commenced, and was gaining ground, to put an end to this 'immodesty' and to introduce the concept of childhood innocence. Among both Protestants and Catholics in France and England texts for children had already begun to be expurgated of sexual reference and a new decorum was being demanded of pupils to avoid indecent or offensive words. Among Jesuits, nakedness was being disallowed and during corporal punishment only the necessary amount of skin was allowed to be revealed so as to facilitate the whipping. Through the seventeenth and eighteenth centuries these practices became widespread. Aries explains the change as one in which '[a]n essential concept had won acceptance—that of the innocence of childhood'.[7]

This early notion created under religious influence was not specifically sexual innocence. Although a child could not be both sexual and innocent within the canonical view the innocence was more metaphysical than bodily. The appearance of a sexual aspect in a child's nature cast a dark shadow over the innocence of the child but it could be forced away by the purity of the child. Childhood innocence rested upon the belief that children were as God made them; they were pure; they were God-like. Their innocence flowed as a metaphysical force. From the seventeenth century, for example, religious iconography featured the infant Jesus. Prayers devoted to holy childhood were framed, and pedagogic literature featured those passages in the Gospel in which Jesus spoke to children.[8] Thus the church valorised childhood innocence as a state into which the child was born but which needed safeguarding against pollution by life and particularly by sexuality. The child's state of innocence provided a metaphysical force which flowed beneficially through society and could, in fact, be used to protect adults. Thus children were sometimes taken on dangerous missions in order to provide a protective aura of innocence and purity.[9]

From the end of the eighteenth century, as metaphysical views were replaced by medical theories, innocence was still a state into which children were born and it could still be corrupted, but it had no mystical power. There was, however, one further difference. For the first time, unambiguously, childhood innocence meant sexual innocence and there developed a strong perception that this sexual innocence was that which defined 'childhood', although until the mid-decades of the nineteenth century this was not universally accepted. Many legislators attempted to find other ways of defining 'the child' through a plethora of inquiries and parliamentary debates.

Commencing in Britain in 1847 a series of Royal Commissions and Select Committees considered the special category of juvenile criminals and pondered over whether they, like other criminals, should be imprisoned, whipped, transported and institutionalised.[10] During a century greatly concerned with discipline, especially of the displaced urban poor who flocked into the new industrial cities, the juvenile criminal had, by the late 1840s, been located as special and had been categorised under the differentiating label of the delinquent.[11] Industrial and Reformatory School legislation, commencing in the 1840s, was designed to bring the children who roamed the streets, the so-called street arabs, under the care and control of the state. Children of vicious parents and those who appeared to have no parents were categorised as 'criminal' and were brought before a magistrate who had the discretionary power either to send them to prison or to reformatory school. Until the twentieth century any child could be legally brought before a magistrate at the age of seven but until the 1870s when registration of births began to be formalised it was impossible to determine a child's age and some children were sentenced to imprisonment under that age.[12]

In both types of institutions the stated object was to 'reform and rehabilitate the children by discipline combined with moral, religious and industrial training'.[13] Segregation of juveniles from other 'hardened offenders' was necessary to keep them innocent or, in the case of already corrupted children, to attempt either to reform them or stop them from corrupting other children. In fact, the Acts proved to be virtually useless except in the case of children detained for criminal behaviour who were then sent to the reformatory school instead of prison. Abandoned, orphaned, and homeless children still either roamed the streets, or provided they were under ten years of age, were taken in by denominational orphanages.[14] Children over ten years of age could be taken in but only in a temporary capacity before they were 'sent out' into domestic and labouring service. This was discontinued during the 1870s when legislation was passed in most colonies to remove children, usually defined as people under fourteen, or sometimes thirteen, from the workforce.[15]

These reports, all utilitarian in reasoning, which sought to change the environmental conditions of the child in order to make them more useful, could not agree on an age parameter of childhood. Within each specific law that which determined their state of 'childhood' was, as the reformists readily acknowledged, an arbitrary age barrier. This led to differing ages being used in each legislation. For example, using the typical case of the colony of Queensland, under the *Industrial and Reformatory Act* (1865), males could be detained until they were almost nineteen years old in what were reformatory schools for children. Females could be detained until they were twenty-one years, again in institutions specifically designed for children. Until 1911 the school leaving age was twelve, after which time the young person was free to enter the workplace as an adult. In 1911 this age was raised by one year. Throughout the nineteenth century the legal age at which a girl could marry with her parents' consent was fourteen years, and for a boy was sixteen years of age. The lack of congruency in age barriers of childhood characterised utilitarian child management because the style of reasoning required no notion that some one thing defined a person as a child. The idea that a natural essential presence, or absence, defined childhood clearly belonged to psychological reasoning, but it was not until the closing decades of the nineteenth century that psychological reasoning began to dominate debates about children.

It was a general perception that there was something incontrovertible about the state of childhood which provided the impetus from the last decade of the nineteenth century, and gaining momentum during the first two decades of the twentieth century, to consolidate all laws relating to children. During the 1890s most colonies passed State Children's Bills which incorporated the Orphanages, Industrial and Reformatory Acts together, creating, for the first time, a state department under the auspices of the Director of State Children whose responsibility it was to act *in loco parentis* to all children whom the state had decided either to remove from, or raise in the absence of, parents. This Act streamlined the process through which the child was placed in state custody, enabling officers employed by the state to remove children from the street or from families, without the child having to appear to be charged before a magistrate.

But this streamlining does not supply any hints of that element which had to be present, or absent, so that a person could be categorised clearly as 'a child'. The laws which finally found a way of defining 'childhood', based upon unarguable natural forces, were those which came to be popularly called the 'age of consent' laws. In the wrangle over fixing a legal age under which it was an offence to have sexual intercourse with a person—and most legislators meant a girl—that which was being fixed was clearly a *natural* age barrier of childhood.

The amendments to the age of consent clauses of the criminal codes of each colony swept though parliaments in the last decade of the nineteenth century following concerted feminist and evangelical campaigning to stop child rape and child prostitution.[16] Reports on child sexual abuse, such as the 1837 Molesworth Committee and the 1847 Committee of the House of Lords on Juvenile Offenders and Transportation[17] had long documented the frequent rape of 'children under seven and eight, and down as low as three and four' in New South Wales. Henry Parkes' 1859–60 Select Committee on the Condition of the Working Classes of the Metropolis in New South Wales supplied further detailed evidence of child prostitution. The rates collector Joseph Clayton, for example, stated:

> I have been astonished lately, more especially during the last five or six months, to see young girls not over twelve years of age upon the town . . . soliciting men. When I was taking the Census I found in one place no less than seven young girls . . . they were children.[18]

The medical practitioner Isaac Aaron was also able to state that he had witnessed some girls 'of not more than ten years of age' who were 'in a state of open prostitution . . . There could be no doubt about it from their appearance and manner'.[19]

It was, however, the evidence of Inspector Charles Edward Harrison which provided the most detailed picture of the juvenile prostitution of Sydney. He was adamant that the trade was booming, estimating that at least one-third of the whole number of prostitutes are 'these young children' of around nine to twelve years.[20] The committee found Harrison's evidence so disturbing that they asked him to withdraw 'that portion of evidence relating to children of tender years', a request with which he obliged. The record of his verbal evidence shows no sign of this omission, nor that the record is a censored account, but Harrison subsequently submitted a written report in which he asked for special permission to mention certain cases which had come to attention. Attached as a Separate Appendix, this evidence contained over twenty case studies of individual prostitutes either under the age of seventeen, or with children who were under that age who lived in one room with them. Many of the children in this latter group were under ten.

There were also cases of children being sold on the streets by their relatives. During an evening shift, for example, while investigating a crime near the markets, he overheard an old man offering a half-a-crown to a woman for her young daughter. He followed the man and the child to 'the dark part of the market', took the child from him, and attempted to locate the woman, who had run away. The girl said she was seven years old. Other children were operating without any adult supervision at all, as in the following case:

> Just before leaving Sydney in 1856, I was in Sussex–street about one o'clock in the morning. I found a little girl about seven years of age standing at the entrance of one of the lanes. She told me that she was waiting for another girl, her companion, who had gone into a house up the lane with a man; that she had no home, her father being dead and her mother in prison. I went to the hovel she pointed out, and looking in between the openings of the boards, I saw a man, about 40 years old, on the bed with a child. I burst open the door, rushed in, and struck the man a blow on the head, which severely wounded him, and threw him down a flight of steps to the rock beneath. When I questioned the girl, she told me she was nine years old.

Harrison's picture of the life of children on the streets was one which depicted a hazardous existence in which the children offered each other little comfort. Young boys, Harrison claimed, met the girls in the streets, and acted 'in an indecent manner towards them'. The girls 'receive[d] this rudeness with laughter and coarse jests'. Harrison was by no means alone in his concern over the inappropriate laughter and language of sexualised children. During the same period in France an 1878 report on street children by Othenin d'Haussonville echoed the same scenes:

> These little vagrants, who in England are called 'Arab boys', congregate at night in the suburbs of Paris. What goes on at these meetings of both sexes, the kinds of obscene remarks that are exchanged during the hours of waiting, the liaisons that are formed, and the demoralising influences that are brought to bear in this corrupting milieu are truly frightening. The sight of these faces of poor girls who have forgotten how to blush is altogether a saddening spectacle.[21]

Like d'Haussonville, Harrison's testimony was sympathetic towards these urban poor children who had been brutally located in the domain of the sexual. Using the example of one child, an eleven-year-old watercress seller, Harrison detailed a typical case witnessed by the toll receiver Mr P. The girl arrived at the bridge one night with her two younger sisters, all of whom supported themselves and their mother selling watercress and by casual prostitution with men and boys. The girl was so tired she sat down and cried and her two sisters left her while she rested. She was then joined by some young boys who 'began pulling the girl about' until Mr P drove them off. Despite her weariness and recent harassment, presumably not unusual experiences, the girl recovered herself enough to tell Mr P 'give me ninepence and you can go with me if you like'.

In the late nineteenth century Social Purity Societies sought to use the steady stream of evidence of child sexual abuse, both in Australia and in Britain, to pressure governments to raise the age of consent in both countries. In the mid-1880s these two leading campaign pressure groups were greatly assisted by the journalistic crusade of William T. Stead whose 'Maiden Tribute of Modern Babylon', printed in the *Pall Mall Gazette*, was a crucial factor in substantially raising the age at which it was legal to have sexual intercourse with a female in Britain and in Australia.[22] Bills designed to do this which had floundered for three years[23] supported only by Social Purity Societies[24] were passed within days of the 'Maiden Tribute' reaching an eager public.

The *Pall Mall Gazette* was one of England's most popular dailies and the pioneer in the United Kingdom of sensationalist, or yellow, journalism.[25] On 5 July 1885 it published the first part of one of the most widely read newspaper articles of the Victorian period. Stead's evocatively entitled article told in graphic detail of the organised selling of virginity as a market commodity in the London sex market. The 'Maiden Tribute' caused a sensation. Its reception in Australia was also spectacular. On the 14 August 1885 a crowd awaited its arrival on the first mail to arrive by P&O shipping company at Adelaide, the first port of call. Their wait was in vain, however, because very few copies had been sent. It was a very timely publication for South Australian legislators because, as a result of pressure from the feminist-evangelical union in the Social Purity Society, the Young Persons Protection (Criminal Law Consolidation) Bill had been reintroduced to the lower house in late June and had been passed by the end of July. The year before a similar Bill had been introduced but had been 'talked out' by opposition members. When the revelations in the 'Maiden Tribute' reached Adelaide the Upper House had already received the first reading of this Bill, designed to raise the age to fifteen years. However, as the House of Assembly received the Bill for its second reading, the 'Maiden Tribute' had been read by all of the honourable members, and thus stirred by Stead's journalistic crusade, the Upper House raised the age of consent to sixteen years. The Bill was passed and given royal assent on 8 December 1885. As in the British legislation it was deemed a reasonable defence that the accused had grounds for believing that the girl was over sixteen. In New South Wales the *Evening News*, the most widely read daily, reprinted 'The Maiden Tribute' in almost complete form, censoring some of the most explicit cases, while in Victoria the major paper *The Age* published a greatly abridged version.[26]

Clearly there are elements of voyeurism and fetishism in both the success of the 'Maiden Tribute' and the effect it had upon parliamentary debates. The lure of 'the forbidden' was the essential aspect which, Stead argued, attracted the depraved buyers of children to their prey. As innocent beings they were forbidden because they were 'out of bounds' or, literally, out of the economy of sexuality. Parliamentarians, despite their concern about 'scheming girls' found themselves unable to resist the pressure of policing the boundaries which kept the innocent safe from the depraved. Yet, inside that legal space, as inside the geopolitical space of the family, the child occupied a very tense place in the sexual map. Throughout all debates over childhood sexuality the tension between their natural lack of sexuality, and their potential to be sexualised, placed all children 'on this side of sex, yet within it, astride a dangerous dividing line'.[27] That tension, born of an ambiguity over whether the child was truly asexual or was the bearer of dormant sexuality, was not created through utilitarian reasoning. It required psychological reasoning and, if parliamentarians displayed a reluctance to accept the working class girl child as innocent, their ambivalence was more than matched among their medical contemporaries.

Stephen Kern's study of late nineteenth century theories of child sexuality has shown that from around the late 1860s throughout Western Europe the sexuality of children was debated.[28] Many theorists, including the prominent English psychologist Henry Maudsley, stated adamantly that childhood sexuality was universal and natural. In 1867 Maudsley's *The Physiology and Pathology of the Mind* argued that:

> . . . [i]t is necessary first to guard against a possible objection that this instinct is not manifested until puberty, with the distinct assertion that there are frequent manifestations of its existence throughout early life, both in animals and children, without there being any consciousness of the aim or design of the blind impulse.[29]

Theories of childhood sexual innocence, he went on to state, were 'poetic idealism and willing hypocrisy by which man ignores realities and delights to walk in a vain show'.[30]

The debate over childhood sexuality produced a wealth of publications on the topic, both as medical, and medico-psychological texts, and also as parent guidance manuals. Unlike Maudsley, the majority of theoretical work during this pre-Freudian period treated childhood sexuality as pathological, with most using environmentalist logic to attribute sexual behaviour in children to the habit of allowing children to sleep with servants, as well to the practice of entrusting the care of the infant to wet nurses. These working-class women were often accused of fondling children's genitals to quiet them.[31] In Australia, Dr James Beaney's 1880 publication, *The Generative System*, warned of the dangers of 'a few viciously trained children, who have learned their first depraved lessons from the herd of immoral servants who infest the houses of the colonists'.[32]

In 1886 Krafft-Ebing's influential *Psychopathia Sexualis* created a core of work which equated childhood sexuality with masturbation, stating that the practice in children 'should always be regarded as an accompanying symptom of a neuropathic constitution condition'.[33] This work represented the bridge from the tense utilitarian view that childhood sexual feelings required an environmental stimulus to be created, and the psychological view which saw it as the product of innate natural forces. Following Krafft-Ebing, so many theorists represented children's masturbation as the sign of pathological and unnatural sexuality that in 1899 a German physician, Hermann Rohleder, produced a 320 page volume *Die Masturbation* devoted entirely to the topic.[34] In 1905 Sigmund Freud's *Three Essays* claimed to be the first text to address the topic of 'the regular existence of a sexual instinct in childhood'.[35] Freud's work set out to show that sexual feelings in children occur before puberty. They are a natural part of the development of sexuality in Man and, from birth, progress sequentially through a series of predetermined stages.

In the early 1880s, when the age of consent laws began to be debated in Western parliaments, neither Freud's theories nor the earlier *Die Masturbation* had been published. Despite the arguments of some theorists, such as Maudsley, the view that childhood sexuality was unnatural was by far the most popularly received and parent guidance manuals overwhelmingly adopted the view that its presence was indicative of pathological abnormality. So, when the age of consent laws commenced their passage through parliaments, normal healthy childhood was characterised by one single factor—the absence of sexuality. In Victoria, for example, philanthropic efforts succeeded in raising the age of consent to sixteen in 1891. The 1891 law did not affect 'improper intercourse with a girl under ten' and this remained a crime punishable by death. All members were in agreement that this category of person was 'a child of tender years'. Such a person could not give consent to engage in activity which their asexuality rendered meaningless to them. In other words there was, by the 1890s, strong opinion among legislators that, due to a natural biological 'fact'—the absence of sexual urges—a girl under ten was clearly 'a child' and, conversely, that that which made her a child was this absence.

By the late nineteenth century the debate about child sexuality was no longer concerned with behaviour as a categorising tool. Led by feminists and evangelicals, each with their own agendas, the debate had moved to the key issue of just when did childhood, and therefore asexuality, end. These two groupings were by no means satisfied that ten years was a reasonable age. The pre-1891 law held that 'the age at which a girl could consent' was twelve years, articulated by most members as the age of puberty, and any person having intercourse with a girl over ten years, but under twelve years, was liable to imprisonment for any term not exceeding ten years, unless the person was a teacher or guardian, in which case the term could range up to fifteen years. This upper age represented different things to different people. To some parliamentarians any age beyond twelve represented one, two or three years of arbitrary legal 'protection' after the onset of puberty had biologically pushed them into the domain of the sexual. Usually this was perceived as 'protection' from either their own silliness or immorality.[36] For others it represented the fixing of a time, after puberty, when 'a girl was sufficiently intelligent to understand the probable consequences of such an act'.[37] Thus the ability to reason was being given time to develop after puberty so that the newly emerged sexuality could be better managed and protected by the young female.

In New South Wales protagonists of extending the age to fourteen years had resorted to the popularly believed social Darwinist biological argument which held that Australia's environment caused different growth patterns to those in England. The hotter climate resulted in 'girls here arriv[ing] at puberty earlier than in England' and were thus physically, but not mentally, 'mature' at an earlier age. This left them in such a vulnerable position that:

> . . . protection of the law should be thrown around them. Many of these girls are the victims of what I may call designing scoundrels . . . I think it is necessary for the sake of the purity of our public life, for the protection of young girls from the machinations of designing men, that we should extend the protection up to the age of fourteen years.[38]

For others the age of consent law represented the state policing of the morality of daughters of the working class who were perceived to be irresponsible parents. One South Australian parliamentarian, for example expressed this view:

The [Social Purity] Society had information which could be relied on testifying that numbers of girls below the age of sixteen years were parading the streets of the city up to 11 and 12 o'clock at night. Most of these girls were engaged in some employment during the day, and he did not blame them so much as their parents and protectors. It was a very sad thing that parents did not exercise proper control, and remember the importance of that control over their children, and especially over their daughters.[39]

Opponents of raising the age, even to fourteen years, worried about the effect of the warm climate, and the hereditary vestiges of convict immorality, still coursing through the veins of even the respectable working class. During the Victorian parliamentary debate of 1890, for example, members insisted that in Australia a girl over twelve years was not necessarily a child as in many cases her sexuality was already well advanced beyond innocence and she was, in fact, often the dangerous sexual disrupter of moral order and not the 'much maligned' boys. As one member stated:

. . . girls arrived at puberty in this part of the world much earlier than in the old country. The law of England fixed the age before which a girl could not give consent at sixteen years. The girls here not only reached puberty early, but were more forward and more precocious than the girls in any other part of the world.

This speaker, a medical doctor, went on to illustrate his point with the following example:

On one occasion when he was attending out-patients at the Melbourne Hospital, a girl of not more than fourteen years came in. She was accompanied by a big fellow, who remained at the door. He asked her who this person was, and she replied—'Oh, that's an old flame of mine.' He did not think, however, that any special protection was required for boys, because boys in the colonies were also very precocious.[40]

Many members were, however, worried about its impact on young men for several reasons. In the first place it was pointed out that there were some 'bad' and, thus, sexualised females under fourteen years and no law could distinguish between a sexual encounter with one of them and the seduction of a virtuous girl. Basically, this side argued, any law would be unfair on young men because:

We often see in the streets girls of thirteen or fourteen making their living by prostitution, and seducing boys and young men, and to say that the law should be such that these young fellows could be brought up for a criminal offence and sentenced to years imprisonment seems to me to be diabolical.[41]

Many members were prepared to spell out the class nature of the ramifications. It was middle class boys and men who made use of sexually active working class girls and they were, in short, worried that they, or their sons, might get caught. For example, a South Australian parliamentarian objected that:

> . . . he as a citizen, but chiefly as the father of two boys who were ripening into manhood, would not be a party to passing legislation which was so unjust to the one sex, and which so unfairly protected the other.[42]

In both England and Australia lobbyists and parliamentarians alike stressed that the law would give ammunition to the designing working class against the middle class. The highly respectable *St James Gazette*, for example, pointed out that:

> Now, so long as the age of the child suffering wrong was under twelve all these conditions were secured; a girl under twelve is a child the evidence of his eyes proved the fact to the intending offender . . . But for every year by which the limit of age is raised—to sixteen, seventeen, or eighteen—one or other of these conditions is weakened. Whatever be the wrong which the girl has suffered it is only by a figure of speech that she can be called a child . . . as the age rises the chance that the law will simply be used by the so-called child or her parents for the purposes of extortion is proportionately increased.[43]

These debates, which brought many varied arguments together, had two basic points of agreement. The first was that there *was* an age—whatever it might be—at which sexuality began and childhood ended and this age was determined by natural human development. The other was that the management of the sexuality of children, whenever it appeared, was clearly the business of the family in its role as the basic unit of society, and of the state in its role as *in loco parentis* of wayward working class children.

While, as we have seen, from the late eighteenth century children were gathered off the streets by the police or taken out of immoral families by middle class philanthropists to be handed over to state or denominational care, during the late nineteenth century a new feature of state care came to the foreground. State children, particularly those who had been removed from vicious parents, found themselves under the constant gaze of their supervisors whose job it was to guard against the appearance of their omnipresent sexuality. Through this process working class children began to be subject to a series of proscriptions which had already permeated middle class child management. From the seventeenth century European and American child-rearing manuals included advice that children should never be left alone, that their sleeping positions should be monitored to make sure they were lying modestly but, of most importance, that the age-old tradition of sleeping several children to a bed be completely discontinued.[44] By the early eighteenth century it was typical of these manuals to issue such instructions as '[p]arents must teach their children to conceal their bodies from one another when going to bed' and '[t]each them to read books in which purity of language and wholesome subject-matter are combined'.[45] Through the eighteenth century, texts concerned with child onanism appeared and, of equal importance, the architectural layout and the rules of discipline of boys' colleges and military schools began to be designed with the primary aim of guarding against boyhood solitary vice.[46]

Following this trend of management of middle class children, during the late nineteenth century the regulations of the various state and denomination homes began to feature the constant supervision of working class children as a vital aspect of their management. The Salvation Army, for example, warned that:

> Under no pretext, or inducement, must children of the lower classes be permitted to engage in any games that necessitate hiding in secluded and dark places. Too great care cannot be exercised, as immorality and vice in so many phases are ever to be feared among this class of children.[47]

From the turn of the century the Annual Reports of the Director of State Children also discussed the importance of the constant surveillance of the wards, although that which was being guarded against was never spoken about. For example, the 1914 annual report of the Queensland Director of State Children, alongside suggestions that state boys would make good soldiers in the war effort, explained in detail the arrangements which facilitated against an unspoken, but obviously vitally important, behaviour in the reform schools. Like military schools, the dormitories of the Reformatories Schools which were only for boys aged between thirteen and eighteen, were, he stated:

> . . . so arranged that all the beds can be seen from the one spot. A warder is on duty all night and dimly lighted lamps are burning in each dormitory. It is therefore impossible for a boy to leave his bed without the warders knowledge. Each boy has his separate bed.[48]

While night-time surveillance was facilitated by the arrangement of the beds in the dormitories, during the daytime strict regulations ensured that the boys could not physically place themselves beyond the gaze of supervision:

> All the boys in each group are constantly under the eye of the warder, and are not allowed to leave the group on any pretence. During periods of recreation there are certain bounds that must not be passed and the warders are on duty with the boys in the yard. They are under supervision during their most private periods.[49]

From the late nineteenth century the emergence of the notion of child asexuality necessitated a new role as sexual guardian for the mother within the middle class family and the dormitory supervisor in the *in loco parentis* family of the state. This determined surveillance was the licit response to the tense positioning of childhood sexuality in the economy of the sexual. The sexual commodification and rape of children was the illicit response to the ambiguities of childhood innocence. The absence of sexuality within childhood was as loud and determining as any presence could have been. It fetishised children in a way that utilitarian perceptions of childhood had not done. For example, the 1837 Molesworth Committee and the 1847 Committee of the House of Lords on Juvenile Offenders and Transportation had both assumed that the frequent rape of young girls in New South Wales was due to a series of interrelated problems in the penal colony. The reports blamed the 'Disproportion of the sexes; "a superstitious Belief" that venereal disease would be cured by intercourse with an innocent child; and the Absence of Marriage'.[50] Except for the metaphysical notion of child purity present in the venereal disease theory, these explanations were built upon an assumption that the child was sexually used in the absence of the real object of desire, woman. Yet, while these early nineteenth century reports made this assumption, late nineteenth century reports assumed otherwise. The children, in the later reports, were perceived to be desired specifically because they occupied an ambiguous space in the grid of sexualities. Late nineteenth century reports assumed that it was the lure of the forbidden, not the unavailability of the permissible, that drew adult men to rape little children.

One indicator of child fetishisation was the dramatic rise in documentation of child prostitution. An 1882 House of Lords report included evidence from a prostitute that the asexual child had become so fetishised that adult prostitutes were now forced to dress up as children to attract clients.[51] Both Stead, in the 'Maiden Tribute', and Harrison, in giving evidence to the Parkes inquiry, had shown that men had bought female children from and, therefore, in preference to adult women. This is the case also in the Victorian pornographic work *My Secret Life*, where it is clearly the lure of a non-sexual sexualised ideal which draws Walter into an underground chamber to rape brutally a very young girl.[52]

The sexuality of children is a presence which problematises the modern family unit. That unit which is the basis of bourgeois order, around which reconceptualisation of the lower orders into the working classes took place, seems therefore to rest upon a site of potential disorder. The very notion of the child as a separate type of human with a special place inside the family, and outside in society, came into existence dependent upon a notion of sexual innocence, so it is not surprising that late nineteenth, and twentieth century preoccupation with this construct revolved primarily around their problematical sexuality.

The mother of the middle class family had a special role, guarding her children's sexuality, but throughout the twentieth century working class families were seen to be deficient in this role. The non-respectable who had left their children to raise themselves in the streets had provided the depraved with a supply of precociously sexualised children, and had left middle class society, primarily through medical science, with the problem of policing the behaviour of these sexual children. In the twentieth century the state removed children from families who failed to accept the proper roles assigned to mothers and fathers inside the familial dynamic. Fathers who failed to discipline children are returned to in chapter seven. They provided the state with the perceived right to whip recalcitrant sons. Mothers who failed to guide their children's sexuality were replaced by institutional care in which specially designed dormitories facilitated correct sleeping arrangements and constant vigilance ensured that sexuality was never provided with the opportunity of revealing itself.

5   Seduction and punishment

Historians of childhood have noted that the discursive construction of childhood innocence played its most important role within middle class morality during the late nineteenth century.[1] Some have argued that even the stifling of language, which will be discussed in chapter seven, can be contextualised as a part of the discursive construction of the child. The inability to speak about sexuality and such bodily functions as menstruation was felt most strongly among Victorian middle class females. Joan Jacobs Brumberg has described this taboo of silence, and the resultant ignorance of girls as 'a source of pride, and probably, middle-class self-definition'.[2] By keeping a female uninformed about sexual activity or reproductive knowledge, the Victorian mother self-consciously sought to extend the period of her daughter's 'childhood'.[3]

As childhood came to be conceptualised by a tense absence or presence of sexuality, the young person who emerged out of childhood also began to be conceptualised as a special category of person. Again it was sexuality—this time newly emerged—which designated them as such. For some, this young person occupied a space framed by the age brackets of ten years to twenty-one years, and for others, intent upon stretching the reaches of childhood until sixteen, occupied a more elastic space ending only in marriage. Historians of sexuality have emphasised the process, through the closing decades of the nineteenth century, of policing the morals and public behaviour of young working class youth. Most have noted that females, in particular, came in for special attention.[4] The crude dichotomy of the good and bad woman assumed most of its meaning in this group; the range of treatments or punishments and the type of institution in which the young working class woman was incarcerated also reflected this dichotomy.

The grouping was a category without a name although, in the post second world war period, the term teenager probably came closest to providing a label.[5] In the nineteenth century, the young female remained unlabelled, primarily because those philanthropic and anti-vice groups who promoted the notion that the grouping constituted a special category deliberately sought to call the person a child, and not a woman, for the same reason that William Stead, in 'The Maiden Tribute', had fudged the boundaries of 'the virgin' and 'the child'. The semiotic loading of sexual innocence attached to the term 'child' was exactly the connotation which these groups wanted to attach to this young person. So rhetorically, she remained both unlabelled and, therefore, the bearer of child-like sexual innocence.

During the late nineteenth century, as the category began to be assigned meaning, a new masculine construct, the seducer, was introduced into discussions of sexuality. The average late Victorian middle class man and woman constantly read in their newspapers, journals, novels, and religious and philanthropic papers that society was under threat from the actions of a group of young men, whose primary role in life was to seduce virtuous young women, by promising them marriage. The permeation through middle class society of this theme was such that politicians were lobbied to do something about it and attempts were made to pass laws making seduction, a crime in some cases, punishable by a two year gaol sentence. Rescue societies, lying-in hospitals, and other charity groups, such as the Royal Society for the Prevention of Cruelty, although set up long before the advent of the seducer, quickly embraced and condemned this construct. Reports from these societies, from the 1880s, overwhelmingly explained the necessity for their existence in relation to seduction. A long-term committee member of Sydney's Benevolent Society, Mr Abigail, for example stated that:

> . . . for fourteen years he had been a member of the committee
> of the Benevolent Society in Sydney, and he had heard girls of
> fifteen and sixteen tell tales of deception of the most dreadful
> character, on the part of men—tales that had made men almost
> cry. Not one or a dozen, but hundreds of these cases, the records
> of the institution would show . . . there were numbers of these
> cases where the unfortunate girls had no parents living, and where

the men had deliberately set themselves to work to deceive them by false promises, and in some cases by even a mock marriage.[6]

Promising marriage, this deviant and classless male preyed upon young working class females, awakening their post-child sexuality and then, having thus 'ruined' them, he deserted them in a hostile world. The seducer's actions were the subject of the speeches of politicians, philanthropists, the clergy and the judiciary.

Before the 1840s seduction of working class girls had been of concern to the state only in so far as it deprived employers of the services of their servants and, of less importance, fathers of the marriage prospects of their daughters. Only in this context could it be legally acted upon.[7] In the second half of the nineteenth century, however, seduction was repositioned, in popular perceptions if not in law, as a moral crime which threatened society. The popular press as well as the publications of morality control groups began conceptualising the actions of the seducer in this light. The findings of the 1882 House of Lords report were used to lend a great deal of weight to this scenario in the United Kingdom and in Australia. The Lords had commissioned a survey of 3076 incarcerated prostitutes about the stated cause of their 'fall'. With one-third of this sample citing seduction under promise of marriage as the cause the data were used to illustrate the havoc wreaked on female lives by 'the seducer'.[8]

A whole scenario began to unfold to explain why regulation of young working class women's sexuality was of vital importance to the social fabric. The necessity to *regulate* was the stressed factor. A self-conscious assertion that bourgeois social order required all sexuality to be accounted for, and assigned a place, is dominant in the literature. Practical concerns about the welfare of illegitimate children were of far less importance in this process. In the nineteenth century the vital task was *regulating*, controlling, and mapping the sexual economy of the entire population. In 1884 the Anglican Bishop of Melbourne, for example, articulated this notion of regulation for the sake of social order:

Trample on women and you trample on your own moral nature. Respect a woman, care for her, work for her, give her knightly shelter, and protection from the human beasts who would wring a moment's pleasure from her ruin, and with continually accelerating force in secret unconscious ways of which we can give no account, you shall find the loftier emotions gaining sway in your heart and touching your life to finer issues. Believe me, the maintenance of purity in the relations of the sexes is vital to national greatness and prosperity.[9]

This speech delivered to an all-male meeting of the Anglican White Cross Society was similar to many others being delivered to young men in the United Kingdom and Australia at the time. Young men were warned of the dreadful wrong they did to young women, to themselves and, of most importance, to society by seducing chaste women.

The previous year the Committee of the New South Wales Social Purity Society, again an all-male gathering, had been even more forcefully questioned by the Reverend Charles Olden:

> . . . will it do for anyone to blindly follow his inclinations? It is one man's inclination to lie; another's to steal; another's to commit murder. Not one of these is worse than the inclination some men have to acts of seduction. It cannot possibly be worse to murder a woman outright than to drag her down to prostitution. We are compelled to imprison some men, and even to put them to death, for following their inclinations. And we shall need to restrain men's desires in this direction, by the force of moral suasion and by the penalties of the law.[10]

Many commentators were prepared to concede that the extreme gullibility and foolishness of young girls made them easy prey to the seducer. The New South Wales parliamentarian, Cohen, to pick one example among many, in an 1883 debate over the age of consent stated that 'many of [these girls] are precocious, and lend too willing an ear to the temptations of the charmer'.[11] The respectable *Westminster Review* in 1850 published the following explanation of the dynamics of relations between males and females which made seduction possible:

> There is in the warm fond heart of women, a strange and sublime unselfishness, which men too commonly discover only to profit by—a positive love of self-sacrifice—an active, so to speak, and *aggressive* desire to show their affection, by giving up to those who have won it something they hold very dear . . . [They] seek to prove their devotion to the idol they have enshrined, by casting down before his altar their richest and most cherished treasures.[12]

The yellow press tended to create more melodramatic constructions, such as the Queensland *Figaro*'s colourful story entitled 'A Heartless Case of Seduction'. It appeared on 17 May 1884, announcing itself as a 'story of Eden and the Serpent; of man's perfidy, of man's unspeakable meanness; and of an innocent girl's misplaced, confiding trust'. The main character was Tilly, a girl who was 'getting into her teens' but still 'no taint of the outer world had reached her young mind then, no knowledge of Dead Sea fruit had come to her lot'. That was before the seducer, the other character, came into the story. This 'slimy, scaly Serpent

. . . invade[d] this Eden of Human Happiness' and swept poor virtuous Tilly off her feet. After some weeks of courtship Tilly disappeared only to return the next year:

> A broken-hearted woman, bearing a child in her arms. Can this be Tilly? The gay-hearted, the blithe Tilly? No, it is not she. It is her dead and departed ghost. Her womanhood has been killed and the blight of social leprosy is upon her. Poor, pale, weeping Tilly.[13]

Seduction was by no means the exclusive domain of the sensationalist press. Accounts of seduction often appeared in late nineteenth century mainstream newspapers all featuring the seducer as a lying cheat who offered marriage to an innocent girl in return for sexual intercourse. For example, the *Daily Telegraph*, a Victorian paper, wrote about a seduction in the following terms:

> When the betrayer of Marjory Robertson hears the story of how she found herself friendless and penniless in the City of Melbourne and how she was driven to commit a felony in her extremity, he will, perchance, realise the great wrong he has done.[14]

When, in February 1884, two young unmarried women, Elizabeth Murphy and Annie Cuthbertson, suicided after becoming pregnant, the media coverage of the cases generated a great deal of public interest. Murphy's case in particular led to large public meetings in her home town of Ballarat, commencing a Victorian campaign to make seduction a crime. Melbourne's *Truth* at first fully endorsed the citizens' initiatives, agreeing that 'no punishment can be too pitiless for the villain who deliberately destroys the body and soul of an innocent girl'.[15] In support of this statement *Truth* went on to devote its cover on 15 March 1884 to a feature on this issue. The full page graphic was of a young woman hurling herself from a bridge to the murky water below. 'One more unfortunate' the caption bluntly stated, and the article went on to ask 'Will the law *Never* reach the seducer?'. The editorial of 12 April, however, did a *volte face* on the whole campaign insisting that such things should not be handled by the law but rather by a return to principles of decency and brotherly protection of sisters. In affecting this about-face the editor was reasserting the belief that while state intervention might be appropriate among the outcast and non-respectable, among the respectable the middle class family was the legitimate manager of the sexual economy.

The New South Wales Social Purity Society might have agreed in principle but they were insistent that the family needed the support of punitive legislation. In 1887, through parliamentarian and Catholic layman James S. Farnell, they introduced into the Legislative Assembly a Seduction Punishment Bill designed to make illegal seduction of a previously chaste female between the ages of fourteen and eighteen years, and of mentally retarded women. The Seduction Punishment Bill was the outcome of Social Purity's attempts to compensate for their failure in the age of consent debates in that state. In New South Wales the age of consent had remained at fourteen years while other states had raised the age to sixteen and seventeen years of age. Protagonists and opponents differed, not over the notion of female innocence, nor that of preying seducers, but rather over whether or not the law should intervene.

Yet, opposition to the Bills acknowledged the overriding 'truth' that what was being discussed and legislated upon was a process in which men sought to trick women into having sex through false promises, usually of marriage. Furthermore, it was not in dispute that women, with the exception of prostitutes and the indistinguishable girls of dubious character, were gullible and trusting and agreed in the hope of delayed gratification in the form of the respectability and possible economic security offered by marriage. Supporters of the Bills acknowledged that there were some 'bad' women but stressed that a far worse problem was the designing man. Farnell, who had introduced the Seduction Punishment Bill, was probably more convinced of this than most members. In defence of his Bill he stated that:

> . . . he did not believe in the arguments as to women seducing men. Women, as a rule, were chaste, and very few went wrong unless they were deluded by some unprincipled vagabond. The crime of seduction was almost equal to that of murder.[16]

Although the Seduction Punishment Bill was defeated in New South Wales, both the discourse of seduction and the right of the state to regulate working class sexuality among the young had in no way been undermined by its demise. According to the Bill's protagonists, similar Bills had been passed in both Canada and the United States in the 1880s, and in both these countries the same scenario of seducers preying upon innocent girls justified the existence of such laws.

During the Seduction Punishment Bill debate only one member argued that the parliament was actually attempting to legislate against a normal aspect of youthful working class life. Wise, a vocal opponent of the Bill, pointed out that sexual activity among the young was common and, in fact, most working class girls' first sexual experiences were not with designing seducers at all, but rather:

> We know on the authority of the police and other people that the larger amount of immorality is between juveniles; we know that a large proportion of the girls are ruined when they are children, and by children of their own age, with whom they work or associate.[17]

He went on to cite a case which 'within the last twelve months [had] come under [his] notice', of a fifteen-year-old girl, and a boy 'of tender years':

> . . . the girl had repeatedly had intercourse with other boys; but her parents took no notice of this sort of thing until this particular boy, against whom they had a strong personal animosity, was found having connection with the girl. It was not until that time that they interfered; they laid an information against the unfortunate lad, and it was only by the jury deliberately straining the law—refusing to administer it—that the lad escaped.[18]

What this member was positing was the view that the working class allowed precocious sexual activity among their children and that, in fact, the problem of illegitimate births and prenuptial pregnancy was the product of a different set of sexual practices.[19] So for this speaker and for others who adhered to this view, the problem was not seduction, but the unwillingness of working class families to regulate the sexuality of their young. Wise's arguments in opposition to this particular Bill, however, did not detract from the perceived right of the middle class to intervene in the family dynamics of the working class. In either scenario, whether the threat came from outside the family in the personae of the seducer, or from inside due to a lack of sexual regulation, the message was clear. It was the duty of the middle class, through philanthropy and the law, to police the sexual economy of the working class.

The effect of creating a space beyond childhood which was brought into play using sexuality as a determining presence was that, increasingly, young working class women found themselves in the gaze of the law and of its *de facto* assistants, charitable institutions and, also, of medical science. Often their crime was simply 'placing themselves at risk'. This included a range of activities, the most common being the normal habit of working class youth of socialising on the streets—a practice probably arising from traditional notions of festival as much as being caused by cramped living conditions. The long-term traditional acceptability of street socialising among the working class represented a double danger to middle class order: the availability of vulnerable unchaperoned young women to seducers and the public displaying of rowdy, unchaste, unnatural, non-middle class behaviour.

Historically, middle class commentators have been quite willing to state a belief that the streets presented working class youth with theatres to display their resistance to middle class order. For example, social outrage at the behaviour of the larrikin pushes during the 1870s and 1880s specifically referred to the fact that they 'outraged decency in all our parks', and 'insulted respectable women in the streets'.[20] As Chris McConville has noted, the 'epithet [larrikin] described boys and girls (sometimes dubbed "larrikinesses") who gathered on street corners'.[21] Similarly, as both Stratton's Australian study and Pearson's British study have shown, from the early nineteenth century to well into the twentieth century, charitable organisations had attempted to get the youth off the streets, to remove them from the contaminating influence at work among their peers who determinedly mingled there.[22]

So it was of great concern to the promoters of the discourse of seduction that young women be completely removed from this traditional breeding ground of vice. They condemned the fact that many working class parents seemed to condone their daughters' socialising on the streets. Parental resistance to middle class intervention into the street activities of the young was the major theme of a speech delivered by Victoria's Chief Justice, Sir John Madden, to the annual meeting of the Carlton Refuge in Melbourne in 1908. Madden, a prominent Catholic layman, was adamant that the reason girls 'fell' was that when 'not under control [they] were allowed to go abroad in the streets at night and mingle with the other sex; often with the least desirable members of that sex . . . Girls should be home at a time when all wisdom said they should be home'.

Yet, when he had tried to point this out to the parents of young women who had been brought before him he was confronted with a resistance he found quite incomprehensible:

> . . . he had asked parents; 'How is it your girls go abroad at
> night with young men who cannot hope to become their
> husbands?'. The reply was: 'When they come home from business
> of an evening you cannot deny them the right of going out' . . .
> Parents seemed to think that a sufficient answer.[23]

Madden was not alone in his condemnation of the lack of guidance displayed, according to middle class viewers, by working class parents. The State Children's Council in 1901 was quite clear about whose responsibility this public behaviour was and also why it was so pernicious:

> Young girls from twelve to sixteen are permitted to parade the streets at late hours, aping the worst manners of their elders, forming undesirable companionships, hearing conversations anything but edifying, and witnessing and participating in conduct calculated to blunt the finer feelings.[24]

The great fear of such moral reformers as articulated here was that public socialisation quickly led to worse behaviour. From the middle of the century complaints could be heard that respectable people could actually happen upon couples engaging in sexual acts in public places. The bailiff in Sydney's Domain, in 1858, felt his job was made more difficult by the fact that at night:

> . . . there are seats all about, and every seat is generally occupied by a couple. I have seen young men taking improper liberties with girls. I have seen men and women in the Domain lying about on the grass at twelve at night, or at one or two in the morning.[25]

Similarly, Adelaide's ample parklands were said to have contributed significantly to South Australia's illegitimacy rates, a point noted by the self-appointed sexual adviser, William James Chidley, in his confessions.[26]

Added to the calls for stricter policing by parents and the state were a range of publications stipulating the rules of correct behaviour and manners in general, and acceptable courtship practices in particular. These etiquette manuals were united in their being adamant that the regulated mingling of the sexes had to take place indoors. A sample of six Australian etiquette manuals produced between the years 1885 and 1919 all displayed an overwhelming bias towards private indoor activity. In twenty-two chapters, Theodosia Ada Wallace's *The Etiquette of Australia* devoted two to outdoor activities and one-half of another to chance encounters in corridors or streets.[27] G.R.M. Devereaux's *Cole's Correct Guide to Etiquette for Men and Women* devoted four chapters out of twenty-two to outdoor activity, but three of these concern themselves with activities in which one was likely to have been an invited guest among friends—'yachting', 'bicycling' and 'visiting in the country'.[28] 'Outdoors' conduct among the public was the concern of only one chapter. Oliver Bruce's eight chapter manual devoted one chapter of five pages to rules while 'In Public'[29]; Mrs Erskine's twenty chapter book was concerned in one chapter only with 'Behaviour in Public'[30]; and Lillian Pyke considered one chapter out of twenty-one on 'Etiquette Away from Home' quite sufficient.[31] An uncharacteristically large etiquette manual published in 1886, entitled *Australian Etiquette or the Rules and Usages of the Best Society in the Australasian Colonies Together With Their Sports, Pastimes, Games and Amusements* comprised forty-four chapters, two of which fell into the category of etiquette while among 'the public'.[32] One was entitled 'Street Etiquette' and the other was concerned with 'Travelling Etiquette'.

Furthermore, the few pages of each manual which did discuss proper procedure in public were full of defensive warnings designed to shield ladies from potential danger. Gentlemen were reminded that:

> . . . when walking with a lady . . . you must be guided by the fact that she must always have the inside of the path. It is your duty to keep as near to her as possible, paying due regard to other ladies who may be walking. It would be very impolite to turn them off that you might remain near your companion.[33]

In a large crowd a gentleman's duty was to 'go first to make a path, in any case try to keep all crushing and pressure from her, and protect her as much as possible'.[34]

Lingering on the streets was viewed by these authors, but also by a range of middle class reformers, as inherently dangerous and immoral. The streets were to be used only as a thoroughfare and not as meeting places. For some philanthropic groups the street socialisation of working class youth lowered the moral character of females so much that they were inseparable from prostitutes. Accordingly, these people used the expression 'on the streets' indiscriminately to describe both practices. When the Victorian branch of the Girls Friendship Society was established in Melbourne in November 1881 its stated aim was 'to maintain among girls a high ideal of moral character and to preserve in the paths of virtue those who are entering on the business of life'. It was their contention that:

> . . . respectable girls are driven onto the streets for amusement because of the overcrowded state of their home. Surely, then it would be wise to open a bright attractive room, where wholesome amusement could be found, and if classes for cookery and house management grew out of it so much the better.[35]

Finding a proper space to train the bodies of the working class to be both useful and disciplined continued the process of surveillance and incarceration which characterised the great institutions of the bourgeoisie—the hospitals, prisons, schools and factories. Getting working class youth into specially provided rooms and off the streets was the stated aim of many philanthropic organisations from the late nineteenth century, and into the twentieth. In 1906, for example, the Brisbane Valley Girls' Club was set up:

. . . to provide a comfortable room where girls may meet each other and pass a pleasant evening together. To instruct girls in cooking, ironing, dressmaking, millinery, plain and fancy needlework, swimming, and gymnastics, and, last but not least—to help girls to become good and useful women.[36]

Similarly, the extremely wordy letterhead of the Brisbane Institute of Social Service, established in 1906, included the slogan:

The swiftest and surest way to graduate our boys and girls from the blighting School of the Street is by the Law of Substitution and give them instead of the street, an attractive Social Rendezvous, where they will find pure, healthy and joyous occupation for both mind and body.

Also included at the top of the page were the aims of:

Formation—not reformation.
To improve the conditions of the Industrial Classes
To provide a Centre for a Higher Social and Civic Life
To Institute and Maintain a place of Wholesome Amusement and
    Clean Recreation
Humanitarian—not sectarian.[37]

The concerns of these twentieth century groups illustrate not simply that the public street socialisation of the youth of the working classes was still being represented as a threat to social and moral order but, also, that the group of girls past the age of consent but too young for marriage were still being targeted as both an identifiable category and, more importantly, as a high priority group whose sexuality had to be organised, ordered, and treated where appropriate. The rooms where the girls were taught to be useful women also provided the opportunity for their middle class reformers to watch them, guarding their latent sexuality, helping the process of mapping it onto the grid of natural sexualities, and tapping their potentialities as the mothers of the nation.

These rooms were part of a complex network of places where the young women of the working class were channelled, ordered, trained, watched and made useful. In the reformatory school, the lying-in hospital, the Lock hospital and the prison, young working class girls who were post-childhood but pre-marriage were detained and watched, and from the first moment that casual juridical observation changed to serious legal surveillance—from the moment of arrest, or medical referral—a case history began to be compiled of the type of sexuality which was being revealed. From their establishment date, the administrators of each institution knew exactly who their clientele were and what type of training was possible for the particular type. The worst offenders who were, for reasons of age, being kept out of prison were detained in industrial schools which set out their aims, the types of behaviours which would constitute their attention, and the types of training they could hope to achieve. The following examples are typical:

> The Parramatta Industrial School is designed to deal with neglected and uncontrollable girls between the ages of thirteen and sixteen years, more particularly that type of girl whose companionships or home associations have resulted in her developing immoral tendencies or criminal instincts. Experience has shown that, as an institution, it is especially valuable to parents whose daughters have, much to their sorrow, got beyond control, and conceived an infatuation for the society of immoral or dangerous companions.
>
> *Period of detention*
>
> All girls committed are under control until they are 18 years of age. The time that a girl spends in the institution after committal depends largely upon her behaviour. Those who conduct themselves well, and come from good homes, may be discharged to them again on condition of good behaviour. Others may be sent to service as indentured apprentices. The balance stay in the institution until they attain the age of 18 years, when they are free to leave.[38]

The Wooloowin Industrial School in Queensland stressed in its annual report of 1914 that their girls could be trained only to a limited degree of usefulness and, like their New South Wales counterparts, were kept on menial tasks:

> . . . girls proved guilty of immoral conduct are sent here. Though it is a Roman Catholic institution managed by the Sisters of Mercy, Protestant girls guilty of such conduct are also sent here. This is the worst type of girl to deal with, and the sisters are at a loss at times to know what really can be done for some of the girls. When a young girl gets down to such a state that she has lost all her self-respect, she is very hard indeed to reform. The girls are employed at laundry work.[39]

Lying-in hospitals also specialised and felt under no obligation to take all cases simply because they were needy. Their aim was not simply to supply relief but to participate in the network of institutions which managed, controlled and retrained the bodies of the potential mothers of the nation. The Carlton Refuge in Melbourne, for example, stated in 1900 that it only took 'hopeful cases', a decision according to the Right Rev. Dr Clarke based upon the belief that 'there was more chance of doing good with the first delinquent than one sunk deep in vice'.[40]

The rigid specialisation of the institutions meant that a whole process of confessions had been elicited before incarceration took place. A young woman's case history often started when a policeman categorised her set of behaviours as worthy of attention or, in the case of a pregnant woman, when she first presented herself for treatment. In the former case the offender, perhaps having committed no greater act than 'placing herself at risk' confessed first to the arresting officer, who recorded the beginnings of her history, then to the magistrate, who made a crude non-medical assessment of the type of sexed female she was— hardened offender, common prostitute, neglected, uncontrollable (a category her parents or guardians had the prerogative of attaching to her), or perhaps she was a first offender. These were all sexual labels, irrespective of the range of activities which had brought her to the policeman's attention in the first place. She was then channelled by the magistrate into the particular institution which catered for her 'type'.

Sometimes demarcation disputes erupted over the detention of particular girls, with the administrators of one institution claiming that the offender's sexuality rendered her more fitting for their control rather than that of the institution into which she was assigned. In these cases the interpreted confessions, recorded as case histories, would be referred to and her range of behaviours and, therefore, her type of sexuality decided the case. Records remain of one such dispute in 1891 between the Convent Sisters of Mercy in Brisbane and the industrial school in Toowoomba over Mary Winifred O'Callaghan who had already served four years of a five year sentence.[41] Mary's age was not mentioned but she was older than twelve being declared 'too old for the orphanage' but obviously under seventeen, having one more year to serve. She was, therefore, clearly in the category of the post-child, pre-marriage 'girl'.

In September 1891 Father Fouley applied to the Colonial Secretary for Mary's transfer into Catholic care since two of her confessors, the superintendent of the industrial school and the police magistrate of Toowoomba, were able to report 'that her conduct while she has been in the institution has been excellent'. Not only this but her aunt had revealed herself to be of good moral character and, despite the fact that she resided in Ireland, this boded well for Mary's potential to be redirected and reformed into a useful woman. The Sisters of Mercy, the priest explained, planned to train her as a dressmaker.

The certificate of transfer was duly signed in October. In November the Reverend Mother reported her anxiety about admitting Mary into her institution. Mary's case history was not clear, her sexuality had not been given a clear bill of health, as 'I have heard from two or three persons that M.W. O'Callaghan is more a subject for the Magdalene Asylum'. Mary's sexuality was being relocated onto the grid of sexualities into the unnatural, for the Magdalene Asylum detained prostitutes. The Superintendent's reply two days later protested. He, too, was unsure about Father Fouley's information that Mary's 'excellent' behaviour and familial, albeit distant, support positioned her sexuality close to the natural centre but he was certain that it should not be positioned 'with the class of Inmates that you have in the asylum' and Mary should not be sent to 'consort' there. The Reverend Mother had judged Mary's sexuality unnatural, however, and four letters later, on 15 January 1892, her sexuality, and that of her absent aunt, stood condemned—'I beg to say that, in consequence of certain information which has reached here with regard to the girl's disposition and antecedents, they decline taking her from the institution'.

The network of institutions for these young girls, or women, played the same role the church had once played through the confessional. From their first confession to the doctor or police officer it was their sexuality which was on trial, its type and species being determined by a range of semi-juridical and medical authorities. In the institutions records were kept which, along with doctors' case reports, all added to 'the lyrical outpouring from the sexual mosaic'.[42] While detained the girls were under supervision, their behaviour, and also the behaviour of their parents or relatives outside the institution[43], was fed back into the system and affected the way they were perceived, and treated; how long they were detained; how useful or reformable they could be; and where their particular sexuality was located in relation to the central core of natural conjugal sexuality. A common set of questions spanned all the institutions, the uniformity ensuring sexuality spoke through a homogeneous grid. It was, as Foucault notes:

> . . . no longer a question simply of saying what was done—the sexual act—and how it was done; but of reconstructing, in and around the act, the thoughts that recapitulated it, the obsessions that accompanied it, the images, desires, modulations, and quality of the pleasure that animated it.[44]

The state funded Adelaide Lying-in Hospital has left a detailed record of the types of confessions collected during the late nineteenth and early twentieth century by the institution. The uniformity of the responses betrays the types of questions asked— the 'how, how often, where, with whom, what thoughts premeditated the act, seduction or rape, pleasure or pain' grid is evident. For example, Ethel K, a twenty-year-old domestic servant, confessed that she:

> . . . does not know the name of the father of her expected child. She was employed at Deacon's Refreshment Rooms in King William Street South near Glenelg Railway Station. He had lunch there two or three times and made an appointment to meet her. She met him one night early in December, and he had connection with her in the South Park Lands.[45]

Ivy G, a domestic servant, was nineteen when she:

> . . . first met [a young man] at the Rotunda one Sunday night in March, there was a Sacred Concert. I was introduced to him by a young man named Alick—whom my sister and I met once before. Before parting that night we made arrangements to meet on the following Wednesday night. We all met on the City Bridge. We sat on a seat in the Rotunda. We met again on Friday night—same place. Met again on Friday 1st April—My sister and I separated. She went off with Alick and I sat down with Defendant on the bank of the river and ultimately Deft had connection with me. It was the first time such a thing had ever happened to me. The next time was when Deft and I went for a drive on a Thursday night—Deft had connection with me another time on the river bank and twice in the one night.[46]

Florence H, a twenty-year-old domestic servant, had a case history which fell into the category of the seduced and abandoned girl but, unlike Ivy, her seduction took place in the context of a courtship:

> I am in trouble and expect to be confined August next. The father of my unborn child is Horace B, about 24. Plasters labourer. Lives 28 Field St, Adelaide with his parents. I have known him 3 years and kept company with him from October 1909. We used to meet at Walkers Corner, King William Street. Went to South Terrace and in the part under some trees. He said 'If I get you into trouble I will either marry you or keep the child.' I said 'All right'. Then he had connection. It occurred again several times. The last time was in November '09. I had my changes in the beginning of November and have not seen them since.[47]

The case history of Frances N, a nineteen-year-old domestic servant, located her outside a pattern of either seduction or courtship, necessitating closer attention to the pleasure and pain grid. She confessed that she had continued to meet Harry after their first outing together, despite the fact that when:

> . . . [s]he first met him one Sunday night outside St Paul's Church, they walked home together and when in the Park Lands he tripped her and had intercourse with her. She met him twice after this and [he] had connection with her in the South Park Lands.

Christina C's case history is similar. She too was a 'victim' of a dominating male, Joseph S, a twenty-one-year-old labourer:

> First had connection with him in May some time. Girl was at his Sister-in-Law's place. S took her in his arms into a room—and committed the offence. His sister-in-law opened the window and threatened to tell her husband—She was angry. Girl states she was helpless. Had connection with S three times—all during the same week.

The institutions for prostitutes employed the same range of confessing stages. From the mid-eighteenth century, when the first rescue home for fallen women was opened in London, the confessions of the inmates were sought and recorded. Like the nineteenth century gaol inmates, who were urged to speak of their behaviours by the 1882 House of Lords Report, the first reports from charitable homes for fallen women show that a particular range of questions were put to them. The questions predetermined the possible range of ways that they could speak of their experiences. The guiding path provided by the questions, in turn, shaped the way in which their case histories could be constructed. One of the first reports from the London Magdalene Hospital, published in 1761, for example, expressed a great deal of concern that the:

> . . . juvenility of the prostitutes was as appalling as their numbers. Of 281 'objects' admitted to the Magdalene Hospital between its opening in August, 1758 and February 1761 'several were very young; shocking to think, even under fourteen years of age'.[48]

While another in 1769 stated that:

> Out of an hundred girls now . . . in the Magdalene House, above a seventh part have not seen their fifteenth year; several are under fourteen; and one third of the whole have been betrayed before that age.[49]

Over a hundred years later the recorded confessions of a group of sentenced, incarcerated prostitutes in London showed that a similar range of questions had been asked of them.[50]

By the end of the nineteenth century, it seems, young women were so used to confessing their sexual acts that from the moment that they found themselves caught in the web of institutions, even illicit ones such as abortionist clinics, they began to confess. Records seized from an abortionist in Sydney in the 1890s, and presented as evidence to the 1904 New South Wales Royal Commission into the Decline of the Birthrate, show exactly the same process of confession. The Birthrate Commission has an entire Appendix of recorded confessions most of which conform to the questioning patterns used to construct the wider map. A 'Broken Hearted Girl', for example, provided the following typical case history:

> I have not seen The Changes for Two Months Last Saturday and I have only Been out With a young once [sic] and He Took me down a lonely Way and Got The Best of Me and he promised me Faithful That If he got me Into Trouble He would stick To Me But Like The Rest When I told Him he Went away and Hear [sic] am Left and don't know to do.[51]

The network of confessing bodies was diverse, although inter-related. From policemen to magistrates, from illicit abortionists to medical practitioners, from ladies' committees to ministers and priests, a whole hierarchy of confessors were positioned at every stage in the construction of the map of sexuality. Who then was to have the ultimate responsibility of interpreting the gathered data? By the time sexology, psychoanalysis and psychology had established themselves, during the first decades of the twentieth century, as legitimate and distinct sciences and the highest bodies of interpretations of confession, the medical practitioner had already fought the battle for them. As a wealth of amateur, philanthropic, religious, and juridical confessing bodies emerged in the second half of the nineteenth century, the organising profession of medicine began its move for control of interpretation.

Their commitment to control was not simply pecuniary. A philosophical tradition had already established that the medical profession alone had the wisdom and science to 'play a decisive role in the organisation of assistance. At the social level at which help was distributed, it was the doctor who discovered where it was needed and judged the nature and degree of the assistance to be given'.[52] As the medical profession organised itself during the late nineteenth century to gain control over social and physical treatment of the population, it was with this overarching vision in mind.

Their battle for the right to interpret the confession of sexuality was but part of their general mobilisation. A late nineteenth century moment in this battle was played out in the 1880s, in the *Argus*, in a very public debate about the screening practices of the Melbourne Lying-in Hospital.[53] According to the protagonists the debate was about a single case in which the Committee of the Lying-in Hospital had refused to admit a young 'girl', identified only as C.L. Within the context of identifying and charting the various species of sexuality the case typified the general disputation about who had the right of authoritive interpretation of confession. Sexuality revealed itself through speech, forced from the bearer of the sexuality through confession to a wide range of bodies such as the church, the law, the reformer, the charitable institution and a variety of state run institutions. The following case illustrates well the process through which the right to interpret the sexuality revealed and recorded bit by bit, confession by confession, was battled out between medicine and 'the rest'.

C.L's case history was constructed as follows. In May she was treated at the Melbourne General Hospital where it was ascertained that she was pregnant. The doctor who treated her elicited the tearful confession that 'she had been keeping company with a young man who promised to marry her, and under this promise had succeeded in seducing her'. In June she was admitted to the hospital suffering from a fever and the next part of her case history was constructed:

> She stated that she had tried in vain to obtain a situation as a servant, and had been endeavouring to support herself by needle-work, but as she could not earn enough to pay for the rent of the room, and to provide the common necessaries of life, she had been reluctantly compelled to walk in the streets in the evening, and resort to prostitution of her person to obtain a little money every week.

Like a puzzle the medical gaze was constructing a picture of the type of sexuality being revealed through these stages of confession. In hospital, under observation, it was reported that:

> . . . she conducted herself with the strictest propriety, and during her convalescence was engaged in attending to the wants of the other patients in the ward, or otherwise employed in sewing and making articles for the Hospital bedding.

She was discharged from the hospital and reappeared in August at the Lying-In Hospital, seeking admission. She had, as was required, a recommendation from a physician, in her case Dr

103

Motherwell of the Melbourne General Hospital who had previously treated her. The Committee of Ladies at the Lying-In
Hospital was her next confessing body. She was 'brought before'
them, and 'was asked a variety of question, such as, "Who was
the father of the child? Where was he? How did she support
herself?".' At this stage, at the first moment that the process of
confession passed out of medical hands, her case history became
cloudy. The Committee decided not to admit her although they
found her confession 'truthful'. The minutes showed that she was
'refused unanimously; very well dressed, and informed the Committee she was living in a gay house'.

Following the decision, Dr Motherwell pleaded her case stating,
according to the Committee's records, that he was astonished at
their decision and pointing out that he was convinced 'that the
young woman wished to alter her way of life, and that poverty
had driven her to the refuge she had sought'. In separate
correspondence Dr Motherwell said he was 'hurt' at the decision,
a choice of words which revealed that his professional reputation
was at stake because the Committee, a non-medical body, had
challenged his expert medical interpretation of her confession.
The committee agreed to re-examine her case. A week after their
first ruling they stated that they were not convinced 'of her desire
to reform' but would give her another chance if she 'agreed to
leave her present abode at once, [to] gain admittance to the
Immigrants' Home'. If she consented 'Mrs — promised to visit
her there, and if she thought fit' she might be admitted. The
young woman had to relocate herself to another institution so
that her confession could be reheard, highlighting again the
bourgeois propensity to equate space with the individual; to
equate a particular institution with a given set of sexualities.

By the end of August the Committee's minutes showed that
Dr Motherwell had still not 'made any more inquiries about her'
so 'the case remained as it was'. His records showed that this
was because he had already agreed to attend her birth at the
brothel, without charge. His decision to do this showed his refusal
to accept either their interpretation of her confession or their
right to decide upon suitable treatment or punishment based on
that interpretation. In September more evidence was added to
her case history. Dr Motherwell attended her, delivering a male
child, and reported that:

> . . . she was in a most abject and pitiable condition. The gay
> clothes which had been given her at this house were hanging on
> the wall, otherwise the wretched apartment in which she lay was
> destitute of furniture. After her accouchement she was procured

admission to the Immigrants' Home. She wrote to the father of her child, stating the fact of its birth, and he at once, to prevent exposure, paid 15s. per week to support it.

'This', Dr Motherwell stated in conclusion, 'is a simple statement of the case'. With this final summation the medical practitioner demanded that his interpretation be acknowledged as authoritative and that his original ruling be recorded as right. The young woman, as he had predicted, was rescuable, her sexuality was not within the range of species which characterised the depraved prostitute.

The establishment of the category of young person who was neither a child nor an adult took place through a series of debates which have been outlined in this chapter. Through the construction of the 'seducer' a popular non-medical dichotomy was established which allowed non-scientific personnel, such as the charity workers, police, magistrates and representatives of the church to begin to hear the series of confessions which would create the myriad of individual case histories. Once located in a particular institution further confessions were encouraged and further details recorded so that, eventually, a picture of the type of sexuality of the girl/woman began to emerge. By the end of the nineteenth century the final right of interpretation had been won by the bourgeois medical profession. The juxtaposition of institution or place with sexuality echoed bourgeois disciplinary processes which, in the factory, school and prison had assigned the individual an individual place.

6 Mothering the population

Female bodies were centrally located within the entire classing process and in middle class intervention into the working class. The sexual axis of the middle class family, the careful management of the sexuality of the post-childhood female and, finally, the psychological and physical training of the female body in preparation for motherhood are all crucial aspects of the process through which the working class was articulated and managed. During a period spanning the eighteenth to the twentieth century, through a concern with maternal fertility and child preservation, the mother of families of all classes fell under the policing gaze of a range of medical and juridical experts. The campaigns, which are discussed in both this chapter and the next aimed to construct a particular notion of motherhood and to assign the mother a range of policing roles within the family.

It is Jacques Donzelot's central thesis that this highly particularised construction of motherhood, in turn, positioned the mother as the link between the state and the family unit.[1] This chapter and chapter seven will build on Donzelot's central thesis and will discuss key campaigns designed to alter the behaviour and morality of the respectable working class. Throughout the eighteenth century medical handbooks designed to help procreation as much as possible reflected the overwhelming belief that national greatness rested on a thriving population. This 'century of Malthus', Paul-Gabriel Bouce notes:

. . . was also a period when depopulation (especially in rural areas) and a supposedly flagging demography haunted the national conscience. Before Malthus's *Essay on the Principle of Population* (1798), most writers, even of fiction—such as Smollett in *Humphry Clinker* (1771)—seem to have been obsessed with a putative decrease of the British population, which would have laid the country open to a French invasion.[2]

Throughout the nineteenth century, despite Malthus' warning that, in fact, overpopulation was the real danger, commentary continued to state that 'the art of fooling nature', which was believed to be common among even peasants and the urban poor, was a threat to national security.

Reproduction and attendant contraceptive practices became, therefore, the legitimate concerns of science, allowing the same sort of detailed intervention into the family unit as the church had once enjoyed. Yet, the family unit of the middle class was, by definition, a private space, relatively safe from the scrutiny of science, until the end of the nineteenth century. Throughout the twentieth century this absolute right to privacy has been eroded. The absence of the non-respectable working class within the traditional utilitarian human sciences facilitated the integration of the working class into a unified, knowable population. In the process motherhood became a publicly accountable notion. In this sense then the middle class family, too, lost its privileged privacy. This chapter is about the public takeover of motherhood, a process which began under the political influence of demography and which brought about detailed intervention into the family unit. It started with the families of the working class and spread throughout all levels of society.

The last two decades of the nineteenth century saw an unprecedented concern, in Britain and its colonies, with the growth patterns of Western populations. At the same time each and every individual within the population, excluding the outcasts among the non-respectable and perverse, became a valuable being. Whereas at one time the birth and survival rate among the poor was of little concern to most commentators, by the end of the century their contribution to population statistics was crucial. Birth control among the working class was a cause for moral panic; maternal mortality became a national tragedy; and infant death was reconceptualised as the loss of a potentially useful citizen.

The two major Australian surveys of this period, both chaired by Octavius Beale, were the Royal Commission on the Decline of the Birth-Rate and on the Mortality of Infants in New South Wales, 1904, and the Royal Commission on Secret Drugs, Cures and Foods, 1907.[3] Both found that the birth-rate was falling and blamed this on a lack of patriotism and natural motherly feeling on the part of women of all classes—though evidence focused primarily on working class women. As with most social problems from the end of the nineteenth century the major authorities in this public takeover of motherhood were the medical profession, whose efforts to stamp out 'quackery' intensified from the 1880s to the 1930s until they were established as the only legitimate healers of the body. The pregnant body, repositioned in medical discourse as 'ill', was included in this appropriation.[4] The campaigns described in this chapter against traditional women healers, midwives, pharmacists, herbalists, and self-styled pedlars of 'nostrums', were carried out with the stated aim of minimalising child and mother wastage but can also be contextualised within the wider process of medical management of the population and of society.

The population surveys united two trends which had been occurring within middle class thought. One was the valorisation of 'the child'; the other was the replacement of the dark unknown of the 'lower orders' with that of the Asiatic and Negroid races. Both these trends reflected the final integration of the working class (and, from this time, this meant only the respectable working class) into the population, making them sufficiently familiar and 'like' the middle class. Anxiety about the falling birth rate was not just explained in terms of its decline but, more importantly, that it was falling relative to, in this case, that of the Asiatic or Negroid races, just as in the eighteenth century the British birth rate was thought to have been falling relative to the French increase.

In the late years of the eighteenth century and until the mid-nineteenth century one of the indicators of difference for the lower orders was that, because of their immorality and lack of reasoning, they, like animals, were prolific 'breeders' even in the Australian colonial scenario. In 1813, for example, Governor Macquarie worried about the 'convict taint' and despaired that female convicts 'have large Families of Children'.[5] A report in the *Moreton Bay Courier*, in what was to become Queensland, showed that this attitude was still strongly adhered to in 1850. When Mary W was charged with 'cribbing gingerbeer bottles', the paper described her as 'carrying in her arms, as most women do in this prolific town, a young squaller'.[6]

By the end of the nineteenth century, however, this perception was replaced with an anxiety that all women, both working and middle class, were not producing enough children. Demographers calculated that the population fertility patterns were decreasing at a rate which could actually result in the demise of the European race.[7] Australian fertility patterns showed a rapid downward swing from the 1860s.[8] Pat Quiggen's study has found that Australian women born during the 1840s and, therefore, having children in the late 1850s and 1860s showed fertility patterns which indicated an absence of any contraceptive or other family limitation practices.[9] Women born a decade later 'had families smaller on average by nearly two children'.[10]

The decline accelerated throughout the rest of the nineteenth century, not just in Australia but also throughout northern Europe, Britain and America. These figures (which reveal that the anxiety was based upon a 'real' trend) do not explain, in themselves, the manner in which the information was received. Birth control practices began to take on a bourgeois history in France from the middle of the eighteenth century, a half-century at least before they were mapped and represented as a 'problem' in Britain. Literature on contraception in France has suggested that the heightened awareness of the practices in the eighteenth century was the product of a change in attitude by the church which had not found fault with some practices until then. P. Biller, for example, has suggested that there is evidence that contraception was widely employed from the fourteenth century.[11] Ironically (considering the earlier British fear of being overtaken by the prolifically breeding French) in France, by mid-way through the nineteenth century, contraception became the source of great alarm and widespread contraceptive practices were being referred to in such terms as being a 'natural threat'. By the end of that century, census reports were carrying dire warnings such as: '[t]he problem of population can only awaken uneasiness and calls attention to a peril that becomes every day more menacing'.[12] By the end of the nineteenth century similar panic had spread to America, Australia and Britain. In May 1906 the *Lancet* warned that 'the birth rate in the Australian colonies and among British-Canadians is little higher than that of France, and unless the British become more fertile it is doubtful whether the British Empire will long remain British in anything but name'.[13]

The literature pertaining to race suicide encapsulates a sense of the unknown which had moved from the lower orders to another, again rapidly breeding, group. President Roosevelt, for example, is quoted in the Australian Commonwealth 1907–8 Report of the Royal Commission on Secret Drugs, Cures and Foods as saying:

Do you know that there are fewer descendants of the
revolutionary forefathers living to-day than there was fifty years

ago? . . . We must either alter our ways or we must make way for the other races, Asiatic or whatever they are, that will certainly replace us.[14]

The Asiatic races are here the 'other', the unknown. The working class no longer is perceived as standing outside, as being different. One woman quoted by Beale in his Commonwealth Royal Commission summed up this changed attitude when she wrote to the editor of the *Lancet*, complaining about advertisements for abortionists and contraceptives:

> If the British race is not to die out, this sort of thing must be stopped. Will no Member of Parliament bring in a Bill making such advertisements criminal? If there is a high class of workman in the United Kingdom it is those for whom the enclosed weekly journal is printed (*The Railway Review*), mostly very intelligent and thrifty, and obliged to be sober owing to their particular employment. It is to the notice of this class that these advertisements are brought, the class which the country requires to increase and multiply, strong in physique and intellect.[15]

Psychological sciences pointed to the 'healthy' sexual dynamics of privatised conjugal relations to illustrate the superiority of the bourgeois family over other family types. In late nineteenth century population surveys, by contrast, the superiority was primarily based upon child preservation. Within this scenario, it was the middle class mother who was considered the key to a healthy population. Medical intervention into the family was so widespread by the end of the nineteenth century that Jill Hodges and Athar Hussain have described the link between the family doctor and the middle class mother as:

> . . . the same as that between the doctor and the subordinates (nurses and Medical auxiliaries); the man of knowledge, the doctor prescribed, while his ally carried out his instruction . . . The mother of the modern family was constituted in the context of the health of the population in general and that of children in particular.[16]

Medical advice was followed by economic advice, all designed to ensure the maximum utility of the nation's resources in order to create the maximum possibility for healthy children. Throughout the late nineteenth century home management texts, a genre of home advice usually written by doctors, included detailed designs for appropriate clothing for the future mothers of the nation. The body of woman, a permissible subject of polite conversation only in terms of its role in nurturing, was to be freed of the constraints of fashion. These texts detailed the effects of tight lacing on those vital female parts pertaining to birth and childbearing.

Throughout the nineteenth century, the medical profession led campaigns against contraceptive or 'family planning' practices which were gaining popularity among middle class women. When, in the late decades of the century, medical and moral attention was turned towards working class women, it quickly became obvious that intervention into their mothering practices required campaigns which reached far deeper into the philosophical understandings of pregnancy itself. Bourgeois discourses of pregnancy contrasted markedly with working class conceptualisations. The bourgeois view prioritised the foetus and saw pregnancy as a period of gestation in the development of a new human. It was a scientific view, locked into the general concern of the human sciences to know Man in all stages of development. The working class woman saw pregnancy as a female condition, and her view brought into play metaphysical notions of female cycles. This traditional view prioritised the woman, and placed very little significance on the foetus, at least until quickening when the woman felt movement. The working class view was that pregnancy was a woman's condition, part of her health patterns, and for this reason maintenance of pregnancy, including its termination, was the business of women.[17] Female management of pregnancy was an aspect of the divided world of working class communities. As Judith Allen has shown, women had little choice but to regard pregnancy as women's business as working class men refused to take responsibility for either contraception or abortion.[18] Coronial depositions bear out Allen's interpretation.

The sexual demarcation which left women to manage the 'ailment' of pregnancy, was particularly clear in the case of thirty-two-year-old Brisbane mother of two, Mary E, who told her wharf labourer husband 'if she did not get fixed up she would throw herself in the river'. Although he gave her all the money he could raise and assisted her to cash in the insurance policy on his life to raise the fee, he repeatedly refused to accompany her to see the abortionist nurse—'I told her that I did not like going up there'. Instead, Mary wrote a note to a neighbour, whom she knew only as Mrs T, asking her '[i]f you are not doing anything this afternoon or tonight could you come down and see me. I would like to speak to you *privately*'. It was Mrs T who then accompanied Mary to the destination where she was met by a 'dark cab', and wrote down the phone number which was to be given to Mary E's husband 'should something go wrong'. The final note Mary E wrote to her husband, as she left to have her abortion, read as follows:

111

> Have gone to see a friend of mine who is sick and if I am late, put the children to bed. Don't worry if I am away all night everything will be alright. Kid.

The next morning her body was found outside a Brisbane girls' school.[19]

The pattern of female responsibility for management of pregnancy was commented on, critically, by many middle class social commentators at the turn of the century. For example, in 1906, in referring specifically to the lead-based abortifacient, diachylon, a British doctor lamented the fact that 'the spread of the evil is principally due to secret information, passed by one woman to another'.[20] From the late 1880s the fact that in cases involving abortion men were either not mentioned or were recorded as having been reluctant to be involved, was given prominence in coronial and parliamentary reports. Males entered these scenes as doctors, police or, in the final role of authority, as the coroner who prised open the secrets of the unnatural mother. In this way the pattern was established of the destructive impact of women on mothering. Rather than being the natural nurturers of children, working class women entered coronial and parliamentary report as members of 'secret' networks which were the organised enemy of the foetus. It is a pattern which provided a moral as well as a medical argument to legitimate the presence of male medical practitioners within a process which was biologically feminine. In the process doctors positioned themselves as the experts, or the natural guardians of the foetus and the child, and mothers were positioned as their offsiders who needed to be educated to treat these precious commodities correctly.

This was a argument which Octavius Beale, in particular, went to great lengths to illustrate. Beale was also in the position of needing to legitimate his intervention in the nurturing stages of pregnancy and he did it through highlighting such cases as the following account. The Report of the Secret Drugs, Cures and Food Royal Commission recorded the case history of a husband whose sad fate it was to be married to an unnatural woman:

> A city merchant in Australia said: I met one of the tenants in our building and observing that the man was pale and nervous, even trembling, asked him what was the matter. 'My wife has made up her mind that she will have no more children. She and her sister, who is also a married woman, have come to that decision together, and I cannot keep them apart. A few days ago I was called home from business, and there was this sister, and a nurse who had operated upon my wife, and she was dangerously ill'. Why does your friend continue to live with a wife who thus

murders their offspring? I put that to him, but his answer was, 'What am I to do with my two poor little children?'[21]

Beale's purposeful insistence here that the foetus and the child were identical, and that abortion and murder were indistinguishable has a very recent history. It was not until the first half of the nineteenth century that modern medical science 'discovered' the embryo, or at least accorded it an importance that was completely new. Within a short space of time the science of embryogenesis, first named in 1830, gave way to that of embryology, first named by Darwin in *The Origin of Species* in 1859. The name change reflected a shift from studying the origin and formation of the embryo—that is watching its biological development—to a broader concern which accorded the developing group of cells a history and a mortality pattern, in short, a case history. From the middle of the nineteenth century the embryo was conceptualised within medical discourse as having a presence in the human condition, as being a type of person. So, for the first time, conditions or states of being could be measured against the embryo. One could, for example, have embryocardia, a condition of the heart in which one had a heartbeat like an embryo. The embryo had become a recognisable type of human, like a child or a 'teenager', and while 'embryocide' never quite made it into the vocabulary, foeticide certainly did, being first mentioned in a medical dictionary in 1844.[22]

Angus McLaren's study of abortion in England illustrates that even the middle and upper classes did not develop modern, or medical, notions of pregnancy as being a gestation stage in the life of a new human until the end of the eighteenth century. It was only during the nineteenth century that there was, through all but the working classes, an adoption of 'the concept of the sanctity of embryonic life from the moment of conception'.[23] Prior to this point, concern rested, not on the embryonic human but, rather, on a more metaphysical notion of 'life'—that is, the pregnant woman was nurturing a God-given 'life', rather than a human with a case history. Soloway, for example, writing of British medical opinion in the late nineteenth century, illustrates this lingering perception, still strongly in currency long after the embryo had been clearly positioned as a type of person:

During a 1879 meeting of the London Medical Society, a neo-Malthusian doctor, Drysdale, tried to explain to one of his colleagues, that abortion was not the same as the prevention of conception. The perplexed physician was unable to see any difference since the goal, the deliberate thwarting of nature, was the same.[24]

For this doctor, both pre- and post-conception practices were indistinguishable and pregnancy represented a process in an abstract natural life cycle. This perception of procreation, which placed no particular importance on the moment of conception, was far more characteristic of the eighteenth century—and the early part of the century at that. Lawrence Stone, for example, shows that within what he calls the propertied classes of Europe in the eighteenth century:

> Coitus interruptus, in which the male withdraws just before ejaculation, was still condemned as the sin of Onan referred to in the Book of Genesis. Not much distinction was made between it and deliberate acts to abort the foetus, or infanticide at or immediately after birth.[25]

Here, semen has a significance as being the essence of life, and its wastage was as sinful as the wastage of 'life' in other forms, such as abortion, killing of the pre-speech infant and contraception. Notions of 'the child', or equating the foetus with the child, did not enter the debate until the end of the nineteenth century, and did not dominate the debate until mid-way through the twentieth. Thus during the eighteenth century, while coitus interruptus was looked upon with horror, coitus reservatus, where no ejaculation takes place, was given official approval.[26]

This Christian-based notion gradually gave way, during the eighteenth century, to a concern with conception, resulting in the legislative reform embodied in Britain's first abortion statute, the Ellenborough Act of 1803. This Act gave legal protection to the foetus for the first time. This legislation did, however, distinguish between 'quickened' foetuses, when the mother felt movement, and unquickened foetuses, with the latter attracting punishment of a fine, corporal punishment, imprisonment, or transportation for up to fourteen years, while the former was punishable by death.[27] In this first anti-abortion Act the feelings or sensations of the mother were given status and until she could actually 'feel' the movements of the foetus, it was not granted legal protection.

This consideration of maternal sensations was removed from subsequent laws. The Ellenborough Act was followed in Britain, in 1837, by a further Act which gave foetuses at all stages equal legal protection.[28] It was this later Act which reflects the degree of acceptance throughout the middle and upper classes of the importance of conception as the point at which 'human-ness' began its biological and moral existence. The medical profession was at the forefront of promoting the view that a potential human was in the making from the moment of conception, irrespective of whether the woman knew she was pregnant or not. As one doctor articulated in defence of the Bill—'[w]hat, it may be asked, have the sensations of the mother to do with the vitality of the child? Is it not alive because the mother does not feel it?'.[29] For this doctor, and for his class, the foetus took on human-ness irrespective of its unviability without the pregnant woman. Yet despite the nineteenth century trend to prioritise and give a case history to the foetus, in the middle of the century, the English *Offences Against the Person Act* and the Australian *Crimes Act* of each colony incorporated Acts relating to abortion into a general economy of management of the body. The whole area of legal rights of a foetus had proven too difficult to manage and certainly too difficult for juries to agree upon. It was far easier to determine whether or not a person had 'unlawfully use[d] any instrument to procure the miscarriage of any woman'.

Long after the passing of the first anti-abortion Act the working class, according to McLaren, continued to adhere to a 'notion that life was not present until forty to eighty days had passed'[30] and, thus, found this Act incomprehensible. It could not be coincidental that this attitude matches early Christian teachings that the soul entered the foetus at forty days for boys, and eighty for girls and, therefore, reflects a concern with spirituality and the essence of life and not human-ness.[31] Rosalind Pollack Petchesky's study of abortion notes that in France, Britain and the United States, throughout the nineteenth century, working class women 'commonly believed that, regardless of the law, there was no baby, hence nothing "wrong" in ending a pregnancy, prior to "quickening" '.[32]

In 1903, the English Birkett Committee still found that among the working class 'mothers seemed not to understand self-induced abortion was illegal. They assumed it was legal before the third month, and only outside the law when procured by another person'.[33] In Australia, too, in 1903, it remained a common police complaint that 'there [was] a very great difficulty in bringing an abortionist to justice' because it was 'very difficult to get a jury to convict, even in the case of clear evidence'.[34]

During the mid-eighteenth century working class women began conceptually to separate infanticide from the range of fertility control practices. During the nineteenth and early twentieth centuries, however, infanticide among the working class was still frequently reported in medical journals. Infanticide has historically been so common among the British working class that in the seventeenth century it was considered the most common form of 'murder'.[35] In 1739 Captain Coram opened London's Foundling Hospital in an attempt to decrease the 'frequent Murders committed on poor Miserable Infant Children at their Birth by their

Cruel Parents'.[36] It was, he reported, a dismal failure for within four years 14 000 infants were left at the gates and, of this figure, which represented a constant stream of some seventy deserted infants a week, more than 10 000 died within a short time of their arrival.[37] In 1894 the *Australian Medical Journal* lamented the loss of infant life in Australia, but supplied no figures.[38] Between 1898 and 1903 there were still on average seven dead newborn infants abandoned each year in Sydney.[39]

While these figures do not in themselves prove that such infants were perceived as valueless and lacking in human-ness, other material does support this concept. Judith Allen has pointed out that the 1907 Commonwealth Royal Commission on Secret Cures, Drugs and Foods found that it was commercially viable for several undertakers to specialise exclusively in the burial of 'stillborn' babies. The babies, buried several to a coffin, often showed signs of strangulation and at least one witness to the Commission reported his shock at being brought a stillborn for burial that was at least two years old.[40] The 1904 Royal Commission on the Decline of the Birth-Rate and on the Mortality of Infants in New South Wales supplied details of professional baby-minders, or baby-farmers as these women were called, who it was alleged specialised in killing infants left in their care. The *Australian Medical Journal* supplied further details of this practice.[41]

British legislation designed to protect infants predated Australian efforts by almost two decades. The *Infant Life Protection Act* of 1872 protected infants until they were twelve months old and made registration necessary, if two or more infants, excluding twins, were taken in by the same paid baby-farmer. The Fourth Report of the Royal Commission on Friendly Societies, 1872–74 represents an important moment in British perceptions of the child, as its intent was to investigate the impact on infant mortality of infant insurance. Although stopping short of claiming that working class parents killed infants for the insurance they could collect, it did show that a large number of children were insured in several friendly societies at the same time, thus more than covering the cost of the funeral expenses. One child was found to be insured 'in eight societies which would have produced £30 at death'.[42] During the next session of parliament, a Friendly Societies Bill was introduced, limiting the number of societies and the amount for which an infant could be insured. An unusually long period lapsed before the first Australian colony followed this British trend, with the Victorian *Infant Life Protection Act* (1890).

Given that substantial numbers of infants were still being killed during the early years of the twentieth century it seems unlikely that the next phase in the medical process of concern with early human existence, the valorisation of the foetus in all stages of its development, had permeated very deeply into working class value systems. Certainly, working class abortion patterns do not suggest that the foetus was accorded very high value. The 1903 Birthrate Commission, in attempting to estimate the number of women who had had one or more abortions, requested the opinion of a number of doctors in the Sydney and Newcastle areas. While most doctors were of the opinion that 'there was a strong tendency for the wives of the working classes to limit the number of their offspring in that way'[43] many also reported that middle class women, or even the 'educated classes occasionally'[44] were also asking for abortions. Dr McKay, whose work was largely among the working class in the industrial city of Newcastle, believed that very few working class women with children had not had one or two spontaneous, or induced, abortions.[45] Spontaneous abortions, or miscarriages as they became known in the twentieth century, occurred naturally, while induced abortions had been brought about by human intervention. It was estimated that 60 or 70 per cent of all abortions were induced and 80 per cent of first abortions were induced.

Dr McKay's observations were supported by figures collected in 1902 by Dr Watson Munro and, later, revealing a remarkably consistent pattern, by a 1937 survey at the Melbourne Women's Hospital by Dr R.G. Worcester.[46] Watson Munro found that of a sample of 1108 married women, 32 per cent of pregnancies ended in either spontaneous or induced abortion. This figure reflects an induced abortion rate among married women of over one in five pregnancies at the beginning of the twentieth century.[47] Worcester's study attempted to calculate abortion ratios in the community. He interviewed one hundred married women who had been admitted to the hospital for reasons other than abortion or pelvic inflammation. These women gave a ratio of one abortion to four births. He then interviewed women admitted following an abortion and found a ratio of four abortions to every five births. Concluding that the ratio of abortion in Melbourne was probably somewhere between these two estimates, Worcester, estimating ratios in 1937, stated that '[o]ne is of the opinion that the actual ratio is about one abortion to every three and a half births'. Using a standard ratio of spontaneous to induced abortions, this figure represents again one induced abortion to every five pregnancies.[48] The emphasis placed upon scrutiny of married women in both these surveys reflects medical concern with the mother as pivot of the family unit.

From the time they entered the demographic campaigns, the medical profession seemed to be aware that discourses of pregnancy were culturally and class specific, although they had little understanding or tolerance of what the working class perception actually was. During their early nineteenth century campaign to upgrade the *Ellenborough Act* to cover equal legal protection to foetuses in all stages of development, medical arguments accommodated both perceptions. In the *Legal Examiner* in 1832 a medical practitioner stated, clearly within a middle class discourse of pregnancy, that a new Act was necessary as 'the mind instinctively recoils at the idea of the destruction of human life, however imperfectly and immaturely it may be developed'. However, in the same article the author also recognised that a different argument was necessary to convince the working class woman of its necessity. This time reconceptualising pregnancy as a female complaint, he stated that the law was necessary to stop women harming themselves and also to ensure sexual restraint.[49]

One of the ways through which working class notions of pregnancy can be traced is through printed matter advertising abortifacients where the idea of pregnancy as a female complaint, rather than the middle class notion of a period of foetal nurturing, is clearly reflected. Within printed advertising pregnancy was not represented in terms of bourgeois conceptualisations. It is important, however, to acknowledge that, commencing in New South Wales in 1899, *Obscene Publications Acts* relating to advertising both abortion and pornography caused printed advertisements to be worded in a circumspect manner. Thus, for example, while before the Act, Mrs W could advertise her 'clinic' as a:

> Private Hospital—Select Home for Ladies. Town and Country during Accouchement. Surgical Cases a Speciality . . . 353 Liverpool St. Darlinghurst. [50]

after the Act was passed, she would be more likely, to state, as Mrs L had done:

> Mrs L, Ladies Nurse, late Liverpool St. Vacancy Call or write. 343 Moore Park Rd. [51]

Although those placing advertisements were forced to be deliberately obtuse, the wording still reveals attitudes to pregnancy, simply because the manner in which abortionists referred to pregnancy was shaped, not just by the law, but also by popular perceptions. That is, the veiled messages had to mean something to their audience. For example, when the convicted abortionist

and baby-farmer Margaret Jackson advertised her trade at the turn of the century she employed a legal firm which she described as being of 'high respectability' to draw up a hand-bill that would not contravene the *Obscene Publications Act.* The hand bill announced a:

> Safe and Unfailing Remedy for Women. Mrs. T. Jackson Begs to Announce that her SAFE and UNFAILING REMEDY is positively the only one in AUSTRALIA upon which strict reliance can be placed. Its efficiency to RESTORE REGULARITY— irrespective of the duration of obstruction—is beyond a question of dispute. It does not in the slightest degree interfere with domestic duties. APPLY WHEN ALL OTHERS FAIL. MRS. T. JACKSON, as MIDWIFE, offers Best Private Accommodation to Ladies during confinement. TERMS LOW. Special advantages offered. For particulars, write and enclose Two shilling stamps to MRS. T. JACKSON, TERRY STREET, TEMPE, SYDNEY.[52]

She circulated this notice on railway platforms and carriages, and letter-boxed houses and gardens. The legal firm may have been highly respectable but they were not particularly skilled as the reference to 'female irregularities' was sufficient ground for conviction and Jackson was fined three pounds.[53]

Despite the fact that Jackson had deliberately, if unsuccessfully, attempted to obscure her intent the crucial concepts were clearly presented for her audience. The perception of pregnancy as 'an obstruction' of varying degrees of duration and the idea that it was synonymous with the simple absence of 'normality' in the menstrual cycle, clearly meant something to the women she targeted. Pregnancy had to be perceived by them in a similar vein for the advertisement to work. Most abortion advertising reiterated these key concepts of pregnancy as either 'an ailment', an 'irregularity', or a 'complaint'. Examples from the *Evening News* in 1899 included the following:

> LADIES—My Female Pills Restore Regularity, no matter what has failed. Box posted 5s 6d. Write Professor W.W.G, Collins St. Melbourne.
> A BOON TO LADIES. Madam B's Famous Female Remedy. For all irregularities. Acts almost immediately, does not interfere with household duties, and will not injure the most delicate. Over twenty thousand cases successfully treated. Results are the true test of value.[54]

These advertisements were typical of hundreds that appeared in the late nineteenth and early twentieth century press. They all presented pregnancy as an ailment, or as a blockage, and they often incorporated testimonials which included references to being 'put right', 'cured', or being 'restored to regularity'. None of the advertisements showed any concession to the bourgeois view of pregnancy as being the gestation of a human being. For example, none were defensive. They did not show any sign of needing to prioritise the mother's health or well-being over the foetus's rights. They showed no sign of needing to justify abortion in any way. It was clearly presented as a woman's business and as something she needed to do in order to be restored to normality. They do, by contrast, reflect female concerns over safety and disruption to domestic duties. In short they reflected, or manipulated, a view which saw pregnancy as a female condition rather than one in which a valued being, a foetus, was involved.

While juridical authorities commenced the processes of policing female management of pregnancy by introducing laws which clearly prioritised bourgeois understandings and which, therefore, made abortion illegal irrespective of the senses and sensations of the mother, the medical profession concurrently began the process of wresting control of the entire birth process from traditional female midwives.[55] Specialisation within the medical profession occurred at the same time and from the 1880s 'gynaecology was becoming a speciality in its own right, and one quite distinct from obstetrics'.[56] By the turn of the century efforts to drive female midwives out of the arena of pregnancy management were so clearly on the political agenda of the medical profession that, in 1902, when a physician politician presented to the New South Wales parliament a Bill which would have allowed for the regulation and registration of midwives, similar to the 1902 British *Midwives Registration Act*, he was opposed by the profession for attempting to 'create and license an inferior type of practitioner, who would be in opposition to the general practitioner'.[57] This licit mobilisation and organisation by the medical profession also had an illicit program. Doctors moved into the abortion networks as one consequence of their general consolidation of the entire field of treating human ailments. Like their campaign against 'quacks' and midwives, their competitive move against traditional abortionists was effected through strategic legislation.[58] Deaths in lying-in establishments had to be covered by a medical certificate. One or more doctors could issue such a certificate. No further checks were necessary and, so long as the stated cause of death was natural, there would not be an inquest. Senior-Sergeant Sawtell testified to the 1904 Birthrate Commission that medical malpractice was rife, and cited this example:

> Only last month I had a case where a girl was operated upon by a medical man. She died in a nurse's home—his own home,

practically, though it was under the name of nurse and a
certificate was given by another doctor, who had not treated her
at all, merely to oblige his fellow practitioner. He gave a certificate
of pleurisy.[59]

With a death certificate duly forged, bodies could go straight to
an undertaker for burial with no post-mortem and it was only
under unusual circumstances that any suspicion could be cast on
the abortionist. The unusual cases when police intervened
occurred because they had been tipped-off. They would receive
information from suspicious bystanders or neighbours, anxious
husbands or relatives, and even from rival abortionists or the
corrupt police they kept on their payroll. Kelvin Churches gives
the example of Eva Manning, a Melbourne abortionist, who fell
from favour (and protection) with the police when she gave an
interview to *Smith's Weekly* in 1927, in which she implied that
the police were on her payroll. She was prosecuted some months
after these allegations appeared.[60] Manning's prosecution was part
of a growing trend to prosecute abortionists. As Judith Allen has
noted female abortionists experienced the greatest backlash from
the law and among those prosecuted, 'qualified doctors were
notable for their absence'.[61]

Despite this discriminatory policing, intervention by doctors in
this illegal manner made abortion a more dangerous practice for
women. It seemed that doctors were more willing to sacrifice the
safety of their patients for their own legal safety than traditional
female abortionists had been. For example, a legal loophole meant
that women could be legally curetted once a 'miscarriage' had
commenced so, in some cases, doctors would partially induce
abortions in one centre and then admit the woman into their
private hospitals for a legal curette. Alternatively, women were
required to bring about their own terminations and then seek
legal medical help. One doctor who was criticised by the profession through the pages of the *Australian Medical Journal* was
Melbourne based Dr Barker. In October 1882 the journal published a lengthy report on 'The Stentt Case' in which 'a young
married woman named Annie Stentt, aged 28 . . . died suddenly
in Dr. Barker's consulting room on August 4th.' Although he
was called to give evidence to the coronial inquiry Barker was
not charged with any offence.[62] Later that same year, another of
his patients, Mary McPhail, died after throwing herself down the
stairs several times while pregnant. Even the medical establishment were suspicious that she had done so under Barker's
instruction, in order to partially induce an abortion so that she
could then have a legal curette with Dr Barker. Mary McPhail

died but, again, Barker was not charged.[63] From the end of last century to the late twentieth century it was easier to practise abortion as a middle class crime than as a working class practice.

The intervention by doctors into the abortion networks not only placed stress upon official attitudes of the medical profession, it also clearly created a great deal of confusion among the working class female networks. Except by word of mouth there was no way of knowing which doctors were willing to perform abortions. Thus the Birthrate Commission gave many examples of indignant doctors reporting that over the preceding ten years there had been a rapid increase in women asking for abortions. Dr Morgan, for example, complained to the Birthrate Commission that these women 'do not see the moral wickedness of it'[64] and he recounted the case of a 'woman coming and asking me, and I said I did not do that sort of thing: and she said "Oh it would be just as well; I have been down twice before to Sydney, but if you do it for me it would not cost so much"'.[65] Working class women, it seems, were increasingly accepting professional medical advice about accouchement and abortion and were turning away from traditional female support networks without realising that doctors' values as regards pregnancy and abortion were fundamentally at variance to their own.

Three decades later, Worcester's figures showed that from the turn of the century working class women were also far more likely to seek admission into hospital for both accouchement and post-abortion treatment. For example, the statistics on married women's abortion rates remained stable from the early to mid-twentieth century but admissions into hospitals for abortion increased radically from the beginning of the twentieth century. In 1900, the ratio of admissions for births compared to those for abortion was eight to one; in 1910 it was five to one; and in 1920 it was two to one. With slight variations this last ratio remained constant up until 1935.[66]

For their part some doctors, too, seemed either not to understand that a completely different attitude towards pregnancy was being displayed by the women who sought out their services, or were intolerant of the possibility that other worldviews were possible. In his evidence to the Birthrate Commission, Dr Skirving, for example, expressed bewilderment as he explained that:

> I know women, who are absolutely good women, in the best sense of the word; and yet there seems to be a twist in them in that way; they do not seem to consider the question of abortion, or any of those things, in as grave a light as even persons not professing to be particularly pious at all would look at them in;

they do not look seriously on the question of either preventing children or unloading children when children are on the way.[67]

By contrast, another witness, Dr Graham had less trouble understanding his female patients' attitudes, as he explained that:

> It is rare to come across a married woman, respectable as she is, who does not think it the correct thing to come to a doctor and ask that she should be 'put regular' because she is pregnant. A sense of the immorality of the thing seems to be an unknown quantity among the majority of them; that is my experience.[68]

The intervention of the medical profession into the traditional networks of women's knowledge meant that increasingly doctors replaced midwives as the dominant practitioners. Consequently, from the 1880s the *Australian Medical Journal* began to advise doctors about safe conduct when treating cases in which they believed abortion to have been procured:

> In every instance it is the best plan to at once demand a consultation with a practitioner of known probity, thus obtaining a sound defence from ugly aspersion and great anxiety . . . such a consultation being refused the case should be at once relinquished.[69]

The movement by working class women away from traditional midwives towards medical practitioners and their attendant institutions, hospitals, was produced only after almost a century of intervention by middle class reformers. Commencing with campaigns, both juridical and educational, to reconceptualise the very notion of pregnancy, and ending in the process whereby birth became something which occurred in hospitals, the motherhood campaigns fitted neatly into the entire process of intervention into working class social practices. In the process the woman within the family was truly being constructed, not as wife, but as mother, for by rearticulating pregnancy as the nurturing of a human being, rather than as a type of female condition, or as part of a woman's health pattern, women were repositioned as being nothing more than bodies-in-waiting. The female body, through the campaigns described in the last chapter and those explored here, was medically appropriated. Through the moral networks and their specific institutions and rooms and through the medical networks and their hospitals and clinics, young working class females became mothers, or mothers-to-be—young women who were all the natural subjects of medical managers.

As the mothers of the nation the individual health patterns of each working class woman became the business of society, their accumulated fecundity and health the concern of the population.

From the end of the nineteenth century, the detailed alteration of attitudes towards pregnancy and abortion played a valuable role in locating the working class family within the networks of normal social order. It was the mother, in that specifically bourgeois location as the central pivot of the family, who was targeted, and through maternal management a general campaign was under way to control and alter the attitudes and behaviours of a whole stratum of society.

7 Speech and silence

In her role as moral linchpin of the modern family, the mother of working class families found herself being introduced, by middle class reformers, to another fundamental task as the nineteenth century merged into the twentieth. In the early decades of the twentieth century, Kerreen Reiger notes, there was 'increasing freedom to talk about sex'.[1] This process 'has been noted, and interpreted by contemporaries and more recently as a positive movement away from victorian prudery'. The conditions of emergence of this 'freedom to talk' are explored in this chapter for it can be seen that it was, again, the mother who was assigned the primary duty to teach her family how to talk about sexuality. The resultant debates about policing language brought into play a role for the father within the moral management of the family.

Reiger shows that sexual reformers, at the time, placed this 'freedom to talk' within a context of the enlightenment project in which, finally, the rationalisation of the body encompassed, also, its sexuality.[2] That there was a change in the language pertaining to the sexual from the middle of the nineteenth century to the 1930s is indisputable, but it is questionable that it was part of a linear path to 'enlightenment'. This chapter places it in the context of replacing one set of references with another—with removing the language of 'the flesh' and introducing that of sexuality. Midway through last century middle class reformers showed a strong interest in language. The inappropriate laughter and language of the children and adults of the non-respectable working class drew strong condemnation from many middle class commentators, such as witnesses to parliamentary inquiries and investigative journalists. The specific components of the children's language which upset these investigators were both the words used and the topics which were spoken about. Giving evidence in 1859 to the Select Committee into the Conditions of the Working Class one witness went so far as to claim that 'in no part of the world I have visited have I ever heard language so obscene and profane as I have from the children of [Sydney]'.[3]

The role of language in the classing process is the subject of this chapter. A set of campaigns, both social and juridical, to eradicate key words from the vocabulary of the working class will be explored. In the first section, as a way of illustrating how fundamental to experience language is, the chapter looks not at sexuality, but menstruation. Words describing acts, behaviours and desires—that is, the language of the flesh—were slowly eradicated from the language of the middle and upper classes from the end of the seventeenth century and campaigns were under way from midway through the nineteenth to effect the same eradication from the language of the working class. The medical profession, especially during the nineteenth century, and medical scientists (including practitioners of the mind and sex-ologists) claimed for themselves the sole licit right to speak about most aspects of the body. All references to such natural bodily phenomena as the menstrual cycle were completely removed from the vocabulary of the respectable while, at the same time, medical practitioners wrote at great length about the body and its natural urges and cycles in the pages of medical journals. There, in the 'right' arena, the 'authorised' voices discussed the role, function, and effects of bodily cycles, especially menstruation.

The second section of the chapter is concerned with words pertaining to the domain of the sexual, noting the processes through which they were removed from respectable language. One way of speaking was replaced by another at the same time as that which was spoken about was being replaced by an entirely different notion. Sexuality, being invisible, can reveal itself only through speech. The chapter, therefore, details the campaigns, commencing at the end of the nineteenth century, to introduce a vocabulary of sexuality into respectable language. It was through these campaigns that the 'freedom to talk', noted by Reiger, was effected. By the end of the century education campaigns were under way to train 'the mother' to speak to her children about the medicalised concept that was sexuality.

The language which accompanied the notion of 'the flesh' was much more concerned with the body than that which accompanied sexuality. The distinction between obscene and polite language was certainly less clear-cut and, in fact, was not clearly present until the eighteenth century. From the middle of the nineteenth century the shift from one notion of sexual presence to another can be found, in the first place, in the loss of the words which described bodily functions. These were first to disappear from polite conversation. From that time it became the case that only within the moral economy of the illicit, still quaintly termed 'swearing', could the respectable describe the biological function performed when 'going to the toilet'.[4] Within common parlance, only rarely would anyone say 'I am defecating or urinating' while 'going to the toilet'.

The stifling of the language pertaining to bodily functions was nowhere as complete or as rigid as references to menstruation, which were gradually removed from polite conversation over a period commencing in the late seventeenth century. Before this time menstruation was a subject which could be discussed by most people, including men. This was because its role in the metaphysical world was, in many senses, public business.

One of the best sources of pre-rational, metaphysical beliefs surrounding menstruation was written in the first century AD by the Roman historian Pliny in his text *Natural History*. Pliny recorded a belief system in which the menstruating woman had both destroying and healing powers, depending on whether she was in or out of harmony with natural events. She had, he wrote, 'the divine gift of kings, for by her touch she can cure not only scrofulous ulcers, but imposthumes of the parotid glands, inflamed tumours, erysipelas boils and defluxions of the eyes'.[5] Her destructive might could cause dogs to run mad and infect humans with rabies, but, in a sympathetic fashion, she could also heal that same disease:

> . . . when a person has been bitten by a dog . . . it will be quite sufficient to put under his cup a strip of cloth that has been dipped in this fluid, the result being that hydrophobia will immediately disappear.[6]

Other sources have recorded that the curative ability of menstrual fluid was often perceived to be more powerful in virgins.[7] This pre-rational pharmacopoeia held that 'the first napkin used by a healthy virgin was preserved for use in cases of plague, malignant carbuncles, and other diseases'. The menstrual cycle, Pliny asserted, had a dual power of creation and destruction upon living things for, in agricultural societies, menstruating women walked among the plants during the night because the menstrual cycle, in harmony with the moon, enhanced growth. By day, however, the same woman would wreak havoc, causing crops to wither and bees to die; 'seeds touched by her become sterile' as her cycle was antipathetic with the sun. Her power over plants extended to animals and humans. In the procreative cycle menstruation signalled non-conception and, by day, both the woman herself and the menstrual fluid became a danger to all foetuses. Pliny noted that, for example, 'a mare big with foal, if touched by a woman in this state, will be sure to miscarry'.[8] One thousand nine hundred years later, in 1915, Dr Morton of Philadelphia reported that the same perception of balance and harmony, contrasted with rupture and disharmony, continued to inform female midwifery knowledge. Female abortionists among some poor working class American communities included catamenial fluid as one of the ingredients in their abortifacient mixtures.[9] In a belief system which accorded such power to the menses, its privatisation was both counter-productive and dangerous. It was truly public business and not the sole business of the women who were, at any given time, menstruating.

This was the case, also, with Christian teaching on the menses, based on the book of Leviticus, which declared the menstruating woman to be unclean. It was written that they should be kept apart from 'the household, the tabernacle and any holy thing for seven days'.[10] Levitical doctrine asserted that impurities collected in women's blood and were discharged in menstrual fluid thus, traditionally, 'to the men of the monasteries menstruation was a symbol of the essential sinfulness and inferiority of woman, polluted alike and polluting'.[11] From the seventeenth century this was no longer rigidly enforced although Patricia Crawford reports that during that century 'there is at least one complaint of a priest refusing to administer communion to a menstruating woman'.[12] The unusual nature of this single complaint illustrates that the church had modified its stance on the subject but, in previous centuries, when the proscription had been policed, menstruation could not possibly have been a private affair. It was spoken about in public and it was the priest's duty to do so. Congregations were, for example, reminded of the Levitical proscription against intercourse during menstruation and, as Crawford has noted, women were expected to absent themselves from holy rituals during this time.[13]

The authority of science and medicine gradually replaced that of the church from the seventeenth century. In line with enlightened pursuits scientific interest in the menses began the quest to find a physiological rationale for this cycle and to find what laws of science were at work to produce it.[14] By the nineteenth century most theories were variations on the theme that menstrual discharge was the release of an excess of blood which had built up and was causing pressure in the vascular system. The periodic spilling of blood was, therefore, righting an unbalanced system. In 1878 Dr George published, in the *Lancet*, an article which summed up the 'state of play' in the menstrual debate. In 'The Rationale of the Menstrual Flow' he maintained that the menstrual cycle had something to do with young girls needing more blood during their relatively rapid early growth. At puberty growth slowed, the blood supply continued and pressure built up. Its release occurred at the 'weakest spot of the vascular system', the uterus.[15] From then on the female system lurched in and out of balance, building up blood and releasing it.

Debates among medical practitioners in medical journals were by no means confined only to scientific or rational theories. The pre-enlightenment beliefs outlined by Pliny no doubt continued to be adhered to by large sections of the population, especially among the working class. While they were increasingly unable to discuss their beliefs except in hushed conversation, the profession who had claimed the right to speak authoritatively in many cases simply moved the same belief system into the pages of scientific journals. Articles were published in professional journals through the nineteenth and early twentieth centuries debating pre-rational beliefs about the power of bodily cycles. These reports pertained not simply to the metaphysical power of menstruation but also to other beliefs such as maternal impressions. Articles about this phenomenon were common in the *British Medical Journal* until the beginning of the twentieth century. Practitioners published their findings, framing their arguments in scientific terms, reporting the significance of experiments or collated statistics which lent weight one way or the other to the presence of maternal impressions. For example, on 14 July 1877, a letter by W. Smyth showed that he had attended 'a clear-cut case' where a woman 'when about seven months pregnant . . . was knocked down in the street by a bull, and in the fall she hurt her right leg against a box'. The mark on her leg stayed for a long time, and the child was born with a mark in the same place which 'bore a most striking resemblance to the profile of a bull'.[16] The next week, on 21 July, William Sedgwick replied that:

> Some years since, an attempt was made at one of our charitable institutions to note down the most remarkable impressions which had affected, during the earlier months of pregnancy, women about to become mothers. But the result of the inquiry, which was, I think, too limited to be regarded as conclusive, was not favourable to the belief that maternal impressions lead to congenital defects in the offspring.

This letter also called for a systematic inquiry to prove once and for all whether the phenomenon were true, or 'founded on popular fallacy'.[17]

The next year the journal hosted a debate over the vexed question of whether menstruating women soured hams, with some doctors reporting their tests had shown that they did[18], and others reporting that they did not.[19] In 1920 Alois Czepa published an article in *Umshcau* referring to evidence collected by Professor B. Schick, of the Medical Society of Vienna, which 'proved' that menstruating women wilt flowers. Schick had inadvertently given a menstruating servant a bunch of roses to arrange in a vase and, on finding them wilted in the morning, had questioned the servant. She confessed that she had foreseen what would happen but had not spoken about it beforehand, probably due to modesty. Schick then set up a control experiment with two servants and found that flowers handled by the menstruating girls drooped and withered after twenty-four hours. 'Menotoxin', the agent to which Schick attributed this strange phenomenon, was also found to impair the leavening power of yeast.[20]

Both these debates over pre-rational theories and those based on rational notions of the body-as-machine, which simply attempted to solve the mystery of the natural workings of the system, are relevant here because they were carried out by a group who claimed for themselves the sole right to speak about menstruation. At the same time as the church's authority gave way to that of science there occurred an attendant silencing in public discussion about this and other bodily functions. Priests had interpreted and policed God's will on the menses and, thus, congregations were frequently instructed on matters relating to it. Science, by contrast, was operating within a completely different system of thought in which there was no necessity to police attitudes to menstruation. When the church lost its authority to science it became no longer the business of anyone but scientists and doctors to speak of the menstrual cycle. The menstrual cycle was discursively constructed as 'private' or secret only as it was appropriated as the property of science. Menstruation, as Sophie Laws' work has shown, remains a completely unacceptable topic of conversation and continues to be a meaningful topic of the illicit economy of ribaldry.[21]

By the mid-nineteenth century a rigidly enforced silence about the menses had descended on the middle class. Even in the privacy of their own diaries many middle class women did not mention it nor even, it seems, mark the dates of their menstrual cycle. The 1890 diary of Clotilda Bayne is probably typical of private accounts kept by young middle class women. Clotilda was the daughter of an English clergyman. Entries in her diary commenced as she prepared to emigrate to Australia to join her fiance. Daily visits to friends, shopping trips and, to a lesser extent, her anxiety about her forthcoming trip formed the basis of her entries. The only possible references to menstruation were on Tuesday January 14, when she noted 'distracted in mind . . . Lay down on bed a long time. Felt rather better, but very bad'. This entry was accompanied by an asterisk. Two months later a similar sign accompanied the entry on Tuesday, 11 March 1890 which ended with the words 'bad night'.[22]

In 1873 Dr Edward H. Clarke, a Harvard academic, published an influential text, *Sex in Education*, which asserted that mental exertion in girls caused the uterus to atrophy. Clarke's profession as a professor of medicine authorised him to write and speak about the topic. Medical practitioners who rejected his hypothesis debated with his supporters through medical journals until 1920. The *British Medical Journal* published a statistical refutation in 1874 which reported that the American Bureau of Education had collected data from the forty-six colleges and high schools then open to students of both sexes, specifically to ascertain whether Clarke's work had any basis in fact. The fact that they did so illustrates how widespread the text's influence had become. The Bureau's findings were that:

> From all these and from other institutions statistics have been drawn, intended to show that the health of the girls compares very favourably with that of the young men in similar circumstances, and the rate of mortality, so far as it can be estimated from inquiries into the subsequent career of the students, is somewhat lower in the case of the women than in that of the men . . . Of the female graduates it appears that three-fourths have since married, and four-fifths of these were, two years ago, mothers.[23]

In 1874, the prominent British sexologist Henry Maudsley, who was a strong Clarke admirer, reproduced in the *Fortnightly Review* Clarke's central thesis but adapted it to accommodate English conditions. This was not a medical journal and he felt compelled to plead that the subject was so important that it should also be read by non-medical people.[24] Dr Elizabeth Garrett Anderson, who was completely opposed to Clarke's theory, did not agree. She recorded her annoyance at having to discuss the subject in other than a medical text, adding '[w]e cannot but suggest that there is grave reason for doubting whether such a subject can be fully and with propriety discussed except in a professional journal'.[25]

Her assumption that menstruation was 'such a subject' which should be discussed only by medical experts was not a personal peculiarity. Rather, she was stating an obvious and understood social 'etiquette of silence' which had permeated through the middle class.[26] Dr Helen Kennedy's survey of American school children in 1896 is further compelling evidence of this. She found that of one hundred and twenty-five female pupils at a selected school, thirty-six were completely ignorant about menstruation at the time of their first menses and a further thirty-nine had only vague knowledge about it.[27] Havelock Ellis, in a 1922 publication, reported having found a strong trend of trauma among pubescent girls who had been horrified at the onset of a menarche they knew nothing about. By way of illustration he cited the example of a fifteen-year-old girl whose case had been reported in the French newspapers some years before:

> [She] threw herself into the Seine at Saint-Ouen. She was rescued, and on being brought before the police commissioner said that she had been attacked by an 'unknown disease' which had driven her to despair. Discreet inquiry revealed that the mysterious malady was one common to all women and the girl was restored to her insufficiently punished parents.[28]

The absence of any reference to menstruation within the middle class household continued well into the twentieth century. The following two examples concern women who reached the age of menarche in the 1910s. The first, C, a middle class woman who shared her bedroom with a younger sister, started menstruating when she was about fifteen. She recalled the experience as follows:

> So many things we did on Sunday. My sister and I with our new costumes went for a walk on Sunday, and my back ached like mad, all the time, and that night when we were going to bed I discovered the stains. And I said to her, I said, 'What on earth is this?'. 'Oh', she said, 'that's all right. That'll happen every month'. Two years younger than me. She's had it and we shared a room. We were together all the time. How she got away with that I don't know. She told me what she knew and the next day she said 'We'll have to get something to wear'. I don't know what she'd been doing all that time. So we wrote a little note to Mother and caught her in the far corner of the washing place, laid it down beside her and scuttled out to the tool shed. She had, oh eyes, and they can flash, anger, and gave us towels. No more discussion.[29]

Another woman who commenced menstruating when she was seventeen was not told of its existence by either her wealthy grandmother, with whom she lived, nor her friends, who presumably had experiential knowledge of it:

> I remember the first night that I took my pants off, I called [my grandmother], and I said 'Look at my pants, there's all blood in them'. And then she told me that was natural and I'd be giving that every month, that I'd developed into womanhood . . . It was never discussed in those days. Never talked about.[30]

By the turn of the century and, probably, for at least forty years before that, the same discursive pattern and its effects was to be found in the respectable working class. L, an English woman who worked in a textiles factory, recalls experiencing her menarche, aged eleven, in the 1910s, as a complete surprise:

> . . . the very first day when I went to ask, from school, you know, I asked to go to the toilet and of course . . . I see this blood and, of course, it sort of give me a bit of a shock but, anyhow, all I did—because we were always told to be moral . . . not frightened. You know it's your own private affair . . . when I came home I told my mother . . . I did worry. But when I went home—I went home—and told my mother and she said, 'Oh, that's all right' and she sat me down and got me this cloth and everything. We didn't have those bought ones you have today and she got this piece of cloth, you know, the diapers as we called them and she had this band—of course she had always them prepared because she had the girls before. There was two. You know even my own sister never discussed it—till it happened.[31]

The effective removal of a way of speaking about this feminine cycle occurred simultaneously, and as a part of the same process, with the disempowering of women's networks. A campaign was under way to replace one way of conceptualising menstruation— and, more importantly, the female body itself—with another conceptualisation. Practitioners within rational science, who represented the body as a machine, repositioned the female body as a powerless and fundamentally flawed system. Once women had controlled the networks of knowledge about menstruation's metaphysical power. By the end of the seventeenth century, among the middle and upper classes, women were subject to campaigns which encouraged them to understand and relate to their bodies in the medical, middle class, enlightened way. From the middle of the nineteenth century these campaigns began to affect the attitudes and beliefs of working class women.

At the same time the body was being confined from view. This process began to permeate European society in the seventeenth century, commencing with the upper classes and moving slowly down through the lower classes. In Germany, for example, 'the sight of total nakedness was the every day rule up to the sixteenth century. Everyone undressed completely each evening before going to bed, and likewise no clothing was worn in the steam baths'.[32] As the body became concealed so, too, did conjugal sexuality. Throughout the nineteenth century the privatisation of the bedroom and, therefore, of sexual intercourse, was accompanied by the stifling of language which referred even to the act of going to bed, let alone to having sex.

From the end of the eighteenth century a whole area of educational mechanisms, social mores, and prescriptive juridical tools ensured that only the authorised discussed sex, and even these 'experts' were more comfortable engaging in discussion in their journals rather than in spoken conferences. Only within scientific discourses could these subjects be discussed and only using the correct scientific terms. Others risked being charged with obscenity if they dared enter into the dialogue. William Chidley's case history illustrates well the danger for the uninitiated in wandering into this chartered land. Chidley, an uneducated self-styled sexologist, believed that 'natural' sexual intercourse should occur when the penis was flaccid, when the females' sexual excitement would cause her vaginal muscles to draw the penis inside. Penetration by an erect penis, he believed, would cause the female 'shocks of coition'. To his dying day he believed that this is what had killed his *de facto* wife, Ada. He published his theories in a book entitled *The Answer*, which was found by the Crown Solicitor to be indecent on the ground that:

> The book in question does contain passages which are indecent in themselves, and is evidently the work of a crank who thinks he has a mission to reform the relation of the sexes. The work so far as I can judge appears to be a bona fide attempt to contribute to the science of human physiology, with a view to removing what the writer believes to be evils the result of present day ideas and practices in sexual matters . . . The work is not written or published in the usual style of a medical treatise, the language being mainly untechnical. The book appears to be regarded by the author as a work of physiological research, however crude or mistaken he may be.[33]

Chidley's crime was not just that he spoke about sexuality but, also, that he spoke about it in the wrong way. He used the wrong words and he spoke to the wrong people. By contrast, some nineteenth century medical sexual theorists lapsed into Latin when describing what they considered to be particularly sensitive aspects of case histories. In this way educated and medical readers could follow the graphic details, while the amateur reader whose

134

access to the text was restricted in the first place, was prevented from sharing in the secret.[34]

As in the case of menstruation, through the nineteenth century, the creating of a space for the new official discourses to emerge resulted in the reality that, except for doctors and scientists, people did not have a day-to-day language with which to speak about sexuality. Among the middle class from the early years of the nineteenth century it became increasingly difficult to make any reference at all to sexual intercourse. Although a whole field of historiography has debated how deeply this permeated the middle class[35], its significance lies in the fact that the inability of members of the class to talk about sexual intercourse was the normative situation. By the mid-Victorian period to at least the 1920s, some portion of two generations of women and men married without having a language in which to know about sexual intercourse. Ada, William Chidley's *de facto* wife, of lower middle class background, was one.[36] Another was Charlotte Carmichael who was married at the age of thirty-nine. She was the mother of sexologist Marie Stopes.[37] She, in turn, passed on no information about sexual intercourse to her daughter, Dr Stopes.[38] Of the same generation, born in Australia in 1897, was D, who described her ignorance in the following way:

> I was married at twenty-nine and the woman who became the mother of my sister-in-law said to me 'Do you know what's going to happen the first night?'. I said 'No, I haven't any idea of anything'. And she said 'Please put a clean piece of cloth in your bed and sleep on it'. I said 'Why?' She said 'You'll find out'. It was a whole enigma and I was twenty-nine.[39]

For this woman's entire pre-marriage existence, reference to sexual activity and to genitalia was completely absent. 'I didn't know the two figures of people', she explained. 'I knew my figure. I didn't know what the figure of a man was'.

Although evidence on male ignorance about sexual intercourse is less documented than that of female lack of awareness, Peter Botsman has cited a letter written around 1920 in New South Wales, which indicates the author had not been given any details about sexual matters, either by his parents or friends. The author believed that he had contracted venereal disease by masturbating:

> . . . if I had only been told and given intelligent instructions on sexual matters this awful thing would never have happened. Oh why is not circumcision compulsory and why is not every boy given a book such as 'what a young boy ought to know'. I am quite sure that if such was the case that there would be no sexual maniacs such as I in the world. Parents will *not* do their duty in

these matters so why does not the state do so, as there would be very little disease and such as I would not be exist.[40]

It was middle class reformers who led the campaign to remove the language of the flesh from respectable vocabularies. In a process commencing at the end of the seventeenth century, this removal spread through the middle class, culminating in the stifled language, or prudery, which many historians have claimed characterised the Victorian period. From the mid-nineteenth century a concerted attempt was made to stifle also the language of the urban working class. The reports of the first wave of middle class surveys in the late 1850s show the clash of two cultures, with a crucial part of the clash being over middle class observers' horror at the common speech of the people they observed. The direct and explicit reference to sexual activity was commented on by many of the witnesses. The New South Wales Select Committee into the Conditions of the Working Classes, for example, was told by one witness that:

> So offensive are the conduct and language on these occasions that on returning from Chapel with any of the female portion of my family, I am compelled to go round by Elizabeth street; and even, when alone, it is most unpleasant to pass along the walk.[41]

Working class youth socialising on the streets were the cause of his distress. Another witness expressed his horror at overhearing the eleven-year-old brother of a thirteen-year-old casual prostitute tell his sister that '[t]wo men were coming down who wanted a —'.[42] Whatever word the boy used, represented only by the ambiguous dash, the perceived need for the censorship immediately placed his language in the realm of the obscene.

That the working class had words to discuss sex is recorded in a variety of historical accounts. Folklorists have recorded the rural tradition of bawdy songs that accompanied important rites of passage, including weddings.[43] The text of the anonymous Victorian pornographic text, *My Secret Life*, is scattered with accounts of direct reference to sex by working class women.[44] The same ability to speak is reflected in the 1858 evidence of a young Irish woman, Mary Murphy.[45] While in prison Mary became pregnant and blamed the gaol warden, Mr Allen, an elderly man whom, she alleged, forced her to have sex with him. Mary's testimony has been edited by the middle class recorders of her deposition but, nonetheless, her account is worth studying for the way in which her narrative is constructed. Although throughout the text the phrase 'to have connection' is used, what the evidence records is a series of acts, positions, conversations, and feelings:

The first time that Mr Allen had connection with me, was during
the absence of Mrs Allen in Sydney for about a week—this was
some time before Christmas, and on a Saturday evening—it took
place in the kitchen—at the oven, and in a standing position,
while leaning against the Oven, it was about dusk in the evening,
one of the other females in the house had gone to the wing for
muster, and the other, was on the green with the children—Mr
Allen had been previously talking to me for about half an hour,
before the connection took place—no person entered the kitchen
during the time Mr Allen was there—during the time he was in
conversation with me, he asked two or three times to allow him to
have connection with me, and I told him I had an objection as I
was anxious to get out of my present trouble before I got into
more. He said he would not get me pregnant, as he was too
old—he then had connection with me, and I made no noise, nor
any struggle.

Her deposition included several other equally detailed accounts
in which they had sex 'in a standing position against the wall'
or 'on the stairs' and 'on his own bed on which he threw me
back'. All of the accounts were presented with a precision that
reveals that reference to sex was still a common part of her
vocabulary or, to put it another way, she could clearly speak
about sex. The last account further illustrates this:

The next occasion was on the top of the stairs about three weeks
or a month after the last—I was coming from the dining room
with a waiter in my hand, when Mr Allen put his arms around
me, and pulled me down on the steps, he then sat down beside
me, and asked me to let him have connection with me, I said no,
we will be caught, but he replied that there was no one down
stairs—I remained with him for about half an hour, and was lying
on the top of the stairs all the time he had connection with me.

Not only could Mary clearly speak about the act of intercourse
but a witness, Boyle, who claimed to have seen her having sex
with another man, could also speak quite explicitly. His lack of
embarrassment at watching them shows, as one would expect,
an absence of any perception of sexual activity as private. Indeed,
Boyle even told the court that he called another man to watch
the pair also. Boyle, who could sign his own name but did not
write his statement, is recorded as saying:

I looked through the windows, and saw Mary Murphy lying on
her back on the ground near the Table, and Mr Bowen on her
person, and apparently in the act of having connection with her.
Murphy's petticoats were up, and Bowen's trousers were down.

Murphy's and Boyle's accounts can be contrasted with that of a young state ward recorded in Margaret Barbalet's study, *Far From a Low Gutter Girl*. Barbalet's research into state ward children has shown that by the end of the nineteenth century it was not uncommon for these working class children, raised entirely in middle class institutions, to be as ignorant about sexual matters, and as unable to speak about sex, as their middle-class counterparts. The following example illustrates both these points, presenting a striking contrast with the testimony of Mary Murphy:

> Mr Braun pulled my clothes and did something else. Something did happen. Mr Braun put his hand between my legs and he put something that was between his own legs into me. That was the first time such a thing ever happened to me.[46]

The campaign to remove the language of the flesh from the vocabulary of the working class often brought into being extremely harsh policing methods. This can be illustrated in the debates over the 1883 amendments to the criminal code of New South Wales. One of the amendments introduced flogging into statutory law. The arguments in favour of its introduction presented it as complementary to parental discipline inside the family:

> If Honourable members would look back to the days of their own boyhood they would remember, as most of us could, that the timely whippings administered by their parents had stopped them from continuing in a course which might have led to serious results. There was a great deal of difference between the whippings administered by parents and those given by the hands of the public flogger. A parent whips for offences committed within the family circle; but the public whipper flogged for offences against the laws of the country.[47]

It was clear to all supporters that flogging was a fitting punishment only for the sons of non-respectable parents. As one member specifically stated: 'If he thought the sons of respectable men were likely to be whipped at the hands of the public flogger, he would not support the clause'.[48] Flogging was, therefore, only for that class of people where the father—and, here we can recognise the role of the father within the modern family—was not acting as the bourgeois social order thought he should, as the link between public bourgeois morality and the family. The necessity to introduce flogging was specifically due to the lack of paternal responsibility among the non-respectable working class. It was self-consciously perceived that in these instances of direct intervention, the state, for all its amorphous ambiguity, acted as a *de facto* parent.

The primary misbehaviour specified in the debate as requiring flogging was 'obscene language'. Other offences were covered in the bill but the members' preoccupation with the elimination of language referring to sexuality was clear. As one member said:

> It provided for the punishment of persons who wrote disgusting words upon the walls of public buildings . . . That filthy language would be seen and read by large numbers of school children, and would flogging be too great a punishment for the wretch who wrote it?[49]

An opponent of flogging also made clear that the eradication of 'obscene language' was the major preoccupation of the amendment. He went on to protest that what the reformers were trying to do was to eradicate an integral aspect of the language of the working class:

> Probably there was scarcely a person who would walk home to-night who would not use obscene language in the public street, and to say that those people should be liable to be flogged was to go to an absurd extreme.[50]

While these members debated the feasibility of whipping in the campaigns to eradicate the language of the flesh from the vocabulary of the working class, prison records also show that incarceration had been employed for some time for this same purpose. The Annual Reports of the Comptroller-General of Prisons in the Queensland, show that between the 1870s and the first decade of the twentieth century, obscene language was increasingly given as the reason for imprisonment, particularly among females. Over this period most reports grouped this charge together with a variety of other charges such as wife desertion but, of those that do not, as Table 7.1 shows, the percentage of total charges represented by obscene language steadily increased until, in 1902, it constituted the largest single category:

Table 7.1 Obscene Language—percentage of total charges

Year	Males	Females
1873	2% of all charges	
1880	8	13
1902	13	29
1906	14	24

Source: Report of the Deputy Comptroller-General of Prisons for 1874; Report of the Comptroller-General of Prisons for 1881; 1903; 1907. Queensland Parliamentary Papers.

In the last two decades of the nineteenth century emphasis shifted from eradication of one set of linguistic terms to the introduction of another. Reformers began to concentrate not on the need to eradicate obscene language among the working class but, rather, on the need to provide mothers of the modern family unit with the necessary vocabulary of sexuality. By the late 1880s some social reformers were expressing concern that the eradication of all reference to sexual and bodily matters had been so successful that the ignorance of the young was exposing them to moral danger and venereal disease. From the 1880s the major concerns about sexuality involved 'the child' and young working class unmarried women. The former, it was believed, were at risk specifically from white slave traders in search of young children for the specialist sex market of the depraved aristocracy, while the latter were the target of unscrupulous seducers. As William T. Stead wrote in 'The Maiden Tribute of Modern Babylon' in 1885:

> . . . girls often arrive at the age of legal womanhood in total ignorance, and are turned loose to contend with all the wiles of the procuress and the temptations of the seducer without the most elementary acquaintance of the laws of their own existence . . . the culpable refusal of mothers to explain to their daughters the realities and the dangers of their existence contributes to fill the brothels.[51]

During the early twentieth century a series of texts appeared instructing mothers about how to discuss sex with their children. The sole responsibility to speak of sexuality lay with the mother. It was assumed that she, and not the father, would be the link between the medical profession and the family unit, and that she would be the teacher of the new ways of speaking. Yet, it was not sufficient simply to urge mothers to 'do their duty by their daughters, and let the girls be instructed, warned, and protected by knowledge'.[52] The deployment of sexuality required that a whole new way of describing sexual practices be introduced. This involved a whole new vocabulary and it was mothers who had to learn this new language. A whole new dialogue written from within medical discourse was therefore introduced which aimed to provide the actual scripts through which mothers learnt a way of speaking about sexuality.

Texts, such as the Mothers Perplexity Series, illustrate the early efforts to talk to children about sex. Through the central character, Alyce, mothers were advised to commence the 'program' when the child was six years old to avoid the danger of 'the beautiful story [being] marred by the boy next door'.[53]

The 'boy next door', like Chidley's text, spoke of the wrong, the untaught, the vulgar and unacceptable set of references. The second part of the program occurred when the child was nine years and the third part at twelve years when young Alyce then 'on the Threshold', was to be more explicitly informed as follows:

'Now, daughter, when I said that you were nearing womanhood, I meant that you were approaching that period of young womanhood when seeds would begin to grow in your body.'
'Then I'm exactly like the flower', said the young girl thoughtfully.
'Yes, dear, and our Love-bud is turning into a blossom; very fast. That is the reason you feel languid at times, and quite unlike your usual self because of the changes which are taking place in your body. Generally when a girl enters the "Teen Country" seeds begin to form in her body, and then pass out into the world.'[54]

The same equating of the reproductive process with that of the rest of the biological world permeated the literature of the social hygiene movement. Differing from the philanthropists, the social hygienists believed that sex education should be introduced into schools and not left to 'unscientific' mothers. Written in 1918, the social hygienist text, *Sex Hygiene and Sex Education*, warns in the introduction that:

In this book we speak plainly about matters connected with sex. Public opinion, for a time at any rate freed from false modesty and prudish sentiment, recognises that something must be done to check immorality and sexual disease, and we propose to strike while the iron is hot . . . We have endeavoured by a progressive system of initiation to expound the necessary knowledge of human sex-relations clearly but with delicacy, avoiding the shock which so many people quite reasonably dread.[55]

The text then went on to explain, without a shred of false modesty, the reproductive cycles of the sweet pea; the king salmon; the lumpsucker, a North Sea fish; the bee; and the May fly, before finally arriving at the 'Development of Human Sex Function'. This same chapter also explained physical changes at puberty by referring to animals.[56]

Marie Stopes, whose text *Married Love* was published in 1918, but who went on to become a major figure in sex reform through the 1920s and 1930s, wrote about sexual intercourse in exactly the same manner. Her research into sex commenced through her efforts to understand why, after two years of marriage, she was not pregnant. She discovered it was because her marriage had never been consummated.[57] Seeking to help other women who were equally ignorant she went on to write what was considered to be a frank instruction manual, although it could be said that it ranged from the coy to the evasive. In the former category was her description of female orgasm as:

> Welling up in her are the wonderful tides, scented and enriched by the myriad experiences of the human race from its ancient days of leisure and flower-wreathed love making, urging her to transports and to self-expression.[58]

In Australia, Jessie Street's Social Hygiene Association, formed in New South Wales in 1916, was specifically interested in taking sexual knowledge into the working class. Based upon her contact with domestic servants, Street believed that working class women were often ignorant about the link between sexual intercourse and reproduction.[59] Advertisements and cover designs of the Association's Annual Reports featured the respectable working class. The 1929 Annual Report showed a young couple, both blindfolded, heading towards a chasm opening in the ground beneath their feet. 'The lack of preparation for marriage means [this]', the text read, before going on to state: 'we say Knowledge means safety. Give them light'. Another represented the street culture of the non-respectables, with two young lads, cigarettes in mouth, hands in pockets, loitering outside a litter-strewn movie cinema enticing a young respectable boy into their midst. Juxtaposed beside this image was the same boy, seated attentively at his mother's feet. 'How does your boy get his knowledge of Life?', the text asked.[60] Marion Piddington's 1925 publication *Tell Them!* also provided a sample conversation in which the mother informed the child about 'the earthly story with a heavenly meaning'.[61]

In this chapter it has been argued that one of the key ways through which the ideas of the working class were shaped was through control of language. This was achieved through a process in which the vocabulary of sexuality was taught through written texts, to mothers and sometimes to teachers. In this way society at all levels and, in particular, the working class learnt the correct way of speaking and the correct way of understanding the notion that was sexuality. As one set of words was removed so, too, were the concepts and ways of perceiving that they described. The earlier working class discourse which reflected an understanding of the sexual as the urges of the flesh relied upon a corporeality which was absent from middle class conceptualisations of sexuality. Thus the first campaigns to eradicate key terms from the language of the working class related to bodily functions not just specifically the sexual aspects of the body. The body was removed from discourse as the language relating to it was removed from respectable narratives until the body seemed not to exist, except in medical treatises. Sexuality, unlike sex, is not corporeal as it exists independently of the individual body. It must be spoken of, for it reveals itself in no other way than through speech.

The mother's role in this process was clearly constituted. She was forever on duty guarding against the presence of inappropriate childhood sexual urges. She also had the primary role of introducing the correct language into the family. During the nineteenth century one of the measuring instruments used by the social surveyors which assigned a family a place in the classed society had been the language of the children. Their language—the words used and the topics discussed—was an indicator of the morality of the mother and, thus, of the whole family unit. Historians of Victorian morality have posited the process through which words were removed from the vocabulary of the respectable as being a stifling brought about by repression. As Foucault has noted, however, power is not just restrictive, it is also creative, and the processes discussed in this chapter show precisely this. It was not a stifling process which reduced the sum amount of permissible words, but a constructive process which replaced one set of words and their attendant understandings and behaviours with another set and another way of relating to the body. It was, in short, an integrative process which recognised the power of language in modes of behaviour and, when the middle class reformers began the process of teaching the mothers of working class families a complete new language, they signalled the final integration of the respectable working class into society. At the same time they signalled, too, the inextricable interweaving of the two discursive constructs—the working class and sexuality.

Conclusion

The working class is a discursive construct which came into existence at a given moment in history, through a particular range of practices and understandings, and which emerged only in relation to particular ways of thinking. It has been the central argument of this book that, from the middle of the nineteenth century, the notions of morality and then, later, sexuality, provided the means through which the middle class constructed that discursive category. Inherent in this argument is the claim that the category of the working class, being of middle class production, assumed meaning only because this politically dominant group gave it meaning and that, in the first instance, it was not a meaningful category to the people who were being thus organised. To put this another way, in the first stages of its emergence the category of the working class had no meaning outside of the consciousness of the middle class who were articulating it. Later, because discourse has effect, the category and its associated concerns became meaningful to the people who were positioned within 'the working class'.

Having been subject to middle class intervention based upon reasoning which brought the category into play, these people responded to the categorisation which had been imposed upon them. The effect of these people's accommodation of the discursive concerns of the category was that they became a part of a more general bourgeois construction, society. The various overlapping sections of what had previously been conceptualised as the lower orders responded to their new categorisation as the working class and gave the term a meaning of their own. This process has been noted in traditional Marxist studies, and has been identified as a stage in history which saw the development of working class consciousness. Traditionally, in Marxist theory, working class consciousness is said to come about when a class shifts from being a class in itself to being a class for itself. The analytical tools of genealogical analysis point to a different, but related, explanation. From this point of view the working class become aware of themselves as a class—that is, acquired working class consciousness—when those people fixed inside the embracing term, the working class, accepted the discursive construct 'working class', giving it their own meaning. The result was that what these people understood to be 'the working class' was, and is, not the same construct as that which middle class reasoning articulated.[1]

The quest of labour and social history to find the 'real' working class, and to give them a voice, makes sense only within this context. That is, what they are doing is separating the two constructions and focusing upon the working class understanding of a discursive articulation—a project which is complicated by the manner in which the middle class construction politically, historically, and philosophically overlays that constituted by the working class themselves. This book has been concerned with uncovering the conditions of emergence of the middle class construction of the working class. It has shown that the idea of a single working class emerged at the end of the nineteenth century. Previously, from the middle of the century, through the influence of the emerging discipline of sociology, the more indefinite notion of the lower orders was reorganised into one which identified two working classes, which have been described through this book as the respectable and non-respectable. These labels equate with a series of related terms used by a variety of nineteenth century theorists covering a broad range of ideological persuasions: Marx's *lumpenproletariat* and proletariat; temperance societies' sober and inebriated; evangelicals' quiet and rowdy; liberal utilitarians' notion of those who chose squalor and those who had squalor imposed upon them; and the authors of etiquette and manners manuals who distinguished between those who looked to the middle class for models of behaviour, and those who, they thought, wilfully ignored middle class behavioural modes.

The division of a section of society into distinct groupings had both philosophical and political underpinnings. The very notion, society, came into being during the nineteenth century. Society was thought of as fundamentally rational and as a measurable concept. Its class demarcations provided for a more scientific dissection than the indeterminate numerous ranks of the earlier formulations of social order. The bourgeois conceptualisation of a society comprising of two working classes, a middle class and an upper class (left over from feudalism but still very powerful) was one in which everyone had their own place and their own range of behaviours and expectations, and was very much in keeping with utilitarian rationalism, as well as bourgeois strategies of order.

The bourgeois institutions of the hospitals, factories, schools and the modern army allowed for precise control over the individuals within these institutions. Everyone was mapped and ordered, the organisation of individuals was made to equate with the organisation of space.[2] In the schools, for example, the pupils sat in the same place, the same row, every day; they had been allocated to the space according to graded merit. The equating of place with individual reflected the type of student they were; in some schools the 'best' sat at the front, in others the 'worst'.[3] Similarly, in the factories each worker returned to the same place in the assembly lines each day. Added to the juxtaposing of place with individual is the attendant strategy of surveillance exemplified by modern prisons, but present in all bourgeois institutions. This was a theme focused upon in chapter four in relation to the organisation of industrial schools, and chapter five in relation to charitable asylums. These bourgeois institutions were microcosms of bourgeois society, neatly and rigidly divided.

However two classes—the upper class or aristocracy and the non-respectable working class—were sites of tension within the ordered representation. The former, although merging with the new industrialists throughout most of Western Europe, nonetheless fitted uneasily within the rational ordered society of the bourgeoisie. To utilitarian theorists they were the vestiges of irrational and superstitious feudalism[4] and they were lambasted for being politically irresponsible and fundamentally immoral by the middle class who were frustrated at being politically constrained by the continued economic strength of this landed class.[5] Yet, it was not utilitarian logic but psychological scrutiny which, in theory if not in fact, tamed the excesses of the upper class, identifying their behaviours as symptomatic not of depravity and conscious manifestations of excess, but of pathological sexual disorders. The political effect of this classification remains to be studied. The same process of psychological scrutiny, when applied to the non-respectable working class filled the lunatic and destitute institutions of late nineteenth century society.[6] This class, too, was conceptualised as the vestiges of past times by many social analysts including Marx and Engels, whose *lumpenproletariat* provided an irrational and counter-revolutionary presence among the rational proletariat:

> Of all the classes that stand face to face with the bourgeoisie today, the proletariat alone is a really revolutionary class . . . The 'dangerous class' [the *lumpenproletariat*], may, here and there, be swept into the movement by a proletarian revolution, its conditions of life, however, prepare it far more for the part of a bribed tool of reactionary intrigue.[7]

Witnesses to such inquiries as the New South Wales Select Committee on the Condition of the Working Classes of the Metropolis in 1859–60, echoed their sentiments, complaining that over a decade after transportation had ceased, the old convict class, and especially the female elements within it, were still a major contaminating influence among the working classes.[8]

Within the utilitarian style of reasoning, the non-respectable were located as an out-group existing on the fringes of ordered society—indeed, in many texts, they were called 'the out-cast'. Within psychological reasoning, these people were classified as the sick, feeble-minded and insane. In utilitarian notions of ordered society the non-respectable were identified through use of the notion of morality. Observable behaviours, such as drinking and non-conjugal sexual activity, were referred to as evidence of immorality, as chapter two discussed. Within utilitarian rationalism intemperance deprived men (*sic*) of the ability to reason (in the process making them more like beasts than men) and positioned them as sites of disorder, and robbed women of control of their sexual urges.[9]

Within psychological reasoning it was the late nineteenth century construction of sexuality which provided the grid through which individuals were fixed within 'their' class category. Had the discourse of sexuality not emerged at this time, the working class as a distinct knowable entity would have emerged as a fundamentally different construct. Conversely, had the working classes not already been articulated as sites for middle class scrutiny and intervention, sexuality would have emerged in relation to a different discursive order. The discourses of sexuality and of the working class were deployed together, each one feeding the other, each overlapping and interrelating. They emerged together, at the same moment in history, with their joint articulation being based upon the same ways of knowing.

The banishing of the language of sexuality from licit conversation took place at the same time as the non-respectables, reconceptualised as the sick and pathological, were banished from the sociological gaze. As medical science, including psychology and psychoanalysis, claimed for itself the role of hearing and interpreting the confessions of sexuality, these new scientific disciplines also laid claim to the minds and bodies of the non-respectable.

This book has provided a framework within which to contextualise the process of banishment of one of the working classes—and, in the process, to understand why Hugo's *Les Misérables* is an untranslatable term. The main focus of the book, however, has been the articulation of the discursive grouping which was left in the sociological gaze—the respectable working class. The process by which the two working classes first emerged over a fifty year period and then one disappeared over the following two decades is just the *beginning* of the story.

While the intervention into the lives of the non-respectables and the stifling of their culture (which had links back to the peasant cultures of pre-industrial times) really took place, and was clearly experienced as repressive, the feelings of these people about the processes have not been discussed here. Rather the concentration has been upon what the discursive articulations and the modes of intervention reveal about the bourgeois world-view. The processes described here are the ways in which the middle class organised knowledge about two inter-related categories—sexuality and the working class. When the middle class invaded the working class family with their charity workers, doctors and, eventually, social workers they did not just record information about family dynamics inside the working class but, rather, they told a story about middle class family dynamics.

The range of inquiries about the sexual practices which fell within the modern notion of incest and which occurred within the working class really revealed very little about working class family sexual dynamics. These inquiries did, however, reveal a great deal about middle class anxiety over sexual dynamics inside the middle class family. Practices revealed in social surveys horrified the middle class viewer, not because they were foreign to their own experience, but because they were too familiar—they pointed to an inherent tension in the sexual economy of the middle class family. Working class men brought before courts, charged with sexually using their daughters, stood condemned for failing to resist a clearly present tension in the modern family. The unbalanced sexual dynamics and the ambiguous place of the father in the guarding of the sexuality of children were highlighted as men like Charles Neuman (whose case was discussed in chapter three) were called upon to explain their failings.

In the same vein, when the sexuality of working class children was placed under the spotlight during the last two decades of the nineteenth century, they were understudies for the real actors who were the daughters of middle class families. Unlike utilitarian styles of knowing, psychological reasoning, which was emerging alongside the concern over the sexuality of children, did not respect class barriers. While the impact of environmental conditions might provide the wherewithal to argue that working class children, unlike their middle class equivalents, were trained into precocious vice, the internal drives of sexuality, if present in one child, were present in all. As chapter four explored, the debates about whether sexuality in children was normal or deviant did not posit that it was normal in the children of one class and deviant in the children of another. The essences of humans, such as intelligence and sexuality, could be *affected* by environmental conditions but were not *determined* by them. In order for the middle class family to consolidate its central position as the only site of normal conjugal sexuality, children had to be positioned inside it as sexless beings. The determination to illustrate, through social surveys and through law, that children stood outside the discourse of sexuality, clearly illustrated that point by concentrating upon working class children. What was revealed, in the process, was very little about working class children but a great deal about the middle class mapping of sexuality within their own ranks.

The organisation of the 'problematical' sexuality of pre-marriage daughters of the working class outside the family can also be similarly contextualised. Debates about the sexuality of children of tender years had predated the late nineteenth century and early twentieth century popularisation of the seducer but both were linked within the discourse of sexuality. The sexuality of these young girls or women within all classes represented the last frontier of an exploratory process in which knowledge about the species of sexuality was increasingly mapped and ordered by psychological theorists. The political processes through which attention was turned on the young males of the working class employed, among other strategies, the notion of the seducer to legitimate intervention. This male construct was deployed, however, to explain not male sexual behaviour but, rather, female sexual behaviour. The seducer was the construct around which the case was built to control the entire sexual economy of the unmarried young of the working class. The state provided the mechanism of surveillance in which sexuality itself was undergoing its final mapping. The organisation and institutionalisation of the female youth of the working class completed the deployment of sexuality, and articulated the final category through which the working class was constructed. This category was given a name—teenager—only by the mid-twentieth century. As the young women of the working class were ordered and mapped, both the articulation of the working class as a discursive category and the deployment of sexuality was completed.

Notes

INTRODUCTION

1 Norman Denny, 'Introduction' to Victor Hugo *Les Misérables*, tr. N. Denny, Penguin, Middlesex, 1976, p. 9.
2 E.H. Carr, *What is History*, Penguin Books, Middlesex, 1961, p. 8.
3 Jeffrey Weeks, 'Foucault for Historians', *History Workshop*, Issue 14, Autumn, 1982, pp. 106–19.
4 Phil Bevis, Michele Cohen and Gavin Kendall, 'Archaeologizing genealogy: Michel Foucault and the economy of austerity', *Economy and Society*, vol. 18, no. 3, 1989, p. 327.
5 Benedetto Croce, *History Its Theory and Practice*, tr. Douglas Ainslie, Russell & Russell, New York, 1960, pp. 11–26.
6 Diane Macdonell, *Theories of Discourse: An Introduction*, Basil Blackwell, Oxford, 1986, p. 27.
7 Louis Althusser, 'Ideology and Ideological State Apparatuses. (Notes towards an Investigation)', in *Lenin and Philosophy and Other Essays*, tr. Ben Brewster, New Left Books, London, 1971, pp. 152–5.
8 See, for example, Jeffrey Minson, *Genealogies of Morals. Nietzsche, Foucault, Donzelot and the Eccentricity of Ethics*, Macmillan, London, 1985, p. 9.
9 Jacques Donzelot, *The Policing of Families*, Pantheon Books, New York, 1979, p. 8
10 Kerreen M. Reiger, *The disenchantment of the home. Modernising the Australian family 1880–1940*, Oxford University Press, Melbourne, 1985.
11 Michel Foucault, *Discipline and Punish. The Birth of the Prison* [1975], tr. Alan Sheridan, Penguin, Middlesex, 1975, p. 250.
12 See, for example, I. Zeitlin, *Ideology and the Development of Sociological Theory*, Prentice-Hall, New Jersey, 1968.

13 See, for example, Paul Hirst, 'Psychoanalysis and Social Relations', *m/f a feminist journal*, no. 5–6, 1981. pp. 91–114.

14 Asa Briggs, 'The Language of "Class" in Early Nineteenth-Century England', in *History and Class. Essential Readings in Theory and Interpretation*, ed., R.S. Neale, Basil Blackwell, Oxford, 1983, p. 3.

15 A. Briggs, 'The Language of "Class"', p. 10–11.

16 Harold Perkin, 'The Birth of Class', in *History and Class*, pp. 166–7.

17 Frederick Engels, *The Condition of the Working Class in England*, Panther, Herts, 1976.

18 R.W. Connell and T.H. Irving, *Class Structure in Australian History. Documents, Narrative and Argument*, Longman Cheshire, Melbourne, 1980, pp. 14–15.

19 Connell and Irving, *Class Structure in Australian History*, p. 15.

20 Some key works in this wordy, but inconclusive, debate were Heidi Hartmann, 'The Unhappy Marriage of Marxism and Feminism: Towards a More Progressive Union', in *Women and Revolution*, ed. Lydia Sargent, South End Press, Boston, 1981, pp. 1–43; Juliet Mitchell and Ann Oakley, eds, *The Rights and Wrongs of Women*, Penguin, Harmondsworth, 1976; Veronica Beechy, 'Some Notes on Female Wage Labour in Capitalist Production', *Capital and Class*, no. 3, 1977, pp. 45–66. The Domestic Labour Debate was also a key debate within this effort to bring together marxism and feminism. It included over fifty papers, most of which revolved around trying to show that women's labour power could also be located within the hidden economy of capitalist production as housework. The debate ground to a halt when Maxine Molyneux pointed out that at no point had anyone explained why women, and not men, were engaged in domestic labour. See Maxine Molyneux, 'Beyond the Domestic Labour Debate', *New Left Review*, no. 116, 1979, pp. 3–27.

21 The labour theory of value has a central place in Marx's theorisation of the commodification of labour power. See, for example, Karl Marx, 'Wages, Prices and Profit', in Marx and Engels, *Collected Works*, vol. 1, Progress Publishers, Moscow, 1950. Debate around the validity of the labour theory of value includes Joan Robinson, *An Essay on Marxian Economics*, Macmillan, London, 1966; Michel De Vroey, 'On the Obsolescence of the Marxian Theory of Value: A critical review', *Capital and Class*, Summer, 1978; Erik Olin Wright, 'The Value Controversy and Social Research', *New Left Review*, no. 116, 1979. A critique of the theory can be found in Maurice Dobb, *Theories of Value and Distribution since Adam Smith, Ideology and Economic Theory*, Cambridge University Press, Cambridge, 1973.

22 A point noted by Jeffrey Weeks, *Sex, Politics and Society. The Regulation of Sexuality since 1800*, Longman, London and New York, 1980, p. 41.

23 M. Foucault, 'Preface to Transgression', in *Language, Counter-Memory, Practice: Selected Essays and Interviews*, ed. D.F. Bouchard [1976], tr. D.F. Bouchard and S. Simon, Basil Blackwell, New York, 1977, p. 50.

1 POPULATION AND SOCIETY

1 David Harvey, *The Condition of Postmodernity. An Inquiry into the Origins of Cultural Change*, Basil Blackwell, Oxford, 1989, p. 27.
2 William J. Lines, *Taming the Great South Land. A History of the Conquest of Nature in Australia*, Allen & Unwin, Sydney, 1991, p. 20.
3 Michel Foucault, *The Order of Things. An Archaeology of the Human Sciences*, [1966], Vintage Books, New York, 1973.
4 Foucault, *The Order of Things*, p. 344.
5 Norman Hampson, *The Enlightenment*, Penguin, Harmondsworth, 1982.
6 Zygmunt Bauman, 'The Social Manipulation of Morality: Moralising Actors, Adiaphorizing Action', *Theory, Culture and Society*, vol. 8, 1991, p. 148.
7 Foucault, *The Order of Things*, p. 345.
8 Foucault, *The Order of Things*, p. 345.
9 B. Benjamin, 'Foreword' to J. Graunts, 'Natural and Political Observations mentioned in a following index, and made upon the bills of mortality. With references to the government, religion, trade growth, ayre, diseases, and the several changes of the said city', 3rd ed, reprinted in *The Journal of the Institute of Actuaries*, vol. 90, no. 384, 1964, pp. 4–61.
10 Peter R. Cox, *Demography*. 4th edn, Cambridge University Press, London, 1970, pp. 296–7.
11 J. Graunts, 'Natural and Political Observations', p. 4.
12 Malthus's *Essay* is written as a debate with the key figures of demography of the period. Throughout the text he takes up points raised by, and disagrees with, Hume, Godwin, Condorcet, Susmilch, Wallace, Adam Smith and Price. T.R. Malthus, *An Essay on the Principle of Population*, reprinted Macmillan, New York, 1909.
13 Foucault, *The Order of Things*.
14 For a detailed study of the findings of colonial and post-colonial population surveys, see Gordon A. Carmichael, 'So Many Children. Colonial and Post-Colonial Demographic Patterns', in *Gender Relations in Australia. Domination and Negotiation*, eds Kay Saunders and Raymond Evans, Harcourt Brace Jovanovich, Sydney, 1992, pp. 103–38.
15 Colin Forster and Cameron Hazlehurst, *Australian Statisticians and the Development of Official Statistics*, Australian Bureau of Statistics, Canberra, 1988, p. 2.
16 T.H. Hollingsworth, *Historical Demography*, Hodder & Stoughton, London, 1969, pp. 72–4.
17 Sir James Watt, 'The Colony's Health', in *Studies From Terra Australis to Australia*, eds John Hardy and Alan Frost, Highland Press and The Australia Academy of the Humanities, Canberra, 1989, p. 139.

18 Phillip to Grenville, 17 July 1790. *Historical Records of Australia*, Series 1, vol. 1, 1788–96, The Library Committee of the Commonwealth Parliament, Sydney, 1914, p. 196–7.

19 Karl Marx, *Capital Volume One*, Engish edition 1887, Progress Publishers, Moscow, 1977, p. 612.

20 For more details on Governor Phillips' records on malnutrition see Watt, 'The Colony's Health', pp. 142–3.

21 Phillip to Grenville, *HRA*, p. 197.

22 Portia Robinson, *The Women of Botany Bay: a reinterpretation of the role of women in the origins of Australian society*, Penguin, Ringwood, 1991, p. 44.

23 Robinson, *The Women of Botany Bay*, p. 45.

24 Robinson, *The Women of Botany Bay*, p. 45.

25 Jill Julius Mathews, *Good and Mad Women. The Historical Construction of Femininity in Twentieth-Century Australia*, George Allen & Unwin, Sydney, 1984, pp. 74–82

26 Michel Foucault, *The History of Sexuality, Volume 1: An Introduction* [1976], tr. Robert Hurley, Allen Lane, London, 1978, p. 104.

27 Robert Hughes, *The Fatal Shore. A History of the Transportation of Convicts to Australia, 1778-1868*, Collins Harvill, London, 1987, p. 244. See also Gill Davies, 'Foreign Bodies: images of the London Working Class at the end of the Nineteenth Century', *Literature and History*, vol. 14, no. 1, Spring, 1988, p. 75.

28 Robinson, *The Women of Botany Bay*, p. 13.

29 Robinson, *The Women of Botany Bay*, p. 11; See also Marian Aveling, 'Bending the Bars. Convict Women and the State' in Saunders and Evans, *Gender Relations in Australia*,

30 Ann Gratton. Diary kept on board the ship *Conway* during the voyage from Birkenhead to Melbourne. June to September, 1858, mss 9367, LTL.

31 Mrs King's Journal of her second Voyage to New South Wales, commenced 20th November, 1799, C185, ML.

32 Details of the progress of eugenics in Australia can be found in Carol L. Bacchi, 'The Nature–Nurture Debate in Australia, 1900–1914', *Historical Studies*, vol. 19, 1980, pp. 199–212; also Mary Cawte, 'Craniometry and Eugenics in Australia: R.J.A. Berry and the Quest for Social Efficiency', *Historical Studies*, vol. 22, no. 86, 1986, pp. 35–53.

33 Ann Curthoys, 'Eugenics, Feminism and Birth Control: The Case of Marion Piddington', *Hecate*, vol. XV, no. 1, 1989, p. 79.

34 For more details on the various female emigration schemes to colonies see Charlotte. J. Macdonald, 'Ellen Silk and her Sisters: Female Emigration to the New World', in London Feminist History Group, *The Sexual Dynamics of History*, Pluto, London, 1983, pp. 66–86.

35 See, for example, letters dated 12 October 1842 and 1 July 1845 from the Colonial Land and Emigration Office, Doc. A1297, ML.

36 Carter and Bonus letter dated 18 April 1845, A1297, ML.

37 Dispatches by Bourke, 1833, A1267/5, ML.

38 Rev. Samuel Marsden, *A few Observations on the Situation of the Female Convicts in New South Wales*, 1806. mss18, micr. no. 1923, ML.

39 Christopher Hill, *Society and Puritanism*, Secker & Warburg, London, 1964, p. 443.

40 Jon Stratton, *The Virgin Text. Fiction, Sexuality and Ideology*, The Harvester Press, Sussex, 1987, p. 42.

41 Stratton, *The Virgin Text*, pp. 40–44.

42 Historians have challenged the sociological thesis that the modern nuclear family is small and the pre-industrial family was large or extended. For example Peter Laslett has shown that the average household from the late sixteenth century to the present contained 4.75 persons. Cf. Peter Laslett, *Family Life and Illicit Love in Earlier Generations. Essays in Historical Sociology*, Cambridge University Press, Cambridge, 1977; the subsequent debate is summarised and contextualised in Rayna Rapp, Ellen Ross and Renate Bridenthal, 'Examining Family History', *Feminist Studies*, vol. 5, no. 1, Spring, 1979.

43 Norah Smith, 'Sexual Mores and attitudes in Enlightenment Scotland', in *Sexuality in eighteenth-century Britain*, ed. Paul-Gabriel Bouce, Manchester University Press, Manchester, 1982, p. 47.

44 Stone, *The Family, Sex and Marriage*, p. 35.

45 Weeks, *Sex, Politics and Society*, p. 24.

46 Katrina Alford, *Production or Reproduction? An Economic History of Women in Australia, 1788–1850*, Oxford University Press, Melbourne, 1984, p. 43.

47 Alford, *Production or Reproduction?*, p. 41.

48 *HRA*, vol. 1, no. 6, p. 202.

49 Alford, *Production or Reproduction?*, p. 41.

50 Select Committee into the Laws affecting the Solemnisation of Marriage, VLC, *V&P*, 1857–8, p. 15.

51 J. Bernard, *The Future of Marriage*, Penguin, Harmondsworth, 1972, p. 122.

52 David Tait, 'Respectability, Property and Fertility: The Development of Official Statistics about Families in Australia', *Labour History*, no. 49, November, 1985, p. 88.

53 1881 Census Report, VLC, *V&P*, 1882, p. 224.

54 On the differences between British social survey forms of sociology and the theoretically based French and German version of the discipline see Perry Anderson, 'Components of the National Culture', *New Left Review*, no. 50, 1968, pp. 3–58; and Philip Abrams, *The Origins of British Sociology 1834–1914*, University of Chicago Press, Chicago and London, 1968.

55 Peter Bailey, '"Will the Real Bill Banks Please Stand up?" Towards a Role Analysis of Mid-Victorian Working Class Respectability', *Journal of Social History*, vol. 12, no. 3, 1979, pp. 336–53.

56 Cited in H.J. Dyos, 'The Slums of Victorian London', *Victorian Studies*, vol. 11, no. 1, 1967, pp. 14–15.

57 Henry Mayhew, *The London Labour and the London Poor. Volume 1, The London Street-Folk*, Griffin, Bohn & Company, London, 1861.
58 W.C. Mearns, *The Bitter Cry of Outcast London; An Inquiry into the Condition of the Abject Poor*, reprinted by Portway, Bath, 1969.
59 Charles Booth, *Life and Labour of the People in London*, Macmillan, London, 1902.
60 Graeme Davison and David Dunstan, '"This Moral Pandemonium" images of low life', in *The Outcasts of Melbourne*, eds Graeme Davison, David Dunstan and Chris McConville, Allen & Unwin, Sydney, 1985, pp. 29–57.
61 W.S. Jevons, *A Social Survey of Australian Cities--Remarks upon a Social Map of Sydney, 1852*, mss B846. ML.
62 R.D.Collinson Black, 'Foreword' in W.Stanley Jevons, *The Theory of Political Economy*, Penguin, Middlesex, 1970.
63 Report from the Select Committee on the Condition of the Working Classes of the Metropolis, 1859-60, NSWLA, 1860.
64 Davison and Dunstan, 'This Moral Pandemonium', pp. 29–33.
65 Michael Cannon ed., 'Introduction', *Vagabond Country. Australia's Bush and Town Life in the Victorian Age*, Hyland House, Melbourne, 1981.
66 *The Vagabond Papers. Sketches of Melbourne Life in Light and Shade*, George Robertson, Melbourne, Sydney, Adelaide, 1876.
67 Cited in Raymond Evans, 'Soiled Doves, Prostitution and Society in Colonial Queensland--An Overview', *Hecate*, vol., 1, no. 1, 1975, pp. 8–9.
68 L.T. Hergenhan ed., *A Colonial City. High and Low Life. Selected Journalism of Marcus Clarke*, University of Queensland Press, St. Lucia, 1972.

2 TWO WORKING CLASSES

1 Cited in H.J. Dyos, 'The Slums of Victorian London', *Victorian Studies*, vol. II, no. 1, 1967, pp. 5–40.
2 Dyos, 'The Slums of Victorian London'.
3 Frederick Engels, 'Letter to Sorge, 7 December 1889' in *Marx-Engels on Britain*, Progress Publishers, Moscow, 1953, pp. 522–3.
4 Karl Marx and Frederick Engels, *Manifesto of the Communist Party*, Progress Publishers, Moscow, 1977, p. 44.
5 Karl Marx, 'The Eighteenth Brumaire of Louis Bonaparte', in *Selected Works, Vol 1*, Karl Marx and Frederick Engels, Progress Publishers, Moscow, 1977, pp. 136–7.
6 For more details on the methodology and findings of Parkes' 1859 select committee see A.J.C. Mayne, *Fever, Squalor and Vice. Sanitation and Social Policy in Victorian Sydney*, University of Queensland Press, St Lucia, 1982, especially chapter 7.
7 SCCWCM, p. 8.
8 SCCWCM, Dr Aaron's evidence is on pp. 1316–1322.
9 SCCWCM, p. 9.

10 See for example the evidence of James Hugh Palmer, SCCWCM, p. 68.

11 SCCWCM, p. 10.

12 *Medical and Surgical Review*, August 1859, p. 4.

13 SCCWCM, p. 68.

14 See, for example, C.T. Stannage, 'Uncovering Poverty in Australian History', *Early Days. Journal and Proceedings (Royal Western Australian Historical Society)*, vol. 7, no. 7, 1975–76, pp. 90–106; Shurlee L. Swain, 'Destitute and Dependent: Case Studies in Poverty in Melbourne, 1890–1900', *Historical Studies*, vol. 19, no. 74, 1980, pp. 98–107.

15 Michel Foucault, *The History of Sexuality, Volume 1: An Introduction* [1976], tr. Robert Hurley, Allen Lane, London, 1978; Foucault, *The Use of Pleasure, The History of Sexuality, Volume 2* [1984], tr. Robert Hurley, Viking, Middlesex, 1986; *The Care of the Self, The History of Sexuality, Volume 3* [1984], tr. Robert Hurley, Pantheon Books, New York, 1986.

16 The significance of this shift is addressed in Arnold I. Davidson, 'Sex and the Emergence of Sexuality', *Critical Inquiry*, Autumn, 1987, pp. 16–48.

17 Davidson, 'Sex and the Emergence of Sexuality', pp. 16–48.

18 Jeffrey Weeks, *Sex, Politics and Society. The Regulation of Sexuality Since 1800*, Longman, London and New York, 1981, particularly chapter six.

19 Sander L. Gilman, 'Freud and the Prostitute: Male Stereotypes of Female Sexuality in *fin de siècle* Vienna', *Journal of the American Academy of Psychoanalysis*, vol. 9, 1981, pp. 337–60.

20 See, for example, Sander L. Gilman, 'Black Bodies, White Bodies: Toward and Iconography of Female Sexuality in the Late Nineteenth-Century Art, Medicine, and Literature', *Critical Inquiry*, Autumn 1985, pp. 204–42.

21 Joseph F. Kett, 'Adolescence and Youth in Nineteenth Century America', in *The Family in History. Interdisciplinary Essays*, eds Theodore K. Rabb and Robert I. Rotberg, Harper Torch Books, New York, 1973; R.P. Neuman, 'Masturbation, Madness and the Modern Concepts of Childhood and Adolescence', *Journal of Social History*, Spring, 1975, pp. 1–25.

22 Foucault, *History of Sexuality, Vol One*, p. 60.

23 SCCWCM, p. 12.

24 Evans, 'The Hidden Colonists', pp. 74–100.

25 R.L. Evans, 'Charitable Institutions of the Queensland Government to 1919', MA Thesis, 1969, University of Queensland.

26 Cited in A. Davidson, 'Sex and the Emergence of Sexuality', p. 40.

27 Davidson, 'Sex and the Emergence of Sexuality', p. 34–5.

28 Elaine Showalter, *The Female Malady, Women, Madness and English Culture, 1830–1980*, Virago, London, 1987, p. 94.

29 Further details of the findings and methodology of Jevons' 1858 study can be found in John Ramsland, *Children of the Back Lanes:*

Destitute and Neglected Children in Colonial New South Wales, New South Wales University Press, Sydney, 1986,

30 W.S. Jevons, *A Social Survey of Australian Cities—Remarks upon a Social Map of Sydney, 1858,* B864, ML, p. 20.

31 Jevons, *A Social Survey,* p. 19.

32 Peter Carl Botsman, 'The Sexual and the Social: Policing Venereal Diseases, Medicine and Morals', PhD thesis, University of New South Wales, 1987.

33 Botsman, 'The Sexual and the Social', p. 342.

34 Cited in Evans, 'The Hidden Colonists', p. 76.

35 Report of the Royal Commission to Inquiry into and Report upon the Operation and Effect of the Wine and Spirits Sale Statute, *VPP,* LA. 1867, vol. 5, Hereafter RCEWS

36 RCEWS, p. 1.

37 RCEWS, p. 6.

38 RCEWS, p. 12.

39 RCEWS, p. 7.

40 *Report of the Board of Inquiry into the General Management of the Gaols, Penal Establishments and Lockups of the Colony, QPP, V&P,* 1887, vol. 1, p. 679.

41 RCEWS, p. 11.

42 RCEWS, p. 7.

43 RCEWS, p. 8.

44 RCEWS, p. 8.

45 RCEWS, p. 8.

46 RCEWS, p. 8.

47 Eugenics, which was introduced into scientific discourses in 1883, asserted that human characteristics were carried genetically, and were therefore produced inside the individual and were not a product of social conditions. Both the word and the political notion of scientifically improving genetic stock has been attributed to Francis Galton. This *Inquiries into Human Faculty and its Development* appeared in 1883 and introduced into the human sciences the notion that social science should 'give the more suitable races or strains of blood a better chance of prevailing speedily over the less suitable than they otherwise would have had'. Nikolas Rose, 'The Psychological Complex: Mental Measurement and Social Administration', *Ideology and Consciousness,* no. 5, 1979, pp. 5–67.

48 Psychology which emerged during the period between 1875 and 1925 introduced the idea of 'intelligence', a scientifically measurable component of the individual mind. Rose, 'The Psychological Complex', pp. 12–15.

49 See, for example, Raymond Evans's study of the treatment of the feeble-minded, the lunatic, and the pauper in Raymond Evans, 'The Hidden Colonists: Deviance and Social Control in Colonial Queensland', in *Social Policy in Australia: Some Perspectives,* ed. Jill Roe, Cassell Australia, Melbourne, 1976, pp. 74–100.
In a study which shows that these groupings were largely the same group of people, Evans quotes from the *Worker,* in 1891, in which

William Lane had written that the pauper 'was "vermin" who should not "breathe the same air, or eat the same food, or do aught else that is done or thought by free men" ', p. 88.
50 William Dick, *A Bunch of Ratbags*, 2nd edn, Ringwood, Victoria, Penguin, 1984.
51 Janet McCalman, *Struggletown, Public and Private Life in Richmond, 1900–1965*, Melbourne University Press, Melbourne, 1984, p. 130.
52 McCalman, *Struggletown*, p. 133.
53 Julia Sheppard, *Someone else's Daughter: The Life and Death of Anita Cobby*, Ironbark Press, Bondi Junction, 1991.

3 SEXUALITY AND THE MODERN FAMILY

1 V. Bailey and S. Blackburn, '*The Punishment of Incest Act* 1908: A Case Study of Law Creation', *Criminal Law Review*, 1979, pp. 708–18.
2 A. Wohl, 'Sex and the Single Room: Incest Among the Victorian Working Classes', in *The Victorian Family*, ed. A. Wohl, Croom Helm, London, 1978, p. 209.
3 Lawrence Stone, *The Family, Sex and Marriage in England 1500–1800*, Weidenfeld and Nicolson, London, 1977, p. 491.
4 Stone, *The Family, Sex and Marriage in England*, pp. 221–68.
5 Norah Smith, 'Sexual Mores and Attitudes in Enlightenment Scotland', in *Sexuality in eighteenth-century Britain*, ed. Paul-Gabriel, Manchester University Press, Manchester, 1982, pp. 47–73.
6 Stone, *The Family, Sex and Marriage*, pp. 144–5; 631–3.
7 Stone, *The Family, Sex and Marriage*, p. 221.
8 Stone, *The Family, Sex and marriage*, p. 221.
9 Michel Foucault, *The History of Sexuality, Volume 1: An Introduction* [1976], tr. Robert Hurley, Allen Lane, London, 1978, pp. 37–40.
10 Alan Sheridan, *Michel Foucault. The Will To Truth*, Tavistock Publications, London and New York, 1982, p. 173.
11 Sheridan, *The Will To Truth*, p. 173.
12 Stone, *The Family, Sex and Marriage*, p. 519.
13 Cited in Pierre Darmon, *Damning the Innocent. A History of the Persecution of the Impotent in pre-Revolutionary France* [1979], tr. Paul Keegan, Viking, New York, 1986, p. 4.
14 Nicholas De Venette, *The Mysteries of Conjugal Love Reveal'd*, Charles Carrington, Paris, 1906, 8th edn, reprint of the 3rd edn. London, 1712.
15 Paul-Gabriel Bouce, 'Some sexual beliefs and myths in eighteenth-century Britain', in *Sexuality in eighteenth-century Britain*, ed. Bouce, p. 30.
16 Darmon, *Damning the Innocent*, p. 3.
17 Stone, *The Family, Sex and Marriage*, pp. 144–5.
18 Frederick Engels, 'The Origin of the Family, Private Property and the State', in *Selected Works*, K. Marx and F. Engels, Progress Publishers, Moscow, 1977, p. 498.

19 Jacques Donzelot, *The Policing of Families*, Pantheon Books, New York, 1979.
20 Foucault, *History of Sexuality, Volume 1*, p. 108.
21 Eric Trudgill, *Madonnas and Magdalenes. The Origins and Development of Victorian Sexual Attitudes*, Heinemann, London, 1976, pp. 51–4; p. 120.
22 Marion Piddington, *Tell Them! or the Second Stage of Mothercraft. A Handbook of Suggestions for the Sex-Training of the Child*, Moore's Bookshop, Sydney, 1925, p. 48.
23 Piddington, *Tell Them!*, p. 49.
24 Stone, *The Family, Sex and Marriage*, pp. 144–5.
25 I. Origo, 'The Merchant of Prato' cited in Jon Stratton, *The Virgin Text. Fiction, Sexuality and Ideology*, The Harvester Press, Sussex, 1987, p. 20.
26 Stratton, *The Virgin Text*, p. 21.
27 Fonssagrives, a nineteenth century French philanthropist cited in Donzelot, *The Policing of Families*, p. 43.
28 Stratton, *The Virgin Text*, p. 20.
29 Donzelot, *The Policing of Families*, p. 44.
30 SCCWCM p. 4.
31 SCCWCM, pp. 32–3.
32 SCCWCM, p. 33.
33 *QPD*, LA, Vol XIX, 1875.
34 Cited in Victor Bailey and Sheila Blackburn, '*The Punishment of Incest Act* 1908', p. 710.
35 Report from the Select Committee of the House of Lords on the Laws Relating to the Protection of Young Girls, *BPP*, House of Lords reprinted in *Crime and Punishment, Juvenile Offenders*, vol. 5, Shannon Irish University Press, p. 92.
36 SCLRPG, p. 93.
37 SCLRPG, BPP, House of Lords, 1882, p. 37.
38 Beatrice Webb, *My Apprenticeship*, cited in A. Wohl, 'Sex and the Single Room', p. 203.
39 Wohl, 'Sex and the single room', p. 310. (My emphasis).
40 Bailey and Blackburn, '*The Punishment of Incest Act* 1908', p. 708; see also Bryan Strong, 'Towards a History of the Experiential Family: Sex and Incest in the Nineteenth Century', *Journal of Marriage and the Family*, vol. 33, no. 3, 1973, pp. 457–66.
41 Bailey and Blackburn, '*The Punishment of Incest Act* 1908', pp. 708–18.
42 Bailey and Blackburn, '*The Punishment of Incest Act* 1908', p. 712.
43 *VPP*, LC and LA, June 25, 1890, vol. XLIII, p. 439.
44 *VPP*, LC and LA, June 25, 1890, vol. XLIII, p. 439.
45 For example, the *Age* reported a case of incestuous rape of a twelve-year-old girl by her father on 28 March, 1889.
46 *VPD*, LC and LA, vol. LXIV. 1890, p. 1289.
47 *VPD*, LA and LC, vol. LXIV, 1890, p. 1287.
48 *VPD*, LC and LA, vol. LXIV, 1890, p. 1287.

49 Sct/CC116 *R V. Neumann,* QSA. My thanks to Anne-Maree Collins for bringing this case to my attention.
50 Sct/CC no. 195 of 1900, May, 1900, QSA.
51 Sct/CC no. 57 of 1898, February, 1989, QSA.
52 Progress Report From the Select Committee on Prevalence of Venereal Diseases, NSW*PP,* LA and LC, 1915–16, vol. 5.
53 SCPVD, Bray's evidence appears on pp. 36–41.
54 SCPVD.
55 See, for example, Peter Carl Botsman, 'The Sexual and the Social: Policing Venereal Diseases, Medicine and Morals', PhD thesis, University of New South Wales, 1987.

4 THE INNOCENCE OF CHILDREN

1 Philippe Aries, *Centuries of Childhood,* Penguin, Harmondsworth, 1973; J.H. Plumb, 'Children: the Victims of Time in *The Light of History,* ed. J.H. Plumb, Houghton Mifflin Co., Boston, 1973. See also A. Skolnick ed., *Rethinking Childhood,* Little Brown, Boston, 1976.
2 Aries, *Centuries of Childhood,* pp. 125–30; Plumb, 'Children: the Victims of Time'.
3 Plumb, 'Children: the Victims of Time', pp. 153–4.
4 Lawrence Stone, *The Family, Sex and Marriage In England 1500–1800,* abr. edn, Penguin, London, 1977, pp. 76–89.
5 Aries, *Centuries of Childhood,* pp. 112–15.
6 Aries, *Centuries of Childhood,* pp. 98–130; Elizabeth W. Marwick, 'Childhood History and Decisions of State: The Case of Louis XIII', in *The New Psychohistory,* ed. Lloyd de Mause, The Psychohistory Press, New York, 1975, pp. 199–244.
7 Aries, *Centuries of Childhood,* p. 108.
8 Aries, *Centuries of Childhood,* pp. 120–1.
9 Aries, *Centuries of Childhood,* p. 121.
10 The Select Committees and Royal Commissions into Juvenile crime have been republished by the Irish University Press in a Series entitled *Crime and Punishment Juvenile Offenders.* It is a six volume collection. See, for example The First and Second Reports from the Select Committee of the House of Lords on Juvenile Offenders and Transportation BPP1847, vol. VII, pp. 9–468. *Crime and Punishment Juvenile Offenders,* vol. 1, The Select Committee on Criminal and Destitute Juveniles, 1852.
11 Margaret May, 'Innocence and Experience: the Evolution of the Concept of Juvenile Delinquency in the mid-Nineteenth Century', *Victorian Studies,* vol. 18, 1973, pp. 7–29; G. Pearson, *Hooligan: A History of Respectable Fears,* Macmillan, London, 1983.
12 The 1847 Report of the House of Lords, for example, from Governor of the House of Correction, Tothill Fields, cited the case of a child who was five-and-three-quarters years old, committed by a magistrate who was both short-sighted and deaf and who had, therefore, not

noticed the extreme youth of the child. Select Committee of the House of Lords on Juvenile Offenders and Transportation, p. 200.

13 Lorraine Goldman, 'Child Welfare in Nineteenth-Century Queensland 1865-1911', MA (Qual.) thesis, University of Queensland, 1978, p. 128.

14 'The Orphanages', *QPD*, vol. XIX, 1875, p. 1054.

15 For more details on the passing of this Act in New South Wales, see David McDonald, 'Child and Female Labour in Sydney 1876–1898', *ANU Historical Journal*, vols 10/11, 1973/4, pp. 40–49.

16 Sheila Jeffreys, *The Spinster and Her Enemies. Feminism and Sexuality, 1880–1930*, Pandora, London, 1985.

17 First and Second Reports From the Select Committee of the House of lords on Juvenile Offenders and Transportation, Minutes of Evidence, 1847, pp. 464–5.

18 SCCWCM, *NSWPP*, LA, 1859–60, Minutes of Evidence, p. 12.

19 SCCWCM, p. 12.

20 All of Harrison's evidence is contained in separate Appendix A, pp. 179–81.

21 Jacques Donzelot, *The Policing of Families* [1977] tr. R. Hurley, Pantheon Books, New York, 1979, p. 79.

22 The speed of the Bill's passage in Britain was particularly rapid following the publication of the 'Maiden Tribute'. On 9 July the Home Secretary announced that it had been decided to resume debate on the second reading of the Bill. The same day it passed its second reading. On 13 July it was moved in committee for two weeks, by 30 July it came back for its third reading. The Bill passed its final reading by 179 votes to 71, and was returned to the House of Lords on 7 August. The Commons' amendments were considered and agreed to by 10 August, and it received the royal assent on 14 August. The age of consent became sixteen.

23 Deborah Gorham, 'The Maiden Tribute of Modern Babylon Re-examined. Child Prostitution and the idea of childhood in Late-Victorian England', *Victorian Studies*, vol. 21, no. 3, Spring, 1978, pp. 358–9; Glen Petrie, *A Singular Iniquity. The Campaigns of Josephine Butler*, Macmillan, London, 1971; Ann Stafford, *The Age of Consent*, Hodder and Stoughton, London, 1964, pp. 167–229; Eric Trudgell, *Madonnas and Magdalenes. The Origins and Development of Victorian Sexual Attitudes*, Heinemann, London, 1976, p. 195.

24 Interest in the House of Lords Report had been high in Australia, and had quickly resulted in the formation of Social Purity societies, the first and most vocal being formed in 1882 in South Australia.'The society for the promotion of morality', *Argus*, 18 March, 1885.
By the end of the year it had branches in almost 'every township of any importance', and throughout that year hundreds of people petitioned both Houses of parliament to effect the recommendations of the 1881 House of Lords Report to raise the age of consent to sixteen in South Australia. *SAPD*, 7 July 1885, p. 186.
By October 1883 a further 8000 adults, out of a total South Australian adult population of 137 000, *Census Report of 1881*, had

signed, and in 1884 another 2000 signed. In many of the smaller towns almost every adult female had signed the petition. Figures calculated from 'Notices of Petitions', *SAPD*.

25 *Age*, 17 August 1885.

26 'The Great London Scandal', *Age*, 21 August 1885.

27 Michel Foucault, *History of Sexuality, Volume 1: An Introduction* [1976], tr. Robert Hurley, Allen Lane, London, 1978, p. 104.

28 Stephen Kern, 'Freud and the Discovery of Child Sexuality', *History of Childhood Quarterly*, Summer 1973, vol. 1, no. 1, pp. 117–41.

29 Kern, 'Freud and the Discovery of Child Sexuality', p. 118.

30 Kern, 'Freud and the Discovery of Child Sexuality', p. 135.

31 R.P. Neuman, 'Masturbation, Madness, and the Modern Concepts of Childhood and Adolescence', *Journal of Social History*, vol. 8, Spring, 1975, p. 9

32 Kerreen M. Reiger, *The disenchantment of the home. Modernising the Australian family 1880–1940*, Oxford University Press, Melbourne, 1985, p. 180.

33 Dr Richard von Krafft-Ebing, *Psychopathia Sexualis: A Medico-Forensic Study*, tr. Harry E. Wedeck, G.P. Putnam's & Sons, New York, 1965, p. 254.

34 Kern, 'Freud and the Discovery of Child Sexuality'.

35 Kern, 'Freud and the Discovery of Child Sexuality'.

36 See, for example, The Hon. H. Cuthbert, 'Criminal Law Amendment Bill, 27 August 1880, *VPP*, vol. LXIV, 1880, p. 1286.

37 Hon. H. Scott, *Protection of Young Persons Act*, 7 July 1885, SAPD, p. 186.

38 *NSWPD*, LA, 1883, p. 1139.

39 Hon. J. Colton, 'Social Purity—Withdrawal of Strangers', 10 October 1883, *SAPD*, 1883.

40 Criminal Law Amendment Bill, 2 September 1890, p. 1335, *VPD*, vol. LXIV.

41 Criminal Law Amendment Bill, *VPD*, p. 1336.

42 Hon. Rees, 'Social Purity', 10 October, *SAPD*, 1883, p. 1286.

43 Cited by the Hon. J. Colton. 'Social Purity', 10 October *SAPD*, 1883, p. 1286.

44 Aries, *Centuries of Childhood*, pp. 106–7; Priscilla Robertson, 'Home as Nest: Middle Class Childhood in the nineteenth century in Europe, in *The History of Childhood*, ed. Lloyd De Mause, Basic Books, New York, 1976.

45 Aries, *Centuries of Childhood*, p. 113.

46 Foucault, *History of Sexuality, Volume 1*, p. 27.

47 Cited in Lorraine Goldman, 'Child Welfare in Nineteenth-Century Queensland', p. 151.

48 *Annual Report of the Director State Children Department for the Year 1914*, QPP, 1915–16, vol. III.

49 *Annual Report of the Director State Children Department for the Year 1914*.

50 First and Second Reports From the Select Committee of the House of Lords on Juvenile Offenders and Transportation, Minutes of Evidence, 1847, pp. 464–5.

51 Report From the Select Committee of the House of Lords on the Law Relating to the Protection of Young Girls, *BPP*, House of Lords, 1882, p. 734.

52 Cited in S. Marcus, *The Other Victorians. A Study of Sexuality and Pornography in Mid-Nineteenth Century England*, Weidenfeld and Nicolson, London, 1966, p. 57.

5 SEDUCTION AND PUNISHMENT

1 See, for example, Deborah Gorham, *The Victorian Girl and the Feminine Ideal*, Indiana University Press, Bloomington, 1982; Martha Vicinus ed., *Suffer and Be Still: Women in the Victorian Age*, Indiana University Press, Bloomington, 1972; Noeline Williamson, 'Hymns, Songs and Blackguard Verses: Life in the Industrial and Reformatory School for Girls in New South Wales, 1867–87', *Journal of the Royal Australian Historical Society*, vol. 67, no. 4, 1982, pp. 375–87; Keith Thomas, 'The Double Standard', *Journal of the History of Ideas*, April, 1959, pp. 195–216.

2 Joan Jacobs Brumberg, '"Ruined" Girls: Changing Community Responses to Illegitimacy in Upstate New York, 1890–1920', *Journal of Social History*, Winter, 1984, p. 250.

3 Brumberg, '"Ruined" Girls', pp. 248–50.

4 Michael Sturma, 'Seduction and Punishment in Late Nineteenth Century New South Wales', *Australian Journal of Law and Society*, vol. 2, no. 2, 1985, p. 76.

5 For more on the emergence of the construct of the teenager, and the way in which the discursive articulation of the category determined styles of policing, see Jon Stratton, *The Young Ones. Working-Class Culture, Consumption and the Category of Youth*, Black Swan Press, Perth, 1992.

6 *NSWPD*, 1887–88, p. 239.

7 *NSWPD*, 1887–88, pp. 1240–4. One member cited the case of an employer who had been awarded damages for the loss of his servant's labour after she became pregnant but the woman herself was not entitled to any money despite having a child to raise.

8 SCLRPG, Appendix B, p. 548.

9 'The Bishop of Melbourne's Address to the Young Men of the White Cross Army', *Register*, 11 October 1884.

10 Rev. Charles Olden, 'Immorality: Its Fascinating Temptations, its Awful Consequences, and the Way to Avoid it. A lecture Delivered to Men only, in the Protestant Hall, Sydney, October 8th, 1883, G.W. Walker Papers, mss11, ML.

11 *NSWPD*, 28 March 1883, p. 1139.

12 *Westminster Review*, July 1850, p. 56.

13 'A Heartless Case of Seduction', *Figaro*, 17 May 1884, p. 387.

14 Quoted in *Truth*, 3 May 1884.
15 *Truth*, 11 March 1884.
16 *NSWPD*, LA, 1887–88, p. 2391.
17 'Seduction Punishment Bill, *NSWPD*, LA, 1887–88, p. 2394.
18 'Seduction Punishment Bill, *NSWPD*, LA, 1887–88, p. 2394.
19 For the historiography which debates this view cf. Carol G. Pearce, 'Some Aspects of Fertility in the mid-Victorian Community', *Local Population Studies*, vol. 10, 1973, pp. 25–9; Cissie Fairchild, 'Female Attitudes and the Rise of Illegitimacy: A Case Study', *Journal of Interdisciplinary History*, vol. VIII, 1978, pp. 627–67; P.I.H. Hair, 'Bridal Pregnancy in Rural England in Earlier Centuries', *Population Studies*, vol. 20, 1966, pp. 233–43; Edward Shorter, 'Illegitimacy, Sexual Revolution, and Social Change in Modern Europe', *Journal of Interdisciplinary History*, vol. 11, 1971, p. 240.
20 *NSWPD*, 1883, vol. IX, p. 1185. One of the ways in which these larrikins insulted young women was 'standing on street corners and the steps of hotels or other public places and boldly scrutinising every lady who passes', p. 1185.
21 Chris McConville, 'From "Criminal Class" to "Underworld"', in *The Outcasts of Melbourne*, eds Graeme Davison, David Dunstan and Chris McConville, Allen & Unwin, 1985, p. 72.
22 Stratton, *The Young Ones*, chapters one and two; G. Pearson, *Hooligan. A History of Respectable Fears*, Macmillan, London, 1983.
23 *Age*, 26 July 1908.
24 Cited in Kerry Wimshurst, 'Control and Resistance: Reformatory School Girls in Late Nineteenth Century South Australia', *Journal of Social History*, Winter, 1984, pp. 273–87.
25 SCCWCM, p. 135.
26 S. McInerney ed., *The Confessions of William James Chidley*, University of Queensland Press, St. Lucia, 1977, p. 53.
27 Theodosia Ada Wallace, *The Etiquette of Australia. A Handy Book of the Common Usages of Everyday Life and Society*, Dymock's Book Arcade & Circulating Library, Sydney, 1909.
28 G.R.M. Devereaux, *Cole's Correct Guide to Etiquette For Men and Women*, Book Arcade, Melbourne, 1873.
29 Oliver Bell Bruce, *Don't. Direction For Avoiding Improprieties of Conduct and Common Errors in Speech and 200 Maxims on Conduct, Habits, and Manners*, E.W. Cole Book Arcade, Melbourne, 1919.
30 Mrs. Erskine, *Etiquette in Australia*, William Brooks & Co., Sydney, 1911.
31 Lillian M. Pyke, *Australian Etiquette*, E.W. Cole Book Arcade, Melbourne, 1913.
32 Anon., *Australian Etiquette or the Rules & Usages of the Best Society in the Australasian Colonies Together With Their Sports, Pastimes, Games and Amusements*, People's Publishing Co., Melbourne, 1886.
33 G.R.M. Devereaux, *Cole's Correct Guide*, pp. 28–9.
34 G.R.M. Devereaux, *Cole's Correct Guide*, p. 29.
35 A Friend of Girls, 'Letter to the Editor', *Argus*, 5 May 1885.

36 Extract from the annual report of the president Mrs W.H. Carvossa quoted in the *First Annual Report*, Brisbane Institute of Social Service, 12 May 1908, OM72–21, JOL.

37 OM72–21, JOL.

38 The Parramatta Industrial School Official Handbook 1910, Q364.72/2, ML.

39 *Annual Report*, Director State Children For the Year 1914, *QPP*, vol. III, 1915.

40 Minutes of the Annual Meetings, 7 June 1882 to 23 February 1938, ms 10052, LTL.

41 Letters dated: September 1891, 21 October 1891, 24 November 1891, 26 November 1891, 30 November 1891, 10 December 1891, 12 December 1891, 15 January 1892, Col. Sec., COL/A684, QSA.

42 Michel Foucault, *History of Sexuality, Volume 1: An Introduction* [1976], tr. Robert Hurley, Allen Lane, Harmondsworth, 1979, p. 64.

43 Under the *Industrial and Reformatory Act*, if it was found that a girl 'reaching the age of 18 years is unable to really take care of herself, or that her parents or relatives who have recently taken an interest in her are of very bad characters, in order to protect the girl, by the approval of the Minister she is kept under control for a longer period, that may be extended to the age of 21 years. This provision has been of great benefit to several girls of the industrial schools'. *Annual Report*, Director of State Children Department for the Year Ending 1914.

44 Foucault, *History of Sexuality, Volume 1*, p. 63.

45 Letters and Memoranda, 1876–1926, GRG28/31, 5 August 1910, SAA.

46 Letters and Memoranda, 1876–1926, GRG 28/31, 12 July 1910, SAA.

47 Letters and Memoranda, 1876–1926, GRG28/31, 1 August 1910, SAA.

48 Report quoted in *The Shield*, October 1913, p. 94.

49 *The Shield*, p. 94.

50 SCLRPG, Appendix B. The records showed the following:
Age at which seduced (3076 cases):

At 11 years	3
12	5
13	16
14	79
15	189
16	184
17	247
18	221
19	297
20	280
21	256
22	227
23	132
24	164

25	152
26	128
27	176
rest	320

51 RCDB, p. 289.
52 Michel Foucault, *The Birth of the Clinic: An Archaeology of Medical Perception* [1963], tr. A.M. Sheridan, Tavistock, London, 1973, p. 41.
53 The entire set of correspondence to the *Argus* was reproduced in the Lying-in Hospital's *Annual Report* to Subscribers that year, MS, LTL (no manuscript number).

6 MOTHERING THE POPULATION

1 Jacques Donzelot, *The Policing of Families* [1977] tr. R. Hurley, Pantheon Books, New York, 1979.
2 Paul-Gabriel Bouce, 'Some Sexual Beliefs and Myths in Eighteenth-century Britain', in *Sexuality in Eighteenth-Century Britain*, ed. Paul-Gabriel Bouce, Manchester University Press, Manchester, 1982, p. 37.
3 For details on the history, methodology and findings of these reports see R. Pringle, 'Octavius Beale and the Ideology of the Birth-Rate, The Royal Commissions of 1904 and 1905', *Refractory Girl*, Winter, 1973, pp. 19–27; Judith Allen, 'Octavius Beale re-considered. Infanticide, baby-farming and abortion in N.S.W., 1880–1939', in *What Rough Beast*, eds Sydney Labour History Group, Allen & Unwin, Sydney, 1982; Lyn Finch and Jon Stratton, 'The Australian Working Class and the Practice of Abortion 1880–1939', *Journal of Australian Studies*, no. 23, November, 1988, pp. 45–64; Judith Allen, *Sex and Secrets. Crimes Involving Australian Women Since 1880*, Oxford University Press, Melbourne, 1990.
4 See, for example, chapter four in Kerreen M. Reiger, *The disenchantment of the home. Modernising the Australian family, 1880–1940*, Oxford University Press, Melbourne, 1985.
5 Macquarie to Bathurst, 28 June, 1813, *HRA*, vol. 1, no. 7, p. 781.
6 Cited in Libby Connors, 'Local History, Social History and the Law: An Introduction to the Study of Criminal Records in Queensland History', Paper presented at Joint Masters in Local History/Brisbane History Group Seminar on Archives at the University of Queensland, June, 1987.
7 Linda Gordon, 'Race Suicide and The Feminist Response: Birth Control as a Class Phenomenon in the U.S, Part I', *Hecate*, vol. 1, no. 2, July, 1975, pp. 40–53, and Part 2, *Hecate*, vol. 2, No. 1, January, 1976, pp. 41–51; Daniel Scott Smith, 'Family Limitation, Sexual Control and Domestic Feminism in Victorian America: Towards a History of the Average American Woman', *Feminist Studies*, Winter/Spring, 1973–74; J.A. and Olive Banks, *Feminism and Family Planning in Victorian England*, Liverpool University Press,

Liverpool, 1964; Linda Gordon, 'Why Nineteenth Century Feminists Did Not Support "Birth Control" and Twentieth Century Feminists Do: Feminism, Reproduction and the Family' in *Rethinking the Family: Feminist Questions*, eds B. Thorne and M. Yalom, Longmans, New York, 1982; Angus McLaren, 'Women's Work and the Regulation of Family Size', *History Workshop*, no. 4, Autumn, 1977, pp. 70–9; Angus McLaren, *Birth Control in Nineteenth Century England*, Croom Helm, London, 1978.

8 J.C. Caldwell and L.T. Ruzicka, 'The Australian Fertility Trition; an Analysis', *Population and Development Review*, vol. 4, no. 1, 1981.

9 Pat Quiggen, *No Rising Generation. Women and Fertility in Late Nineteenth Century Australia*, Australian Family Formation Project, Canberra, Monograph No. 10, 1988.

10 Quiggen, *No Rising Generation*, p. 20.

11 P.P.A. Biller, 'Birth control in the West in the thirteenth and early fourteenth centuries', *Past and Present*, no. 94, February, 1982, pp. 3–26.

12 Cited in *Royal Commission on Secret Drugs, Cures, and Foods*, CPP, 1907, p. 37.

13 *Lancet*, May 1906, p. 137.

14 RCSDCF, p. 26.

15 RCSDCF, p. 253.

16 Jill Hodges and Athar Hussain, 'La Police des Familles', *Ideology and Consciousness*, no. 5, 1979, p. 96.

17 This point was illustrated by Rosalind Pollack Petchesky, *Abortion and Woman's Choice*, Verso, London, 1986, pp. 53–4.

18 Allen, 'Octavius Beale re-considered'.

19 Coronial Report, BCC, no. 526/38, 1938, QSA.

20 Dr Hall, *Pharmaceutical Journal*, March 1906 p. 251.

21 RCSCDF, p. 28.

22 All information on the etymology of these words from the *Oxford English Dictionary*.

23 McLaren, 'Women's Work and the Regulation of Family Size', p. 75.

24 R.A. Soloway, *Birth Control and the Population Question in England, 1877–1930*, Croom Helm, London, 1982, p. 117.

25 Stone, *The Family, Sex and Marriage*, pp. 644–5.

26 Stone, *The Family, Sex and Marriage*, p. 645.

27 R. Sauer, 'Infanticide and Abortion in Nineteenth-Century Britain', *Population Studies*, vol. 32, 1978, p. 84.

28 Sauer, 'Infanticide and Abortion in Nineteenth-Century Britain', p. 84.

29 Angus McLaren, 'Birth Control and Abortion in Canada, 1870–1920', *Canadian Historical Review*, vol. LIX, no. 3, 1978, p. 334.

30 McLaren, 'Women's Work and the Regulation of Family Size', p. 75.

31 Jennifer Craik, 'Reflections on the Feminine', *Cambridge Anthropology*, vol. 5, no. 3, 1979, p. 118. It is also extremely interesting that these time-frames match exactly the experiments of the Egyptian gynae-

cologist, Cleopatra, whose experiments upon female slaves found that a foetus could be clearly identified as having male genitalia at forty days, and female genitalia, at eighty days. Joseph Needham, *A History of Embryology*, 2nd edn. Cambridge University Press, Cambridge, 1986, p. 80.

32 Rosalind Pollack Petchesky, *Abortion and Women's Choice. The State, Sexuality, and Reproductive Freedom*, Verso, London, 1986, p. 53.

33 McLaren, 'Women's Work and the Regulation of Family Size', p. 75.

34 RCDB vol. II, p. 117; see also Judith A. Allen, *Sex & Secrets*, pp. 67–73.

35 R. Sauer, 'Infanticide and Abortion in Nineteenth-Century Britain', *Population Studies*, vol. 32, 1978, p. 86.

36 R.H. Nichols and F.A. Wray, *The History of the Foundling Hospital*, Nicholson & Watson, London, 1935, p. 16.

37 'Infant Life Protection Act', *AMJ*, 20 November 1895, p. 16.

38 'Infant Life Protection Act', p. 513.

39 *The Age*, 26 July 1908.

40 Allen, *Sex and Secrets*, p. 69.

41 See, for example, 'The Care of Illegitimate Children in Victoria', *AMJ*, 20 May 1894, pp. 246–9; 'Infant Life Protection Act', *AMJ*, 20 November 1895, pp. 512–14.

42 Report of the Royal Commission on Friendly Societies, 1872–74, *BPP*, 1875.

43 RCDB, vol. II, p. 53.

44 RCDB, vol. II, p. 50.

45 RCDB, vol. II, pp. 104–6.

46 R.G. Worcester, 'The Problem of Abortion', Appendix 2 to Report of the National Health and Medical Research Council 3rd Session, November, 1937, *CPP*, Canberra, 1937.

47 Dr Watson Munro was Assistant Surgeon, Out-door Department, Diseases of Women, at Prince Alfred Hospital. His evidence to the Birth-rate Commission is contained in paragraphs 2650–802, RCDB, vol. II.

48 Worcester, 'The Problem of Abortion'.

49 Sauer, 'Infanticide and Abortion in Nineteenth-Century Britain', p. 84.

50 RCDB, vol. II, p. 307.

51 RCDB, vol. II, p. 305.

52 RCSDF, p. 32. Some time later she was charged with manslaughter and sentenced to six years imprisonment after a woman whose pregnancy she had terminated, later died. Both she and her husband had previously been convicted, and served one year jail sentences, for baby-farming.

53 RCSDF, p. 85.

54 Excerpts from the *Evening News* reprinted in the RCSDF, pp. 80–90.

55 See, for example, Winifred Adcock, *With Courage and Devotion. A History of Midwifery in New South Wales*, Anvil Press, Wamberal, 1984.
56 Reiger, p. 104.
57 Sir James Graham, Lecturer in Midwifery at Sydney University, evidence to RCDB, vol. II, pp. 111–17.
58 Evan Willis, *Medical Dominance: the Division of Labour in Australian Health Care*, Allen & Unwin, Sydney, 1983.
59 RCDB, vol. II, p. 54.
60 Kelvin Churches, '120 Years of Abortion in Melbourne, a social, medical and legal history', *The Age Review*, 24 April 1976, p. 13.
61 Allen, 'Octavius Beale Reconsidered', p. 122.
62 'The Stentt Case', *AMJ*, October 1882, pp. 457–21.
63 'The McPhail Case', *AMJ*, November 1882. Dr Barker introduced a certain black humour into the Coroner's Court by claiming in his defence that 'He had told her to take exercise, but not exercise of that sort', p. 503.
64 RCDB, vol. II, p. 27.
65 RCDB, vol. II, p. 27.
66 Worcester, 'The Problem of Abortion', p. 25.
67 RCDB, vol. II, p. 98
68 RCDB, vol. II, p. 113.
69 'The Stentt Case', *AMJ*, October 1882, p. 463.

7 SPEECH AND SILENCE

1 Kerreen M. Reiger, *The Disenchantment of the Home. Modernising the Australian Family 1880–1940*, Oxford University Press, Melbourne, 1985, p. 178.
2 Reiger, *The Disenchantment of the Home.*
3 SCCWCM, *NSWPP*, LA, 1859–60, p. 89.
4 Except, interestingly, when adults talk to children. Mothers may still tell children to 'do a poo-poo'.
5 Pliny, *Natural History*, cited in R.Crawford, 'Of Superstitions Concerning Menstruation', *Proceedings of the Royal Society of Medicine (Section Historical Medicine*, vol. 9, 1915, p. 55.
6 Crawford, 'Of Superstitions Concerning Menstruation', p. 54.
7 Crawford, 'Of Superstitions concerning Menstruation', p. 56.
8 Crawford, 'Of Superstitions Concerning Menstruation', p. 56.
9 R. Bourke, *Scatological Rites of all Nations*, cited in Crawford, 'Of Superstitions Concerning Menstruation', p. 54.
10 Patricia Crawford, 'Attitudes to Menstruation in Seventeenth Century England', *Past and Present*, no. 91, May, 1981, p. 60.
11 Crawford, 'Of Superstitions Concerning Menstruation', p. 50.
12 Crawford, 'Attitudes to Menstruation in Seventeenth Century England', p. 61.
13 Crawford, 'Attitudes To Menstruation in Seventeenth Century England', pp. 60–61.

14 For a history of scientific theories about the menses see Patricia Vertinsky, 'Exercise, Physical Capability and the Eternally Wounded Woman in Late Nineteenth Century', *Journal of Sport History*, vol. 14, no. 1, Spring, 1987; Janice Delaney, Mary Jane Lupton, Emily Toth, *The Curse*, New American Library, New York, Scarborough, Ontario, 1977.

15 Dr George, 'The Rationale of the Menstrual Flow', *Lancet*, 16 February 1878. It was not Dr George who first postulated that the uterus was a weak vessel which 'broke its banks'. Avicenna, an eleventh century Arab physician claimed menstrual blood flowed out the womb because it is 'the weakest and the last formed organ'. Delaney et al., *The Curse*, p. 41. Also de Graaf, in the seventeenth century, stated that 'the menstrual blood escapes by the feeblest parts of the body, in the same way that wine or beer undergoing fermentation escapes by defective parts of the barrel' *The Curse*, p. 41.

16 *BMJ*, 14 July 1877, p. 67.

17 *BMJ*, 21 July 1877, p. 96.

18 *BMJ*, 2 March 1878, p. 324; 9 March 1878, p. 353; 27 March 1878, p. 633.

19 *BMJ*, 5 October 1878, p. 544; 7 November 1878, p. 714. For the full text of the letters see also Ronald Pearsall, *The Worm in the Bud*, Weidenfeld & Nicolson, London, 1969.

20 Cited in Paula Weideger, *History's Mistress*, Penguin, Middlesex, 1986, pp. 127–28.

21 Sophie Laws, 'The Sexual Politics of Pre-Menstrual Tension', *Women's Studies International Forum*, vol. 6, no. 1, 1983, pp. 19–31; S. Laws, 'Male Power and Menstrual Etiquette', in *The Sexual Politics of Reproduction*, ed. Hilary Homans, Gower, Hants, 1985, pp. 13–29.

22 Clotilda Bayne Diary, ms 2733. ANL.

23 *BMJ*, 17 October 1874, p. 503.

24 Henry Maudsley, 'Sex in Mind and In Education', *Fortnightly Review*, vol. 21, 1874 pp. 466–83.

25 Elizabeth Garrett Anderson, 'Sex in Mind and Education: A Reply', *Fortnightly Review*, vol. 21, 1874, p. 582.

26 On the modern social etiquette of menstruation see Jennifer Craik, 'Reflections on the Feminine', *Cambridge Anthropology*, vol. 5, no. 3, 1979; and Sophie Laws, 'Male power and Menstrual Etiquette'.

27 Dr Helen Kennedy, 'Effects of High school Work Upon Girls During Adolescence', *Pedagogical Seminary*, June, 1896.

28 Havelock Ellis, *Studies in the Psychology of Sex, Volume VI*, F.A. Davis Company, Philadelphia, 1922, p. 66.

29 Interviewed by Lynette Finch, Brisbane.

30 Interviewed by Lynette Finch, Brisbane.

31 Interviewed by Lynette Finch, Brisbane.

32 Cited in Norbert Elias, *The Civilising Process. The History of Manners*, Basil Blackwell, Oxford, 1978, p. 164.

33 MP.341, 11/9182. Australian Commonwealth Archives, Melbourne Branch. CSR, 27 September 19ll.

34 The eminent psychiatrist Richard von Krafft-Ebing, for example, used this technique, and it was not until 1965 that the translated English editions also translated the Latin. The 'exposed' text of his 1892 classic *Psychopathia sexualis* therefore carried the following credits: Dr Richard von Krafft-Ebing, *Psychopathia Sexualis: A Medico-Forensic Study*, translated from Latin by Dr Harry E. Wedeck. First Unexpurgated Edition in English, G.P. Putnam's and Sons, New York, 1965.

35 For example, Peter Cominos, 'Innocent Femina Sensualis in Unconscious Conflict', in *Suffer and Be Still: Women in the Victorian Age*, ed. Martha Vicinus, Indiana University Press, Bloomington, 1972; Carl N. Degler, 'What Ought to Be and What Was: Women's Sexuality in the Nineteenth Century', *American Historical Review*, vol. 79, no. 5, 1974; Peter Cominos, 'Late Victorian Sexual Respectability and the Social System', *International Review of Social History*, vol. VIII, 1963; R.S. Neale, 'Middle-class Morality and the Systematic Colonisers', in *Class and Ideology in the Nineteenth Century*, ed. R.S. Neale, Routledge & Kegan Paul, London, 1972; Peter Fryer, *The Birth Controllers*, Secker & Warburg, London, 1965; F. Barry Smith, 'Sexuality in Britain, 1800–1900', in *Suffer and Be Still*.

36 S. McInerney, ed., *The Confession of William James Chidley*, University of Queensland Press, St Lucia, 1977, p. 156.

37 Ruth Hall, *Marie Stopes: A Biography*, Andre Deutsch, London, 1977, p. 19.

38 Ellen M. Holtzman, 'The Pursuit of Married Love: Women's Attitudes Toward Sexuality and Marriage in Great Britain, 1918–1939', *Journal of Social History*, vol. 16, 1982.

39 Interviewed by Lynette Finch, Brisbane.

40 Peter Carl Botsman, 'The Sexual and the Social: Policing Venereal Diseases, Medicine and Morals', PhD thesis, University of New South Wales, 1987.

41 SCCWCM, p. 38.

42 SCCWCM, Appendix A, p. 180.

43 Such as Martine Segalen, *Love and Power in the Peasant Family*, Basil Blackwell, Oxford, 1983.

44 For example in Stephen Marcus, *The Other Victorians*, Weidenfeld & Nicolson, London, 1966, p. 122–3.

45 Col. Sec. Special Bundle, *Jails Monthly Reports*, December 1856–57, 4/718.2, NSWSA. My thanks to Libby Connors for bringing these documents to my attention.

46 Margaret Barbalet, *Far From a Low Gutter Girl. The Forgotten world of state wards: South Australia. 1887–1940*, Oxford University Press, Melbourne, 1983, p. 91.

47 *NSWPD*, 1883, p. 1185.

48 *NSWPD*, 1883, p. 1185.

49 *NSWPD*, 1883, p. 1185.

50 *NSWPD*, 1883, p. 1183.

51 *Pall Mall Gazette*, 7 July 1885, p. 7.

52 F.C. Richards and S. Richards, *Ladies Handbook of Home Treatment*, Signs Publishing Company, Melbourne, 1912, p. 53.
53 I.L. Austin, *How Alyce was Told at Six, Mothers Perplexity Series, No 1*, ML, 173/5/5. p. 4.
54 I.L. Austin, *Alyce on the Threshold*, ML, 173/5/A, p. 16.
55 Everitt Atkinson MA, MD, ChB, DPH and William J. Dakin, DSc, FLS, FZS, *Sex Hygiene and Sex Education*, Angus and Robertson, Sydney, 1918.
56 Atkinson and Dakin, *Sex Hygiene and Sex Education*.
57 Ellen M. Holtzman, 'The Pursuit of Married Love', pp. 39–52.
58 Marie Carmichael Stopes, *Married Love*, cited in E. Holtzman, 'The Pursuit of Married Love', p. 50.
59 (Lady) Jessie Street, *Truth or Repose*, Australasian Book Society, Melbourne, 1966, p. 85.
60 Graphics reproduced in Peter Sekuless, *Jessie Street. A Rewarding but Unrewarded Life*, University of Queensland Press, St Lucia, 1978, pp. 30–1.
61 Marion Piddington, *Tell Them! or the Second Stage of Mothercraft. A HandBook of Suggestions for the Sex-Training of the Child*, Moore's Bookshop, Sydney, 1925, pp. 65–7.

CONCLUSION

1 This is a point which is discussed by John Docker, 'Popular Culture and Bourgeois Values', in *Constructing a Culture. A People's History of Australia*, eds Verity Burgmann and Jenny Lee, McPhee Gribble/Penguin, Ringwood, 1988, pp. 241–54.
2 Michel Foucault, *Discipline and Punish: The Birth of the Prison* [1975], tr. A. Sheridan, Allen Lane, Middlesex, 1977, p. 143.
3 Foucault, *Discipline and Punish*, p. 146.
4 Keith Thomas notes that festivals to create rain during dry periods would be attended by both peasants and the landed ruling class even in the nineteenth century. Keith Thomas, *Religion and the Decline of Magic*, Weidenfeld and Nicolson, London, 1971, p. 151.
5 Asa Briggs, 'The Language of "Mass" and "Masses" in Nineteenth-Century England', in *The Collected Essays of Asa Briggs. Vol. 1: Words, Numbers, Places, People*, The Harvester Press, Sussex, 1985, pp. 36–7.
6 As Raymond Evans notes in 'The Hidden Colonists: Deviance and Social Control in Colonial Queensland', in *Social Policy in Australia. Some Perspectives 1901–1975*, ed. Jill Roe, Cassell, Stanmore, 1976, pp. 74–100.
7 Karl Marx and Frederick Engels, *Manifesto of the Communist Party*, Progress Publishers, Moscow, 1977, p. 44.
8 SCCWCM, p. 150.
9 Catholic orthodoxy believed that so great were the carnal lusts of women that they became easy prey for the devil. They allowed Satan's influence to fall upon their families, endangering whole

villages. Brian Easlea, *Witch Hunting, Magic and the New Philosophy. An Introduction to the Debates of the Scientific Revolution, 1450–1750*, The Harvester Press, Sussex, 1980, p. 8.

Bibliography

ARCHIVAL DOCUMENTS

Queensland State Archives

Colonial secretary records
Letter 7945. Joseph Whiting, Secretary Social Purity Society to Colonial Secretary, 11 July, 1893. COL/A793. Col. Sec.
Letters from the Industrial School in Toowoomba to the Convent Sisters of Mercy in Brisbane, 1891–1892, COL/A 684. Col. Sec.
Contagious Diseases Matter, COL/165. Col. Sec.
Queensland Prevention of Cruelty Reports and Correspondence. COL/247–427.
Suppression of brothels. COL/A89.
VD Suspects and Prostitution, 1917–1930. COL/A/21955–21994.
Prostitution in Queensland. White Slave Traffic. A/44696–8.
Minute Books, Medical Board of Queensland, 1860–1930. COL/A/38177–38200.
Minute Books, Pharmacy Board of Queensland, 1885–1930, COL/A/38252–73.

Police department records

Larrikinism. POL/J4–8/M95.
Lock Hospital 1891–1936. POL/J35/M796.
Advertisements (indecent) POL/A/44695.
Vagrants, gaming and other offences 1908– . POL/A/44815–A/11932.

Court records

Supreme Court (Brisbane) Records, 1880–1919. SCT/CC40–SCT/CC270.

Supreme Court (Townsville) Records, 1915. SCT/AR48–61.
Coroner's Court (Brisbane) Records, 1880–1940. JUS/1–74
Inquest Register, 1880–1940. JUS/R1–30.
Crown Solicitor Records, 1915–1921. CRS/227/36/3730–1.
Coroner's Court (Mt. Isa) Records, 1937.

South Australian State Archives

Letters and Memoranda of the Adelaide Lying-in Hospital, 1876–1926. GRG
28.31.

New South Wales State Archives

Jails Monthly Reports, 1856–7. Special Bundle. COL/4/718.2. Col Sec.

National Library of Australia

Clotilda Bayne. Diary. 1890, mss 2733.

Australian Archives (Melbourne)

Crown Solicitor's Records, 1911. MP/341/11/9128.

Melbourne University Archives

Dr V.H. Wallace Papers.

Mitchell Library

Mrs King's Journal of her Second Voyage to New South Wales, 1799. C185.
Letters from the Colonial Land and Emigration Office. 1842–1845. Doc. A.
1297.
Letter from Carter and Bonus, 1845. Doc. A1297.
Dispatches by Bourke, 1833, Doc. A1267.5.
Rev. Samual Marsden, *A few Observations on the Situation of the Female
Convicts in New South Wales*, 1806. mss 18. Mcr. No. 192–3.
W.S. Jevons, *A Social Survey of Australian Cities — Remarks Upon a Social
Map of Sydney, 1852*, msB846.
G.W. Walker Papers, mss 11.
I.L. Austin, *How Alyce was Told at Six*. Mothers' Perplexity Series, No. 1,
173/5/5.
I.L. Austin, *Alyce on the Threshold*, Mothers' Perplexity Series, No. 2,
173/5/A.

John Oxley Library

Extract from the Annual Report of the Brisbane Institute of Social Service,
1906–1971, OML 72–71.
Charity Organisation Society Welfare Services, Records and Papers, 1898–
1969, OML OM70–42–3/1.

Ithaca Benevolent Society Records, 1903–1922, OM66–12.
Annual Reports of the Dunwich Benevolent Asylum, 1920, 1922–25, OML OM72–8.
Medical Society of Queensland Records, 1882–1904, OM78–11.
Red Cross Minutes, 1915–1935, OMBH.

La Trobe Library

Ann Gratton. Diary. 1858. mss 9367.
Minutes of the Annual Meeting of the Carlton Refuge, Melbourne, 1882–1938. mss 10052.
Annual Report to Subscribers, Melbourne Lying-in Hospital, n.d. No manuscript number.

OFFICIAL PUBLICATIONS

Parliamentary Papers

1847   First and Second Reports From the Select Committee of the House of Lords on Juvenile Offenders and Transportation. *British Parliamentary Papers* (Lords)
1852–3   Report From the Select Committee on Criminal and Destitute Children *British Parliamentary Papers* (Commons)
1857   Report of the Select Committee of the Legislative Council on the Sale and Keeping of Poisons. *Victorian Parliamentary Papers* (Council)
1859–60   Report From the Select Committee on the Condition of the Working Classes of the Metropolis. *New South Wales Parliamentary Papers* (Assembly)
1867   Report of the Royal Commission to Enquire into and Report Upon the Operation and Effect of the Wine and Spirits Sale Statute. *Victorian Parliamentary Papers* (Assembly and Council)
1874–5   Report of the Royal Commission on Friendly Societies. *British Parliamentary Papers* (Lords)
1873–5   Annual Report on Gaols of the Colony. *Queensland Parliamentary Papers* (Assembly and Council)
1875–90   Annual Report the Commissioner of Police. *Queensland Parliamentary Papers Votes and Proceedings* (Assembly and Council)
1881–2   Report from the Select Committee of the House of Lords on the Law Relating to the Protection of Young Girls. *British Parliamentary Papers* (Lords)
1881   Census Report. *South Australian Parliamentary Papers*
1885   Reformatory for Boys, Lytton: Annual Report of the Superintendent. *Queensland Parliamentary Papers Votes and Proceedings* (Assembly and Council)

1880–1   Census Report. *Victoria Parliamentary Papers, Votes &*
          Proceedings (Council)
1896   Public Statutes of New South Wales. *New South Wales*
          Parliamentary Papers (Council)
1904   Report of the Royal Commission on the Decline of the
          Birth-rate and on the Mortality of Infants in New South
          Wales, Vols. I and II. *New South Wales Parliamentary*
          Papers (Assembly)
1907–8   Report of the Royal Commission on Secret Drugs, Cures
          and Foods. *Commonwealth Parliamentary Papers*
1911–18   Annual Report of the Director of State Children Depart-
          ment. *Queensland Parliamentary Papers* (Assembly and
          Council)
1915   Progress Report From the Select Committee on Prevalence
          of Venereal Diseases. *New South Wales Parliamentary*
          Papers (Assembly)

JOURNAL ARTICLES

Allen, J., '"Mundane" Men: Historians, Masculinity and Masculinism', *His-
torical Studies*, vol. 22, 1989, pp. 617–28
Anderson, E.G., 'Sex in Mind and Education: A Reply', *Fortnightly Review*,
vol. 21, 1874, p. 582
Anderson, P., 'Components of the National Culture', *New Left Review*, vol.
50, 1968, pp. 3–58
Anon., 'The New Criminal Code in Relation to Medical Evidence: Killing of
Unborn Children: Abortion: Rape', *The British Medical Journal*, July,
1878, pp. 106–7
—— 'Infant Insurance and Mortality', *The British Medical Journal*, June,
1875, pp. 784–6
—— 'Baby-Farming', *The British Medical Journal*, January, 1875, pp. 845–6
—— 'Registration of Still-Births', *The British Medical Journal*, April, 1873,
p. 384
—— 'The Stentt Case', *Australian Medical Journal*, October, 1882, p. 463
—— 'The McPhail Case', *Australian Medical Journal*, November, 1882, p.
503.
—— 'Common Law and Common Sense on Trials for Criminal Abortions',
The British Medical Journal, July, 1878, p. 145
—— 'Infant Life Protection Act, *Australian Medical Journal*, November,
1895, p. 16
—— 'The Care of Illegitimate Children in Victoria', *Australian Medical
Journal*, May, 1894, pp. 246–9
Aveling, J.H., 'On the Instruction, Examination, and Registration of
Midwives', *The British Medical Journal*, March, 1873, pp. 308–10
Bacchi, C.L., 'The Nature–Nurture Debate in Australia, 1900–1914', *Histor-
ical Studies*, vol. 19, 1980, pp. 199–212
Bailey, P., 'Will the Real Bill Banks Please Stand up? Towards a Role Analysis
of Mid-Victorian Working Class Respectability', *Journal of Social History*,
vol. 12, no. 3, 1979, pp. 336–53

Bailey, V. and Blackburn, S., '*The Punishment of Incest Act* 1908: A Case Study of Law Creation', *Criminal Law Review*, 1979, pp. 708–18

Bailey, V. and McCabe, S., 'Reforming the Law of Incest', *Criminal Law Review*, 1979, pp. 749–63.

——'The "Age of Consent" Controversy: Age and Gender as Social Practice', *Australia and New Zealand Journal of Sociology*, vol. 19, no. 1, 1983, pp. 96–112

Barber, R., '*The Criminal Law Amendment Act* of 1891 and the "Age of Consent" Issue in Queensland', *Australian and New Zealand Journal of Criminology*, June, 1977, pp. 95–113, 126–145

Baudrillard, J., 'Forgetting Foucault', *Humanities in Society*, vol. 3, Winter, 1980, pp. 87–111

Bauman, Z., 'The Social Manipulation of Morality: Moralising Actors, Adiaphorizing Action', *Theory, Culture and Society*, vol. 8, 1991

Beechy, V., 'Some Notes on Female Wage Labour in Capitalist Production', *Capital and Class*, no. 3, 1977, pp. 45–66

Behar, C.L., 'Malthus and the Development of Demographic Analysis', *Population Studies*, vol. XLI, 1987, pp. 269–81

Benjamin, B., 'Foreword to J. Graunt, "Natural and Political Observations mentioned in a following index, and made upon the bills of mortality. With references to the government, religion, trade growth, ayre, diseases, and the several changes of the said city"', 3rd edn, reprinted in *The Journal of the Institute of Actuaries*, vol. 90, 384, 1964, pp. 4–61

Ben–David, J., 'The Scientific Role: The Conditions of its Establishment in Europe', *Minerva*, vol. 4, no. 2, 1965, pp. 15–54

Berman, M., 'Hegemony and the Amateur Tradition in British Science', *Journal of Social History*, vol. 8, Winter, 1975, pp. 30–43

Bevis, P. et al., 'Archaeologizing Genealogy: Michel Foucault and the Economy of Austerity', *Economy and Society*, vol. 18, no. 3, 1989, pp. 323–43

Biller, P.P.A., 'Birth control in the West in the thirteenth and early fourteenth centuries', *Past and Present*, no. 94, 1982, pp. 3–26

Brumberg, J.J., '"Ruined" Girls: Changing Community Responses to Illegitimacy in Upstate New York, 1890–1920', *Journal of Social History*, Winter, 1984, pp. 247–71

Bullough, V. and Voght, M., 'Women, Menstruation, and Nineteenth-Century Medicine', *Bulletin of the History of Medicine*, vol. 47, no. 1, 1973, pp. 66–82

Caldwell, J.C. and Ruzicka, L.T., 'The Australian Fertility Transition: an Analysis', *Population and Development Review*, vol. 4, no. 1, pp. 81–103

Cawte, M., 'Craniometry and Eugenics in Australia: R.J.A. Berry and the Quest for Social Efficiency', *Historical Studies*, vol. 22, no. 86, 1986, pp. 35–53

Cominos, P.T., 'Late-Victorian Sexual Respectability and the Social System', *International Review of Social History*, vol. VIII, 1963, pp. 18–48, 216–50

Craik, J., 'Reflections on the Feminine', *Cambridge Anthropology*, vol. 5, no. 3, 1979, pp. 77–142

Crawford, P., 'Attitudes to Menstruation in Seventeenth Century England', *Past and Present*, vol. 91, May, 1981, pp. 47–73

Crawford, R., 'Of Superstitions Concerning Menstruation', *Proceedings of the Royal Society of Medicine*, vol. 9, 1915, pp. 44–66

Curthoys, A., 'Eugenics, Feminism and Birth Control: The Case of Marion Piddington', *Hecate*, vol. XV, no. 1, 1989

Davidson, A.I., 'Sex and the Emergence of Sexuality', *Critical Inquiry*, Autumn, 1987, pp. 16–48

Davin, A., 'Imperialism and Motherhood', *History Workshop*, vol. 5, 1978, pp. 9–66

Davis, G., 'Foreign Bodies: Images of the London Working Class at the end of the Nineteenth Century', *Literature and History*, vol. 14, no. 1, 1988, pp. 64–80

Degler, C.N., 'What Ought to Be and What Was: Women's Sexuality in the Nineteenth Century', *American Historical Review*, vol. 79, no. 5, 1974, pp. 625–34

De Vroey, M., 'On the Obsolescence of the Marxian Theory of Value: A critical review', *Capital and Class*, Summer, 1978

Donzelot, J., 'The Poverty of Political Culture', *Ideology and Consciousness*, vol. 5, Spring, 1979, pp. 73–86

Dyos, H.J., 'The Slums of Victorian London', *Victorian Studies*, vol. 11, no. 1, 1967, pp. 5–40

Evans, R., 'Soiled Doves, Prostitution and Society in Colonial Queensland— An Overview', *Hecate*, vol. 1, no. 1, 1975, pp. 6–24

Fairchild, C., 'Female Attitudes and the Rise of Illegitimacy: A Case Study', *Journal of Interdisciplinary History*, vol. VIII, 1978, pp. 627–67

Finch, L., 'Sexuality and Regulation', *Women/Australia/Theory. Special Issue of Hecate*, vol. 17, no. 1, 1991, pp. 43–50

Finch, L. and Stratton, J., 'The Australian Working Class and the Practice of Abortion 1880–1939', *Journal of Australian Studies*, vol. 23, November, 1988, pp. 45–64

Garton, S., 'Sir Charles MacKellar: Psychiatry, Eugenics and Child Welfare in New South Wales, 1900–1914', *Historical Studies*, vol. 22, no. 86, 1986, pp. 21–34

Gilman, S.L., 'Freud and the Prostitute: Male Stereotypes of Female Sexuality in *fin de siècle* Vienna', *Journal of the American Academy of Psychoanalysis*, vol. 9, 1981, pp. 337–60

—— 'Black Bodies, White Bodies: Toward an Iconography of Female Sexuality in Late Nineteenth-Century Art, Medicine, and Literature', *Critical Inquiry*, Autumn, 1985, pp. 202–42

Goldman, R.J. and Goldman, J.D.G., 'The Prevalence and Nature of Child Sexual Abuse in Australia' *Australian Journal of Sex and Family*, vol. 9, no. 2, 1988. pp. 94–106

Gordon, L., 'Incest and Resistance: Patterns of Father–daughter Incest, 1880–1930', *Social Problems*, vol. 33, no. 4, 1986, pp. 253–76

—— 'Race Suicide and the Feminist Response: Birth Control as a Class Phenomenon in the U.S., Part 1', *Hecate*, vol. 1, no. 2, 1975, pp. 40–53

—— 'Race Suicide and the Feminist Response: Birth Control as a Class Phenomenon in the U.S., Part 2', *Hecate*, vol. 2, no. 1, 1976, pp. 41–51

Gorham, D., 'The Maiden Tribute of Modern Babylon Re-examined. Child Prostitution and the idea of childhood in Late-Victorian England', *Victorian Studies*, vol. 21, no. 3, 1978, pp. 358–69

Hair, P.E.H., 'Bridal Pregnancy in Rural England in Earlier Centuries', *Population Studies*, vol. 20, 1966, pp. 233–43

Hicks N., 'Theories of Differential Fertility and the Australian Experience, 1891–1911', *Historical Studies*, vol. 16, no. 65, 1975, pp. 567–83

Hirst, P., 'Psychoanalysis and Social Relations', *m/f a feminist journal* nos 5–6, 1981, pp. 91–114

Hoar, W., 'Masturbation in Children', *The British Medical Journal*, January, 1875, p. 33

Hodges, J. and Hussain, A., 'La Police Des Familles', *Ideology and Consciousness*, vol. 5, 1979, pp. 87–123

Holtzman, E.M., 'The Pursuit of Married Love: Women's Attitudes Toward Sexuality and Marriage in Great Britain, 1918–1939', *Journal of Social History*, vol. 16, 1982, pp. 39–52

James, W.H., 'The Incidence of Illegal Abortion', *Population Studies*, vol. 25, no. 2, 1971, pp. 327–39

Jamieson, J., 'A Sketch of the History of Midwifery', *The Australian Medical Journal*, May 15, 1885, pp. 193–207

Kennedy, H., 'Effects of High School Work Upon Girls During Adolescence', *Pedagogical Seminary*, June, 1896, p. 562

Kern, S., 'Freud and the Discovery of Child Sexuality', *History of Childhood Quarterly*, vol. 1, no. 1, 1973, pp. 117–41

Knight, P., 'Women and Abortion in Victorian and Edwardian England', *History Workshop*, vol. 4, Autumn, 1977, pp. 57–69

Lake, M., 'The Politics of Respectability: Identifying the Masculinist context: Historical Reconsiderations', *Historical Studies*, vol. 22, no. 86, April, 1986, pp. 116–31

Laws, S., 'The Sexual Politics of Pre-Menstrual Tension', *Women's Studies International Forum*, vol. 6, no. 1, 1983, pp. 19–31

Lei, C. et al., 'Menstruation and the Menstrual Cycle: Knowledge and Attitudes of Mothers and Daughters', *Australian Journal of Sex, Marriage and Family*, vol. 8, no. 1, 1987, pp. 33–42

Maudsley, H., 'Sex in Mind and In Education', *Fortnightly Review*, vol. 21, 1874, pp. 466–83

May, M., 'Innocence and Experience: the Evolution of the Concept of Juvenile Delinquency in the Mid-Nineteenth Century', *Victorian Studies*, vol. 18, 1973, pp. 7–29

McCalman, I., 'Unrespectable Radicalism: Infidels and Pornography in Early Nineteenth-Century London', *Past and Present*, vol. 104, 1984, pp. 75–110

McConville, C., 'Rough Women, Respectable Men and Social Reform: A Response to Lake's "Masculinism"', *Historical Studies*, vol. 22, 1987, pp. 432–40

McDonald, D., 'Child and Female Labour in Sydney 1876–1898', *ANU Historical Journal*, vols. 10–11, 1973–4, pp. 40–9

McLaren, A., 'Abortion in England, 1890–1914', *Victorian Studies*, vol. 20, no. 4, 1977, pp. 379–400

181

—— 'Women's Work and the Regulation of Family Size: the question of abortion in the nineteenth century', *History Workshop*, vol. 4, Autumn, 1977, pp. 70–9

—— 'Birth Control and Abortion in Canada, 1870–1920', *Canadian Historical Review*, vol. LIX, no. 3, 1978, pp. 318–40

—— 'Contraception and Its Discontents: Sigmund Freud and Birth Control', *Journal of Social History*, vol. 12, no. 4, 1979, pp. 513–29

Mort, F., 'The Domain of the Sexual', *Screen Education*, vol. 36, Autumn, 1980, pp. 69–84

Molyneux, M., 'Beyond the Domestic Labour Debate', *New Left Review*, no. 116, 1979, pp. 3–27

Neale R.S., 'Working-Class Women and Women's Suffrage', *Labour History*, vol. 12, 1967, pp. 16–33

Neuman, R.P., 'Masturbation, Madness and the Modern Concepts of Childhood and Adolescence, *Journal of Social History*, vol. 8, Spring, 1975, pp. 1–27

Norris, C., 'Postmodernising History: Right-wing Revisionism and the uses of Theory', *Southern Review*, vol. 21, no. 2, July, 1988, pp. 123–40

Pearce, C.G., 'Some Aspects of Fertility in the Mid-Victorian Community', *Local Population Studies*, vol. 10, 1973, pp. 25–9.

Post, J.B., 'Ages of Menarche and Menopause: Some Mediaeval Authorities, *Population Studies*, vol. 25, no. 1, 1971, pp. 83–7

Pringle, R., 'Octavius Beale and the Ideology of the Birth-Rate, The Royal Commissions of 1904 and 1905', *Refractory Girl*, Winter, 1973, pp. 19–27.

Rapp, R. et. al., 'Examining Family History', *Feminist Studies*, vol. 5, no. 1, Spring, 1979

Roberts, M.J.D., 'Making Victorian Morals? The Society for the Suppression of Vice and its Critics, 1802–1886', *Historical Studies*, vol. 21, 1984, pp. 157–73

Rose, N., 'The Psychological complex: Mental Measurement and Social Administration', *Ideology and Consciousness*, vol. 5, 1979, pp. 5–67

Ross, E., 'Survival Networks: Women's Neighbourhood Sharing in London Before World War I', *History Workshop*, vol. 15, Spring, 1983, pp. 4–27

Roth, M.A., 'Foucault's "History of the Present"', *History and Theory*, vol. 20, 1981, pp. 32–46

Rubinstein, A., 'Subtle Poison: The Puerperal Fever Controversy in Victorian Britain', *Historical Studies*, vol. 20, no. 80, 1983, pp. 420–38

Sauer, R., 'Attitudes to Abortion in America, 1800–1973', *Population Studies* vol. 28, no. 1, 1974, pp. 53–67

—— 'Infanticide and Abortion in Nineteenth-Century Britain', *Population Studies*, vol. 32, 1978, pp. 81–93

Shorter, E., 'Capitalism, Culture, and Sexuality: Some Competing Models', *Social Science Quarterly*, vol. LII, 1972, pp. 338–56

—— 'Illegitimacy, Sexual Revolution, and Social Change in Modern Europe', *Journal of Interdisciplinary History*, vol. II, 1971, pp. 237–72

—— 'Female Emancipation, Birth Control, and Fertility in European History', *American Historical Review*, vol. LXXVIII, 1973, pp. 605–40

Showalter, E. and Showalter, E., 'Victorian Women and Menstruation', *Victorian Studies*, vol. 14, no. 1, 1970, pp. 83–9

Skultans, V., 'The Symbolic Significance of Menstruation and the Menopause', *Man*, vol. 5, December, 1970, pp. 639–51

Spencer, G., 'Pre-marital Pregnancies and Ex-Nuptial Births in Australia, 1911–66—A Comment', *The Australian and New Zealand Journal of Sociology*, vol. 5, no. 1, 1969, pp. 121–7

Stannage, C.T., 'Uncovering Poverty in Australian History', *Early Days. Journal and Proceedings (Royal Western Australian Historical Society)*, vol. 7, no. 7, 1975–6, pp. 90–106

Sturma, M., 'Eye of the Beholder: The Stereotype of Women Convicts, 1788–1852', *Labour History*, vol. 34, May, 1978, pp. 3–10

—— 'Seduction and Punishment in Late Nineteenth Century New South Wales', *Australian Journal of Law and Society*, vol. 2, no 2, 1985, pp. 74–81

Swain, S.L., 'Destitute and Dependent: Case Studies in Poverty in Melbourne, 1890–1900', *Historical Studies*, vol. 19, no. 74, 1980, pp. 98–107

Tait, D., 'Respectability, Property and Fertility: The Development of Official Statistics about Families in Australia', *Labour History*, vol. 49, November, 1985, pp. 86–97

Thane, P., 'Women and the Poor Law in Victorian and Edwardian England', *History Workshop*, vol. 6, Autumn, 1978, pp. 29–51

Thomas, K., 'The Double Standard', *Journal of the History of Ideas*, April, 1959, pp. 195–216

Thompson, E.P., 'The Political Education of Henry Mayhew', *Victorian Studies*, vol. 1, September, 1967, pp. 41–64

Tilly L.A. et.al., 'Women's Work and European Fertility Patterns', *Journal of Interdisciplinary History*, vol. VI, 1976, pp. 447–67

Tilly L.A. and Scott, J.W., 'Women's Work in Nineteenth Century Europe', *Comparative Studies in Society and History*, vol. XVII, 1975, pp. 55–8

Tyler, D., 'The Case of Irene Tuckerman: Understanding Sexual Violence and the Protection of Women and Girls, Victoria, 1890–1925', *History of Education Review*, vol. 1, 1986, pp. 52–67

Van Krieken, R., 'Towards "Good and Useful Men and Women": The State and Childhood in Sydney, 1840–1890', *Australian Historical Studies*, vol. 23, no. 93, 1989, pp. 405–23

Vertinsky, P., 'Exercise, Physical Capability and the eternally Wounded Woman in the Late Nineteenth Century', *Journal of Sport History*, vol. 14, no. 1, 1987, pp. 7–27

Weeks, J., 'Foucault for Historians', *History Workshop*, vol. 14, Autumn, 1982, pp. 106–19

Weiss N.P., 'The Mother–Child Dyad Revisited: Perceptions of Mothers and Children in Twentieth Century Child-Rearing Manuals', *Journal of Social Issues*, vol. 34, 1978, pp. 29–45

White, J., 'Campbell Bunk: A Lumpen Community in London Between the Wars', *History Workshop*, vol. 8, Autumn, 1979, pp. 1–49

Williams, B., 'The Birth Rate in Australia', *Medical Journal of Australia*, October, 1943, pp. 306–7

Wimhurst, K., 'Control and Resistance: Reformatory School Girls in Late Nineteenth Century South Australia', *Journal of Social History*, Winter, 1984, pp. 273–87

Wright, E.O., 'The Value Controversy and Social Research', *New Left Review*, no. 116, 1979.
Zaretsky, E., 'Female Sexuality and the Catholic Confessional', *Signs*, vol. 6, no. 1, 1980, pp. 176–84

BOOKS AND MONOGRAPHS

Abrahms P., *The Origins of British Sociology, 1834–1914*, The University of Chicago Press, Chicago and London, 1968
Adcock, W., *With Courage and Devotion. A History of Midwifery in New South Wales*, Anvil Press, Wamberal, 1984
Alford, K., *Production or Reproduction? An Economic History of Women in Australia, 1788–1850*, Oxford University Press, Melbourne, 1984
Allen, J.A., *Sex and Secrets. Crimes Involving Australian Women Since 1880*, Oxford University Press, Melbourne, 1990
Althusser, L. *Lenin and Philosophy and Other Essays*, New Left Books, London, 1971
Anon. *Australian Etiquette or the Rules and Usages of the Best Society in the Australasian Colonies Together With Their Sports, Pastimes, Games and Amusements*, People's Publishing Co., Melbourne, 1886
Aries, P., *Centuries of Childhood*, Penguin, Harmondsworth, 1973
Armstrong, D., *Political Anatomy of the Body. Medical Knowledge in Britain in the Twentieth Century*, Cambridge University Press, Cambridge, 1983
Atkinson, E, and Daken, W.J., *Sex Hygiene and Sex Education*, Angus and Robertson, Sydney, 1918
Bailey, P., *Leisure and Class in Victorian England, Rational Recreation and the Contest for Control, 1830–1885*, Routledge and Kegan Paul, London, 1978
Banks, J.A. and Banks, O., *Feminism and Family Planning in Victorian England*, Liverpool University Press, Liverpool, 1964
Barbelet, M., *Far From a Low Gutter Girl. The Forgotten World of State Wards: South Australia, 1887–1940*, Oxford University Press, Melbourne, 1983
Beechy, V. and Donald, L., eds, *Subjectivity and Social Relations*, Routledge and Kegan Paul, London, 1986
Ben–David, J., *The Scientist's Role in Society*, Prentice-Hall, New Jersey, 1971
Bernard, J., *The Future of Marriage*, Penguin, Harmondsworth, 1972
Booth, C., *Life and Labour of the People in London*, Macmillan, London, 1902
Bouce, P., ed., *Sexuality in Eighteenth Century Britain*, Manchester University Press, Manchester, 1982
Bouchard, D.F., ed., *Language, Counter-Memory, Practice: Selected Essays and Interviews*, tr. D.F. Bouchard and S. Simon, Basil Blackwell, New York, 1977
Boyd, R.M., *Scottish Church Attitudes to Sex, Marriage and the Family: 1850–1914*, John Donald, Edinburgh, 1980
Bruce O.B., *Don't. Directions for Avoiding Improprieties of Conduct and Common Errors in Speech and 200 Maxims on Conduct, Habits, and Manners by the Best Authors*, E.W. Cole Book Arcade, Melbourne, 1919

Bullough, V. and Bullough, B., *Women and Prostitution: A Social History*, Prometheus, New York, 1987
Burstyn, J.N., *Victorian Education and the Ideal of Womanhood*, Croom Helm, London, 1980
Cannon, M. ed., *Vagabond Country. Australia's Bush and Town Life in the Victorian Age*, Hyland House, Melbourne, 1981
Carr E.H., *What is History*, Penguin Books, Middlesex, 1961
Chamberlain, J.I. and Gilman, S.L., eds., *Degeneration: The Dark Side of Progress*, Columbia University Press, New York, 1985
Chidley, W.J., *The Answer: an Essay in Philosophy*. The author, Sydney, 1914
Connell, R.W. and Irving, T.H., *Class Structure in Australian History. Documents, Narrative and Argument*, Longman Cheshire, Sydney, 1980
Cousins, M. and Hussain, A., *Michel Foucault*, MacMillan, London, 1984
Cox, P.R., *Demography*. 4th edn., Cambridge University Press, London, 1970
Croce, Benedetto, *History Its Theory and Practice*, tr. Douglas Ainslie, Russell & Russell, New York, 1960
Daniels, K. ed., *So Much Hard Work. Women and Prostitution in Australia*, Fontana Books, Sydney, 1984
Darmon, P., *Damning the Innocent. A History of the Persecution of the Impotent in Pre-Revolutionary France* [1979], tr. Paul Keegan, Viking, New York, 1986
Davidson, C., *A Woman's Work is Never Done. A History of Housework in the British Isles. 1650–1950*, Chatto and Windus, London, 1982
Davison, G. et al. eds, *The Outcasts of Melbourne*, Allen & Unwin, Sydney, 1985
de Mause, L. ed., *The New Psychohistory*, The Psychohistory Press, New York, 1975
de Venette, N., *The Mysteries of Conjugal Love Reveal'd* [1712], 8th edn, Charles Carrington, London and Paris, 1906.
Delaney, J., Lupton, M.J. and Toth, E., *The Curse*, New American Library, New York, Scarborough, Ontario, 1977
Devereux, G.R.M., *Cole's Correct Guide to Etiquette for Men and Women*, Book Arcade, Melbourne, 1873
Dick, W., *A Bunch of Ratbags*, 2nd edn, Penguin, Ringwood, 1984
Dobb, M., *Theories of Value and Distribution Since Adam Smith Ideology and Economic Theory*, Cambridge University Press, Cambridge, 1973
Donzelot, J., *The Policing of Families* [1977], tr. R. Hurley, Pantheon Books, New York, 1979
Dreyfus, H.L. and Rabinow, P., *Michel Foucault: Beyond Structuralism and Hermeneutics*, The Harvester Press, Brighton, 1982
Easlea, B., *Witch Hunting, Magic and the New Philosophy. An Introduction to Debates of the Scientific Revolution, 1450–1750*, The Harvester Press, Sussex, 1980
Edwards, S., *Female Sexuality and the Law*, Martin Robinson, Oxford, 1984
Ehrenreich, B. and English, D., *For Her Own Good: 150 Years of the Expert's Advice to Women*, Pluto Press, London, 1979
Elias, N., *The Civilising Process. The History of Manners*, Basil Blackwell, Oxford, 1978
Ellis, H., *Studies in the Psychology of Sex*, F.A. Davis Co., Philadephia, 1922

Engels, F., *Marx–Engels on Britain*, Progress Publishers, Moscow, 1953
—— *The Condition of the Working Class in England*, Panther, Herts, 1976
Erskine, Mrs., *Etiquette in Australia*, William Brooks & Co, Sydney, 1911
Fitzgerald, S., *Rising Damp. Sydney 1870–1890*. Oxford University Press, Melbourne, 1987
Flandrin, J., *Families in Former Times. Kinship, Household and Sexuality*, Cambridge University Press, Cambridge, 1979
Forster, C. and Hazlehurst, C., *Australian Statisticians and the Development of Official Statistics*, Australian Bureau of Statistics, Canberra, 1988
Forster, R. and Ranum, O., *Family and Society*, Johns Hopkins University Press, Baltimore, 1976
Foucault, M., *The Birth of the Clinic: An Archaeology of Medical Perception* [1963] tr. A.M. Sheridan, Tavistock, London, 1973
—— *The Order of Things. An Archaeology of the Human Sciences* [1966], Vintage Books, New York, 1973
—— *The Archaeology of Knowledge and the Discourses of Language* [1969], tr. D. Bouchard and S. Simon, Tavistock, London, 1972
—— *Discipline and Punish. The Birth of the Prison* [1975], tr. A. Sheridan, Penguin, Middlesex, 1975
—— *The History of Sexuality, Vol 1: An Introduction* [1976], tr. R. Hurley, Allen Lane, London, 1978
—— *The Care of the Self. Vol. 3 of the History of Sexuality* [1984], tr. R. Hurley, Pantheon, New York, 1986
—— *The Use of Pleasure. Vol. 2 of the History of Sexuality* [1984], tr. R. Hurley, Viking, Middlesex, 1986
Fryer, P., *The Birth Controllers*, Secker & Warburg, London, 1965
Gardiner, J., ed., *What is History Today?*, Macmillan, Houndmills, 1988
Gordon, C., ed., *Power/Knowledge. Selected Interviews and Other Writings 1972—1977*, The Harvester Press, Sussex, 1980
Gorham, D., *The Victorian Girl and the Feminine Ideal*, Indiana University Press, Bloomington, 1982
Grosskurth, P., *Havelock Ellis. A Biography*, New York University Press, New York, 1985
Hall, S., ed., *Fit Work for Women*, Croom Helm, London, 1979
Hall, R., *Marie Stopes: A biography*, Andre Deutsch, London, 1977
Hampson, N., *The Enlightenment*, Penguin, Harmondsworth, 1982
Hardy, J. and Frost, A., eds, *Studies From Terra Australis to Australia*, Highland Press and The Australian Academy of the Humanities, Canberra, 1989
Hartman, M. and Banner, L., eds, *Clio's Consciousness Raised*, Harper and Row, London, 1974
Harvey, D., *The Condition of Postmodernity: An Enquiry into the Origins of Cultural Change*, Basil Blackwell, Oxford, 1989
Hergenhan, L.T. ed., *A Colonial City. High and Low Life. Selected Journalism of Marcus Clarke*, University of Queensland Press, St Lucia, 1972
Herman, H., *Father–daughter Incest*, Harvard University Press, Cambridge, Massachusetts, 1981
Hill, L., ed., *The Management of Scientists*, Beacon Press, Boston, 1963
Hill, C., *Society and Puritanism*, London, Secker and Warburg, 1964

Hirst, P. and Woolley, *Social Relations and Human Attributes*, London and New York, Tavistock, 1982

Holcombe, L., *Wives and Property*, Martin Robertson, Oxford, 1983

Hollingsworth, T.H., *Historical Demography*, Hodder and Stoughton, London, 1969

Homans, H., ed., *The Sexual Politics of Reproduction*, Gower, Hants, 1985

Hughes, R., *The Fatal Shore. A History of the Transportation of Convicts to Australia, 1778–1868*, Collins Harvill, London, 1987

Hugo, V., *Les Misérables*, [1976], tr. N. Denny, Penguin, Middlesex, 1976

Ignatieff, M., *A Just Measure of Pain. The Penitentiary in the Industrial Revolution 1750–1850*, Penguin, Middlesex, 1989

Jeffreys, S., *The Spinster and Her Enemies. Feminism and Sexuality, 1880–1930*, Pandora, London, 1985

Jevons, W.S., *The Theory of Political Economy*, Penguin, Middlesex, 1970

Kirkman-Gray, B., *A History of English Philanthropy*, Frank Cass & Co., London, 1967

Krafft-Ebing, R.F., *Aberrations of Sexual Life: after the Psychopathia Sexualis: a Medico Legal Study of Doctors and Lawyers* [1937], tr. A.V. Burburg, Staples Press, London, 1959

—— *Psychopathia Sexualis: A Medico-Forensic Study*, tr. H. Wedeck, first unexp. edn in English, G.P. Putnam's and Sons, New York, 1965

Kuhn, A. and Wolpe, A.M., eds, *Feminism and Materialism: Women and Modes of Production*, Routledge and Kegan Paul, London, 1978

Laslett, P., *The World We Have Lost*, Methuen, London, 1971

—— *Family Life and Illicit Love in Earlier Generations. Essays in Historical Sociology*, Cambridge University Press, Cambridge, 1977

Lines, W.J., *Taming the Great South Land. A History of the Conquest of Nature in Australia*, Allen & Unwin, Sydney, 1991

London Feminist History Group, *The Sexual Dynamics of History*, Pluto, London, 1983

McCalman, J., *Struggletown. Public and Private Life in Richmond, 1900–1965*, Melbourne University Press, Melbourne, 1984

Macdonell, D., *Theories of Discourse: An Introduction*, Basil Blackwell, Oxford, 1986

Mathews, J.J., *Good and Mad Women. The Historical Construction of Femininity in Twentieth-Century Australia*, George Allen & Unwin, Sydney, 1984

Mahood, L., *The Magdalenes. Prostitution in the Nineteenth Century*, Routledge, London and New York, 1990

Malthus, T.R., *An Essay on the Principle of Population*, Macmillan, New York, 1909

Marcus, S., *The Other Victorians. A Study of Sexuality and Pornography in Mid-Nineteenth Century England*, Weidenfeld and Nicolson, London, 1966

Marx, K., *Capital. Vol. 1*, Progress Publishers, Moscow, 1978

Marx, K. and Engels, F., *Collected Works, Vol. 1*, Progress Publishers, Moscow, 1950

Marx, K. and Engels, F., *Manifesto of the Communist Party*, Progress Publishers, Moscow, 1977

Mayhew, H., *London Labour and the London Poor. Vol 1. The London Street-Folk*, Griffin, Bohn and Co., London, 1861

Mayne, A.J.C., *Fever, Squalor and Vice. Sanitation and Social Policy in Victorian Sydney*, University of Queensland Press, St Lucia, 1982

McInerney, S. ed., *The Confessions of William James Chidley*, University of Queensland Press, St. Lucia, 1977

McLaren, A., *Birth Control in Nineteenth Century England*, Croom Helm, London, 1978

Mearns, W.C., *The Bitter Cry of Outcast London: An Inquiry into the Condition of the Abject Poor*, Chivers, Portway, Bath, 1969

Minson, J., *Genealogies of Morals. Neitzsche, Foucault, Donzelot and the Eccentricity of Ethics*, Macmillan, London, 1985

Mitchell, J., *Woman's Estate*, Penguin, Middlesex, 1971

Mitchell, J. and Oakley, A. eds, *The Rights and Wrongs of Women*, Penguin, Harmondsworth, 1976

Mort, F., *Dangerous Sexualities: Medico–Moral Politics in England Since 1830*, Routledge & Kegan Paul, London, 1987

Neale, R.S., *History and Class. Essential Readings in Theory and Interpretation*, Basil Blackwell, Oxford, 1983

Needham, J., *A History of Embryology*, 2nd edn, Cambridge University Press, Cambridge, 1959

Nichols, R.H. and Wray, F.A., *The History of the Foundling Hospital*, Nicholson and Watson, London, 1935

Pearsall, R., *The Worm in the Bud*, Weidenfeld and Nicolson, London, 1969

Pearson, G., *Hooligan: a History of Respectable Fears*, MacMillan, London, 1983

Petchesky, R.P., *Abortion and Woman's Choice*, Verso, London, 1986

Petrie, G., *A Singular Iniquity. The Campaigns of Josephine Butler*, MacMillan, London, 1971

Piddington, M., *Tell Them! or the Second Stage of Mothercraft. A Handbook of Suggestions for the Sex–Training of the Child*, Moore's Bookshop, Sydney, 1925

Platt, A.M., *The Child Savers—the Invention of Juvenile Delinquency*, University of Chicago Press, Chicago, 1969

Plumb J.H., *In the Light of History*, Houghton Mifflin Co., Boston, 1973

Pyke, L.M., *Australian Etiquette*, W.W. Cole Book Arcade, Melbourne, 1913

Quaife, G.R., *Wanton Wenches and Wayward Wives. Peasants and Illicit Sex in Early Seventeenth Century England*, Croom Helm, London, 1979

Quiggen, P., *No Rising Generation. Women and Fertility in Late Nineteenth Century Australia*, Australian Family Formation Project Monograph No. 10, Canberra, 1988

Rabb,T.K. and Rotberg, R.I., *The Family in History. Interdisciplinary Essays.* Harper Torch Books, New York, 1973

Rabinow, P. ed., *The Foucault Reader*, Pantheon Books, New York, 1984

Ramsland, J., *Children of the Back Lanes: Destitute and Neglected Children in Colonial New South Wales*, New South Wales University Press, Sydney, 1986

Reiger, K.M., *The Disenchantment of the Home. Modernizing the Australian Family 1880–1940*, Oxford University Press, Melbourne, 1985

Richards, F.C. and Richards, S., *Ladies Handbook of Home Treatment*, Signs Publishing Co., Melbourne, 1912

Robinson, J., *An Essay on Marxian Economics*, Macmillan, London, 1966

Robinson, P., *The Women of Botany Bay: a reinterpretation of the role of the women in the origins of Australian society*, Penguin, Ringwood, 1991

Roe, J., ed., *Social Policy in Australia: Some Perspectives*, Cassell Australia, Melbourne, 1976

Saunders, K. and Evans, R., eds, *Gender Relations in Australia. Domination and Negotiation*, Harcourt Brace Jovanovich, Sydney, 1992

Sargent, L., ed., *Women and Revolution*, South End Press, Boston, 1981

Segalen, M., *Love and Power in the Peasant Family*, Basil Blackwell, Oxford, 1983

Sekuless, P., *Jessie Street. A Rewarding but Unrewarded Life*, University of Queensland Press, St Lucia, 1978

Sheppard, J., *Someone else's Daughter: The Life and Death of Anita Cobby*, Ironbark Press, Bondi Junction, 1991

Sheridan, A., *Michel Foucault. The Will To Truth*, Tavistock Publications, London and New York, 1982

Shorter, E., *The History of Women's Bodies*, Basic Books, New York, 1982

Showalter, E., *The Female Malady. Women, Madness and English Culture, 1830–1980*, Virago, London, 1987

Skolnick, A., ed., *Rethinking Childhood*, Little Brown, Boston, 1976

Soloway, R.A., *Birth Control and the Population Question in England, 1877–1930*, Croom Helm, London, 1982

Stafford, A., *The Age of Consent*, Hodder and Stoughton, London, 1964

Stone, L., *The Family, Sex and Marriage in England 1500–1800*, Weidenfeld and Nicolson, London, 1977

Stratton, J., *The Virgin Text. Fiction, Sexuality and Ideology*, The Harvester Press, Sussex, 1987

—— *Writing Sites. A Genealogy of the Postmodern World*, Harvester Wheatsheaf, Hertfordshire, 1990

——*The Young Ones. Working-Class Culture Consumption and the Category of Youth*, Black Swan Press, Perth, 1992

Street, J. (Lady), *Truth or Repose*, Australasian Book Society, Sydney, 1966

Summers, A., *Damned Whores and God's Police. The Colonization of Women in Australia*, Penguin, Harmondsworth, 1975

Sydney Labour History Group, eds, *What Rough Beast? The State and Social Order in Australian History*, Allen and Unwin, Sydney, 1982

Thomas, W.I. and Znaniecki, F., *The Polish Peasant in Europe and America*, University of Chicago Press, Chicago, 1918

Thomas, K., *Religion and the Decline of Magic*, Weidenfeld and Nicolson, London, 1971

Thompson, E.P., *The Making of the English Working Class*, Penguin, Middlesex, 1981

Thorne, B. and Yalom, M., *Rethinking the Family: Feminist Questions*, Longman, New York, 1982

Trudgell, E., *Madonnas and Magdalenes. The Origins and Development of Victorian Sexual Attitudes*, Heinemann, London, 1976

Vicinus, M., ed, *Suffer and Be Still: Women in the Victorian Age*, Indiana University Press, Bloomington, 1972

—— ed., *A Widening Sphere: Changing Roles of Victorian Women*, Indiana University Press, Bloomington and London, 1977

Walkowitz, J.R., *Prostitution and Victorian Society: Women, Class and the State*, Cambridge University Press, Cambridge, 1980

Wallace, T.A., *The Etiquette of Australia. A Handy Book of the Common Usages of Everyday Life and Society*, Dymock's Book Arcade & Circulating Library, Sydney, 1909

Ward, E., *Father–Daughter Rape*, The Women's Press, London, 1984

Weber, H., *The Restoration Rake–Hero. Transformations in Sexual Understanding in Seventeenth Century England*, University of Wisconsin Press, Wisconsin, 1986

Weedon, C., *Feminist Practice and Poststructuralist Theory*, Basil Blackwell, Oxford, New York, 1987

Weeks, J., *Sex, Politics and Society. The Regulation of Sexuality Since 1800*, Longman, London and New York, 1980

Weideger, P., *History's Mistress: A New Interpretation of a Nineteenth-century Ethnographic Classic*, Penguin, Middlesex, 1986

Willis, E., *Medical Dominance: the Division of Labour in Australian Health Care*, Allen and Unwin, Sydney, 1983

Windschuttle, E., ed., *Women, Class and History*, Fontana/Collins, Melbourne, 1980

Wohl, A., ed., *The Victorian Family*, Croom Helm, London, 1978

Zeitlin, I., *Ideology and the Development of Sociological Theory*, Prentice-Hall, New Jersey, 1968

THESES

Barber, R.N., 'Rape and Other Sexual Offences in Queensland: An Historical and Behavioural Analysis', MA Thesis, University of Queensland, 1970

Botsman, P.C., 'The Sexual and the Social: "Policing" Venereal Diseases, Medicine and Morals', PhD thesis, University of New South Wales, 1987

Collins, A., '"Like Roaring Lions Seeking Whom They Could Devour": Rape in Queensland 1880–1919', BA(Hons) Thesis, Griffith University, 1987

Evans, R.L., 'Charitable Institutions of the Queensland Government to 1919', MA thesis, University of Queensland, 1969

Goldman, L., 'Child Welfare in Nineteenth Century Queensland: 1865–1911', M.Qual thesis, University of Queensland, 1978

Ritter, A.L., 'Concepts and Treatment of Juvenile Delinquency in Nineteenth Century England, New South Wales and South Australia', MA thesis, University of New England, 1974

Index

abortion
  advertisements for, 110, 118–20;
  clinic records, 102; doctors and,
  7, 112–15, 117–18, 120–3;
  drugs for effecting, 128; law
  and policing of, 114–15, 118,
  120, 121, 123; middle class
  opposition to, 6, 110, 112–15;
  middle class women, 117;
  mother dying from, 111–12;
  surveys and studies of, 113,
  115, 117, 122; women as
  enemies of foetus, 112, 113;
  working class women, 7,
  111–12, 115, 117, 122, 124
alcohol, *see* drinking

bourgeoisie, *see* middle class

charity, *see* philanthropy
children
  abandoned, 73, 76; age of
  consent, 61, 74–5, 77, 79–82,
  91; age parameters of
  childhood, 73–4; asylums and
  reform schools, 40, 41, 73, 74,
  82, 83–4, 85, 96–7, 98–9, 146;
  baby farmers, 116; child labour,
  71, 73, 74, 81, 97; Christianity
  and, 72, 80; construction of
  discourses of, 52, chapter four,
  86, 87, 108, 149; crime, 36,
  40, 73; discipline of, 72, 73,
  85; family in relation to, 52,
  55, 70, 82, 85, 92, 93–4, 97,
  143, 149; illegitimate, 25, 26,
  27, 88, 92, 94; incest, 50–1,
  58–9, 61, 62–5, 67–9, 70;
  infant mortality, 71, 107, 108;
  infanticide, 114, 115–17;
  innocence and, chapter four
  passim, 86, 87; language of, 14,
  72, 76, 126–7, 143;
  masturbation, 79, 83; medical
  profession and, 67–9, 72, 78–9,
  81, 85; middle class, 71, 82–3,
  84, 149; mothers as sexual
  police of, 55, 70, 84, 85, 86,
  125, 126, 133, 140, 143;
  parliamentary debates and
  legislation, 70–1, 72–3, 74, 77,
  78; prostitution, 36, 37, 46,
  75–8, 81, 84–5, 101;
  psychological reasoning and, 74,
  78–9, 149; separated from
  adults, 52, 71, 85; servants
  accused of corrupting, 79;
  sexuality, 38, 55, 56–7, chapter
  four, 92, 138, 140–2, 149;
  sexually transmitted disease,
  67–9, 84; sold by relatives, 75;
  street children, 36, 73, 74, 76,
  82, 93, 142; surveys of, 10, 12,

191